WORKING MEMORY CAPACITY IN CONTEXT: MODELING DYNAMIC PROCESSES OF BEHAVIOR, MEMORY, AND DEVELOPMENT

Vanessa R. Simmering

WITH COMMENTARY BY

Nelson Cowan

Patricia J. Bauer
Series Editor

MONOGRAPHS OF THE SOCIETY FOR RESEARCH IN CHILD DEVELOPMENT

Serial No. 322, Vol. 81, No. 3, 2016

WILEY

Boston, Massachusetts   Oxford, United Kingdom

WORKING MEMORY CAPACITY IN CONTEXT: MODELING DYNAMIC PROCESSES OF BEHAVIOR, MEMORY, AND DEVELOPMENT

CONTENTS

COMMENTARY

I. WORKING MEMORY CAPACITY IN CONTEXT: MODELING DYNAMIC PROCESSES OF BEHAVIOR, MEMORY, AND DEVELOPMENT

Vanessa R. Simmering

This article is part of the issue "Working Memory Capacity in Context: Modeling Dynamic Processes of Behavior, Memory, and Development," Simmering, Vanessa (Issue Author). For a full listing of articles in this issue, see: http://onlinelibrary.wiley.com/doi/10.1111/mono.v81.3/issuetoc.

Working memory is a vital cognitive skill that underlies a broad range of behaviors. Higher cognitive functions are reliably predicted by working memory measures from two domains: children's performance on complex span tasks, and infants' performance in looking paradigms. Despite the similar predictive power across these research areas, theories of working memory development have not connected these different task types and developmental periods. The current project takes a first step toward bridging this gap by presenting a process-oriented theory, focusing on two tasks designed to assess visual working memory capacity in infants (the change-preference task) versus children and adults (the change detection task). Previous studies have shown inconsistent results, with capacity estimates increasing from one to four items during infancy, but only two to three items during early childhood. A probable source of this discrepancy is the different task structures used with each age group, but prior theories were not sufficiently specific to explain how performance relates across tasks.

The current theory focuses on cognitive dynamics, that is, how memory representations are formed, maintained, and used within specific task contexts over development. This theory was formalized in a computational model to generate three predictions: 1) capacity estimates in the change-preference task should continue to increase beyond infancy; 2) capacity estimates should be higher in the change-preference versus change detection task when tested within individuals; and 3) performance should correlate across tasks because both rely on the same underlying memory system. I also tested a fourth prediction, that development across tasks could be explained through increasing real-time stability, realized computationally as strengthening

Corresponding author: Vanessa R. Simmering, 1202 W. Johnson St., Madison, WI 53706; email: simmering@wisc.edu

DOI: 10.1111/mono.12249

connectivity within the model. Results confirmed these predictions, supporting the cognitive dynamics account of performance and developmental changes in real-time stability. The monograph concludes with implications for understanding memory, behavior, and development in a broader range of cognitive development.

Working memory is a ubiquitous cognitive function that underlies a broad range of behaviors over development, including everyday activities such as following multi step instructions, keeping track of a referent to understand a pronoun, or learning to follow the rules of a game. Extensive evidence has shown that working memory is important for academic performance and everyday functioning; however, the basic cognitive processes subserving working memory through development are still poorly understood. In particular, the theories proposed to explain how working memory functions and develops are disconnected across research areas focusing on infancy, childhood, and adulthood. The aim of this research is to develop a process-oriented theory of working memory and how it develops that can span multiple tasks and developmental periods.

In order to arrive at a general theory of working memory development, it is necessary to understand how behavioral results relate across tasks designed to assess working memory in different age groups. Longitudinal studies have shown that infants' performance on looking tasks predicts later performance on standardized tests of cognitive abilities at 2–3 years and 11 years (Rose & Feldman, 1997; Rose, Feldman, Jankowski, & Van Rossem, 2005). Performance on laboratory measures of working memory correlates with concurrent measures of children's academic performance (e.g., Raghubar, Barnes, & Hecht, 2010) and general intelligence in both children and adults (e.g., Conway, Kane, & Engle, 2003; Cowan, Fristoe, Elliott, Brunner, & Saults, 2006). However, little is known about how infants' performance on looking tasks relate to children's performance on working memory tasks, much less how these lab-based measures relate to higher-level cognitive skills. Are there common processes across tasks and development, or do these results reflect separable contributions to higher level cognitive skills at different points in development?

Inconsistent results from training studies provide further evidence that current theories have not achieved a full understanding of how working memory relates to other cognitive functions. Recent reviews of working memory training studies show mixed results (Melby-Lervåg & Hulme, 2013; Shipstead, Hicks, & Engle, 2012; Shipstead, Redick, & Engle, 2010, 2012; Wass, Scerif, & Johnson, 2012). For example, Shipstead, Hicks, and Engle (2012) reviewed studies intended to improve attention through visuospatial working memory training (e.g., Klingberg, Forssberg, & Westerberg, 2002). Across these studies, Shipstead and colleagues found fairly limited transfer not only to "far" tasks (purported to measure constructs like fluid intelligence) but also to some "near" tasks (other measures of visuospatial working memory), as well as inconsistent replication. They argued that one of the central obstacles to the progress of research in this domain is a lack of theories specifying the cognitive processes involved across tasks (see also Gibson, Gondoli, Johnson, Steeger, & Morrissey, 2012; Hulme & Melby-Lervåg, 2012; Logie, 2012; Melby-Lervåg & Hulme, 2013).

As a first step toward developing a theory that specifies the common processes across tasks, the current monograph builds from two largely disconnected research areas: working memory in children and adults, and visual memory development during infancy. Both of these areas have amassed a sizable knowledge base, but theories have thus far not been integrated to account for how infant memory relates to later assessments of working memory. Indeed, some theorists question whether infant looking behavior reflects working memory at all, or if the cognitive processes underlying correlations between working memory and more general cognitive skills only emerge later in development (see Cowan, 2007, for discussion).

In the sections that follow, I first review research and theories on working memory in children and adults, then describe infant research and how it may relate to later studies of working memory. Finally, I present a new theory designed to take a first step toward bridging these disconnected research areas by developing a specific account of developmental changes in visual working memory capacity. To preview, the theory I propose here extends an existing computational framework to model visuospatial cognition, the Dynamic Field Theory, to capture performance across tasks and development. Model simulations and behavioral results show that the lab tasks used with infants and adults can yield inconsistent capacity estimates even though they rely on the same underlying memory system. Furthermore, developmental changes in these tasks can be explained by a single mechanism: the strengthening of excitatory and inhibitory connections over development. This theory emphasizes the *dynamics* of cognition, that is, how cognitive processes combine in the moment of a particular task to guide behavior (Simmering & Perone, 2013) and presents a new perspective on development, reconceptualizing cognition in terms of *stability*. This approach to understanding cognitive development can be extended beyond the types of tasks captured in the model presented here, with implications for understanding working memory and development more generally.

WORKING MEMORY RESEARCH IN CHILDREN AND ADULTS

The psychological concept of "working memory" emerged with Baddeley and Hitch's (1974) proposal of a model combining short-term stores of domain-specific information (i.e., verbal versus visual) with a combined "central executive" that controlled and manipulated information within these stores. From this perspective, the central executive performed the "work" of working memory (i.e., control of the "slave" sub-systems) and the domain-specific stores were considered short-term memory. Despite Baddeley and Hitch's clear distinction between short-term and working memory, the terms have been used inconsistently throughout the cognitive and developmental science literatures (see Simmering & Perone, 2013, for discussion). In general, *simple* laboratory tasks that require only maintenance of information for recall or recognition (such as repeating a list of digits or pattern recognition) have been considered measures of short-term memory. By contrast, *complex* tasks requiring manipulation of information (e.g., repeating a series of items backward) or switching between storage and processing tasks (e.g., counting sets of dots and storing the results from the series for later recall) have been attributed to working memory. Theorists have taken different analytical approaches to identify processes in common versus separable across these types of tasks, as reviewed in the next section.

Differentiating Short-Term and Working Memory in Children and Adults

One motivation for distinguishing short-term versus working memory is based on their relative predictive power of more general cognitive skills, such as reasoning and general fluid intelligence. In adults, these types of higher cognitive skills correlate more strongly and reliably with performance on complex tasks than simple tasks (see Unsworth & Engle, 2007, for review). This suggests that the processing involved in the complex tasks (i.e., the "work" of working memory) makes a more substantial contribution to general reasoning and intelligence than simple storage.

A second motivation for distinguishing short-term and working memory comes from latent variable analyses showing that simple and complex tasks load on different factors. For example, Kane and colleagues (2004) compared performance across multiple assessments of verbal and visuospatial memory using simple and complex tasks. Their analyses showed that simple tasks loaded to domain-specific storage factors (verbal versus visuospatial short-term memory) while the complex tasks loaded to a domain-general processing factor (which they termed "executive attention"). Analyses of children's performance have indicated comparable separation of processes between the ages of 4 and 15 years (although some complex tasks were too difficult for young children to perform; Gathercole, Pickering, Ambridge, & Wearing, 2004; see also, Alloway, Gathercole, & Pickering, 2006; Alloway, Gathercole, Willis, & Adams, 2004).

These results differentiating short-term and working memory are compelling, but an important question remains: are the same processes operating in similar tasks at different points in development? The similarity in factor loading is consistent with comparable processes, but it is not conclusive: differentiation between simple and complex tasks in all age groups does not necessarily establish the same source of this contrast within each age group. For example, adults may rely heavily on executive attention across complex tasks (as proposed by Kane et al., 2004); for children, however, inhibition (or other cognitive processes) may play a more central role on these tasks, with attention contributing equivalently to simple and complex tasks. It is also possible that the same processes operate across all tasks, but the demands are minimized in simple tasks, reducing the ability to detect correlations. Evidence for this type of limitation comes from studies showing that higher cognitive functions correlate with simple tasks when those tasks were made more difficult. For instance, Unsworth and Engle (2007) found that performance on simple span tasks related more strongly to general intelligence if trials were scaled to be beyond the individual's capacity limit. Similarly, Cowan (2007) reviewed studies showing that children's intelligence correlated with simple digit span performance if children's ability to rehearse was suppressed. Thus, the processes underlying simple span tasks are related to higher cognitive skills, but these relations can be masked when task demands are low.

Another limitation of the latent variable approach to studying working memory is that it is difficult to apply earlier in development. First, it requires participants to complete a large number of tasks to increase the validity of the analysis; this could limit child samples to only those willing and able to perform many lab tasks. Second, the complex tasks that show strong predictive power in older children and adults are difficult for younger children (and impossible for infants). Alloway and colleagues have had some success adapting such tasks for children as young as 4 years (Alloway et al., 2004, 2006). However, their analyses also showed less separability of factors in this youngest age group (i.e., 4–5 years; Alloway et al., 2006), suggesting developmental changes in how cognitive processes combine to support behavior in these tasks. Even studies with adults have shown that the contrast between simple and complex visuospatial tasks depends on which tasks are chosen. For example, Miyake and colleagues found that performance on both simple and complex visuospatial tasks related equally strongly to measures of executive function, leading them to conclude that short-term memory may not be as dissociable from working memory in the visuospatial domain as in the verbal domain (Miyake, Friedman, Rettinger, Shah, & Hegarty, 2001). Thus, relying on the latent variables identified from different sets of tasks may be missing some important cognitive processes as they change over development.

As an alternative approach, the current research uses a process-based computational model to explore how underlying processes combine in specific task contexts. The utility of this approach within the developmental literature is well illustrated by the work of Munakata and colleagues. Their modeling results have shown how active versus latent memory traces compete to drive performance in two tasks in which children show perserverative responding at different ages: the A-not-B task during infancy (e.g., Munakata, 1998) and the dimensional change card sort task during early childhood (e.g., Morton & Munakata, 2002a). This modeling approach can explain why children perform in seemingly inconsistent ways across tasks that purportedly measure the same construct, for example, why infants perseverate in a reaching version of the A-not-B task but not in a looking version of the task (Munakata, McClelland, Johnson, & Siegler, 1997).

One advantage of using process-based computational models is that they can be applied across task types that may be suitable only during limited periods of development. Drawing on the examples modeled by Munakata and colleagues, young infants can be tested in variations of the A-not-B task (see Marcovitch & Zelazo, 1999, for review), but not the card sort task (which can be used with children 2.5 years or older; Zelazo, 2006); A-not-B-type tasks can be adapted for use beyond infancy (e.g., Schutte & Spencer, 2002; Spencer & Schutte, 2004), when children are able to complete the card sort task. A formalized modeling framework can be used to test whether the same processes are sufficient to explain performance in one type of task over development (e.g., comparing A-not-B tasks between infants and pre-schoolers) as well as across tasks during one developmental period (e.g., comparing preschoolers' performance across A-not-B and card sort tasks). Furthermore, successful implementation of these processes within a formalized model can lead to novel predictions regarding performance in other tasks (e.g., extending insights from the A-not-B and card sort tasks to a speech interpretation task, Morton & Munakata, 2002b) or age groups (cf. effects of long-term memory on working memory in early childhood, Schutte & Spencer, 2002, and adulthood, Lipinski, Simmering, Johnson, & Spencer, 2010). Thus, process-based computational modeling can shed light onto the cognitive processes developing over a wide range of ages to support behavior across multiple laboratory tasks.

Theories of Working Memory and Development

There are three general theoretical approaches to describing how working memory, as measured in complex tasks, functions and changes over development. First, as described briefly in the previous section, is Baddeley's multi-component model (Baddeley & Hitch, 1974). This model includes a central executive as a supervisory system that controls subsystems that originally included verbal and visuospatial storage systems, but was later updated to include an episodic buffer that integrated information across modalities (Baddeley, 2000); each of these components has a limited capacity. The majority of evidence supporting this model comes from studies using complex paradigms with adults, as well as studies of adults with cognitive dysfunction (e.g., dementia; see Baddeley, 2001, for review). The multicomponent model was not intended to address developmental change; as described above, evidence for separation of verbal and visuospatial subsystems and a domain-general central executive process has been found in children as young as 4 years (Alloway et al., 2006). Theories focusing on verbal skills suggest that developmental increases in rehearsal speed could support improvements (e.g., Hulme & Tordoff, 1989; but see Cowan, Elliott, et al., 2006).

A second approach is Cowan's (2005) attentional model, which characterizes memory as an embedded process system in which a subset of long-term memory is activated as short-term memory, with a portion of this activated memory held within the focus of attention. Maintaining information in this state of heightened activation, accessible to conscious processes of manipulation, is considered working memory and has a limited capacity of only three to five "chunks" of information. Cowan, Fristoe, et al. (2006) differentiated the scope of attention—how much information could be stored —and control of attention—how information is processed—as partially overlapping but partially independent contributions to performance in complex tasks. In this model, development is driven by increases in both the scope of attention (i.e., capacity) and attentional control (see also, Cowan, Hismjatullina, et al., 2010; Cowan, Morey, AuBuchon, Zwilling, & Gilchrist, 2010). These authors note that developmental improvements in other cognitive processes, such as encoding strategies or rehearsal, also support performance on lab tasks, but argue that such processes cannot fully explain development (see also Cowan, 2013; Dempster, 1981). Critically, Cowan (2013) concludes that, while there is strong evidence for increases in capacity, the mechanism(s) underlying such increases are currently unknown.

A third class of theories describe working memory as an undifferentiated resource that is flexibly allocated to processing and storage, as opposed to the partial independence posited by Cowan and colleagues or the full independence in the multi-component model. In these undifferentiated models, memory in early development is limited by less efficient processing. Some theories focus exclusively on either time-based decay (e.g., Towse & Hitch, 2007) or resource-sharing interference (e.g., Case, 1995), but more recent models combine time- and resource-based factors (e.g., Oberauer & Lewandowsky, 2011), including consideration for processing speed supporting information refreshing in memory (e.g., Barrouillet, Gavens, Vergauwe, Gaillard, & Camos, 2009). Within these models, developmental change is attributed to the factor(s) considered most important for explaining performance limitations: reduced decay or refreshing speed is most relevant for time-based explanations, and resistance to interference is central to resource-based explanations, with both time and resources contributing to development in combined models.

In summary, theories explaining performance on complex working memory tasks differ in the proposed relation between processing and storage, as well as whether developmental improvements arise through changes in processing, storage, or both. Baddeley's (2000) multi-component model proposed total separation of storage and processing, with no specific account for how each improves over development. Cowan's (2013 see also, Cowan et al., 2005; Cowan, Fristoe, et al., 2006) embedded process model suggested partial separation between the scope and control of attention, with an emphasis on developmental increases in scope/capacity. The time- and resource-based accounts (e.g., Barrouillet et al., 2009; Case, 1995; Towse & Hitch, 2007) included undifferentiated processing and storage, but differentially attributed developmental change to resistance to interference, decay, and/or refreshing.

As this section demonstrates, these theories of working memory development were designed to account for performance on complex tasks that require demanding processing with concurrent storage, with much developmental change arising through improvements in balancing processing and storage. These theories can be difficult to apply to simpler tasks that minimize processing demands and emphasize storage, but still show marked developmental improvements (Simmering & Perone, 2013). Furthermore, it is unclear how or whether these theories could account for earlier periods of development, as complex tasks are rarely used with children younger than 6 years of age. This limited application to early development reasserts the question of whether the working memory processes described in children and adults can be measured in infants. The following section reviews infant tasks that correlate with later abilities and theories to explain these developmental improvements.

WORKING MEMORY RESEARCH IN INFANCY

Complex working memory tasks clearly cannot be used for testing infants' memory, which raises the question of how (and whether) working memory can be assessed during infancy. Some theorists have questioned whether infants possess working memory (as opposed to only short-term memory), as infants cannot complete the kind of manipulations that are standard in working memory research with older children and adults (see Cowan, 2007, for discussion). Reznick (2007) argued that it is not possible to empirically differentiate short-term versus working memory, as it is conceptualized in adults, during infancy; he endorsed the term working memory to describe the processes underlying the types of tasks discussed in this section. Cowan (2007) agreed with this description, noting that young children's performance on simple tasks, like digit span, correlates significantly with intelligence; he concluded that infants and young children use working memory to perform simple tasks that later can be attributed to short-term memory. As such, the current monograph uses the term working memory in the context of infant tasks.

Infant visual working memory is primarily assessed through reaching or looking behaviors. The standard reaching paradigm is the delayed response task in which an object is hidden among, for example, three boxes and the infant is allowed to search for the object following a short delay (see Pelphrey & Reznick, 2003; Reznick, 2007, 2009, for reviews as well as discussion of the related A-not-B paradigm). Capacity in this task is conceptualized not only as the number of objects that can be remembered but also the length of time information can be maintained (also referred to as the durability of memory; Pelphrey & Reznick, 2003). The delayed response task can be used with infants as young as 5–6 months of age, as soon as reaching behavior becomes reliable. Results across a host of studies suggest a roughly linear increase in memory durability from 6 to 12 months, with a few studies demonstrating continued increases in durability through the second year (Reznick, 2009).

Feigenson and colleagues developed a search paradigm to assess how much information can be held in memory during infancy by hiding multiple objects in one container, then allowing infants to search after one or more of the objects has been retrieved by the experimenter (Feigenson & Carey, 2003, 2005; Feigenson & Halberda, 2008; Zosh & Feigenson, 2012). Infants' search times after they saw all the objects removed from the container were compared to search times after they saw all but one of the objects removed (note that no objects actually remained in the box, regardless of how many were removed within the infants' view, to ensure that search times were not affected by success at finding objects). Memory capacity of the total number of objects was inferred from longer search times on trials when infants saw all but one object removed. Using this method, infant's memory capacity has been estimated to reach three objects at 12–14 months of age (Feigenson & Carey, 2003). Studies using this paradigm have not compared performance across age groups, and therefore cannot provide information on how performance changes over development.

Results from reaching tasks show that infants can remember the location of a single object by about 5.5 months and over development this information can be retained over increasingly long delays. By the end of the first year, infants have also gained the ability to retain multiple object representations in memory at once. Less is known about improvements in memory between 1 and 3 years of age due to the challenges inherent in testing these age groups with continuity to either younger or older age groups (Reznick, 2007);

reaching tasks are rarely used as an index of capacity beyond 18 months of age. Furthermore, performance on reaching tasks has generally not been compared to other tasks (either concurrently or longitudinally), so it is unknown whether or how it relates to performance on complex tasks or general cognitive skills.

A second common approach to assessing infant visual memory is through looking paradigms. These tasks generally take two forms: habituation tasks in which a single stimulus is presented until the infant's attention decreases to a preset criterion, then a novel stimulus is presented (see Colombo & Mitchell, 2009, for review); and visual paired comparison tasks in which two stimuli are presented together, usually following familiarization to one of the stimuli (e.g., Fagan, 1970). These tasks rely on infants' tendency to look toward a novel stimulus as an index of their memory for the familiarized/habituated stimulus, and both have been shown to predict cognitive skills later in childhood (e.g., Kavšek, 2004; McCall & Carriger, 1993; Rose, Feldman, & Jankowski, 2012).

Early research with the visual paired comparison task suggested that preferences changed developmentally, with young infants (2.5–3.5 months) preferring familiar objects, no reliable preference around 4.5 months, and novelty preferences thereafter (Rose, Feldman, & Jankowski, 2007). However, further studies showed that this sequence of preferences (familiar to null to novel) occurred within a single age group following increasing lengths of familiarization (see Rose et al., 2007, for review). These results indicated that amount of familiarity with a stimulus required to exhibit a novelty preference decreases over development, that is, the speed of encoding increases developmentally. Memory can also be retained for longer periods with age, in parallel to the findings of increased memory durability in the delayed response task described above. In addition, during the first year of life, infants are able to remember more complex visual stimuli and can recognize objects that require some abstraction (e.g., a slightly rotated view or two-dimensional version of three-dimensional object; Rose et al., 2007).

Infant performance in habituation paradigms shows similar developmental changes in speed of encoding, with older infants habituating more quickly than younger infants (Colombo & Mitchell, 2009). In both visual paired comparison and habituation tasks, individual differences within an age group correspond to developmental differences: an infant who shows faster encoding relative to other same-aged infants typically shows a stronger novelty preference (Rose et al., 2007). Furthermore, individual differences in looking tasks have long-term predictive power for higher cognitive functions. Rose and colleagues have shown that infants' performance in paired comparison tasks predicts general cognitive functioning at 2–3 years (e.g., Rose et al., 2005), as well as working memory (along with other executive functions; Rose et al., 2012) and general intelligence at 11 years (see Rose et al., 2007, for

16

review). In particular, infants' processing speed (as indexed by both reaction times and number of trials to reach criterion for a novelty preference) and novelty preferences in paired comparison tasks at 7 and 12 months had significant paths to working memory at 11 years (Rose et al., 2012).

In a meta-analysis, Kavšek (2004) concluded that measures of habituation rate (i.e., number of looks during familiarization) and dishabituation (i.e., novelty preferences following habituation) had a combined predictive validity of 0.34 for later intelligence assessed between 1.5 and 11 years of age. In an earlier meta-analysis, McCall and Carriger (1993) found similar predictive correlations for habituation or recognition memory (0.41 and 0.39, respectively), suggesting similar processes across looking tasks. Taken together, results from these meta-analyses and Rose and colleagues' studies indicate that infants' looking performance predicts a range of later cognitive functions.

How do results like these relate to the findings described above, that performance on working memory tasks relates to measures of intelligence in children and adults (Cowan, Fristoe, et al., 2006)? Three possibilities exist: the variance explained by infants' looking behavior and older children's working memory performance could (1) overlap entirely, (2) overlap partially, or (3) not overlap at all. Although much research has been dedicated to understanding how intelligence is predicted by different laboratory tasks (e.g., looking tasks in infancy, working memory tasks during childhood), little is known about how these various laboratory tasks relate to each other over development. A few studies have shown correlations between looking behavior during infancy and working memory later in childhood (e.g., Marchman & Fernald, 2008; Rose et al., 2012), but the specific tasks used to assess memory vary both within and across age groups, making it difficult to synthesize results across studies.

Theories of infant memory development differ based on the task used to develop the theory, but may provide an avenue for extension to later development. Developmental improvements on the delayed response task have generally been attributed to brain maturation, citing improved functioning within the prefrontal cortex during this age range (see Pelphrey & Reznick, 2003; Reznick, 2007, 2009, for reviews). These explanations generally suggest that developmental improvements in performance arise through more robust working memory representations and/or processes. As discussed further in Chapters 2 and 5, this notion of the robustness of memory has potential to explain a broader range of developmental changes. This requires a deeper understanding of the link between memory and behavior across tasks, which is a central goal of the current monograph.

Similar explanations can be found across theories of infant looking performance. Most theories are grounded in Sokolov's (1963) comparator model, in which memory representations form over time with exposure to the stimulus. As infants encounter a new stimulus, they try to match it to a memory representation; if a match is found, attention is inhibited, but if no match is found, attention remains engaged until the stimulus is sufficiently encoded to no longer appear novel. Rose and colleagues attributed both individual and developmental differences to similar processes (Rose et al., 2007). In particular, they identified processing/encoding speed and attention (as indexed by look duration and rates of switching between displays) as separable contributions to recognition memory in the visual paired comparison task. Similarly, encoding speed in habituation is an important individual and developmental difference (Colombo & Mitchell, 2009). Although encoding speed was the focus of most theories in infant visual memory, McCall (1994) proposed that inhibition might be an equal (and not necessarily independent) contribution to infants' looking behavior.

To formalize these processes of attention, encoding, and inhibition underlying looking behavior, Schöner and Thelen (2006) developed a simple model of performance in habituation tasks; in this model, two nodes built excitation and inhibition, respectively, with exposure to a stimulus. This model showed how individual and developmental differences could arise through the same mechanism by illustrating how performance differed between "fast" and "slow" habituators when tested in one type of habituation task, a violation of expectancy paradigm (e.g., Baillargeon, 1987). Perone and colleagues expanded this type of architecture to account for a broader range of infants' looking performance, including the shift from familiarity to novelty preferences in habituation (Perone & Spencer, 2013b) and visual paired comparison (Perone & Spencer, 2014), as well as capacity estimates from a variant of visual paired comparison, the change-preference task (described further below and in Chapter 2; Perone, Simmering, & Spencer, 2011).

These model implementations, along with similar connectionist accounts (e.g., Munakata, 1998; Westermann & Mareschal, 2004), point to the same brain maturation implicated in delayed response performance as the likely foundation for improving working memory processes underlying looking behavior. Both the Schöner and Thelen (2006) and Perone (Perone et al., 2011; Perone & Spencer, 2013b, 2014) models provide formalizations to show how changes in connectivity within such models can give rise to increases in encoding speed, attention, and inhibition—processes central to theories presented by Colombo and Mitchell (2009), McCall (1994), and Rose et al. (2007).

The previous section argued that working memory theories were difficult to "scale down" to earlier development because they are tied closely to the complex tasks they were designed to explain. A more promising approach might be to "scale up" theories of infant memory to account for later working memory development. A step in this direction is illustrated by the model Perone and colleagues have used to address changes in infant looking behavior. In addition to the increases in encoding speed, attention, and inhibition mentioned above, the strengthening connections within the model lead to memory representations that are more robust. Conceptual theories of development in reaching tasks posited more robust representations leading to improved performance; these parallels across explanations of development suggests that a single underlying developmental mechanism may be sufficient to explain a variety of behavioral changes (discussed further in Chapter 5; see Simmering, Schutte, & Spencer, 2008, for one example). Expanding this type of model could incorporate many of the conceptual explanations for working memory improvements within a single theoretical framework. This monograph aims to do this by starting with simpler tasks, as described in the following section.

VISUAL WORKING MEMORY CAPACITY AND DEVELOPMENT

The current monograph focuses on two tasks designed to measure visual working memory capacity in different age groups. Visual working memory provides a good starting point for expanding theories of development because it can be assessed beginning in infancy, unlike verbal working memory (which requires adequately developed language skills) or performance in complex tasks (which are difficult to use with children younger than 6 years; Simmering & Perone, 2013). Tasks assessing capacity estimates are the focus of this monograph because they are constrained to limit the use of other processes, as described further below.

The first task, change detection, was constructed to minimize verbal recoding or "chunking" items together, therefore providing a more reliable assessment of capacity limits in visual working memory (see Vogel, Woodman, & Luck, 2001, for a description of how the task was developed). This task can be used with children as young as 3 years of age with only minor modifications (Simmering, 2012). Figure 1 shows a standard change detection trial (e.g., Vogel et al., 2001). On each trial, a memory array is presented briefly followed by a short delay. Then, a test array appears in which either all of the objects match the memory array (no-change trials), or the feature(s) of one object changed to a new stimulus value (change trials). The participant reports whether the memory and test arrays were "same" or "different." Performance is typically near ceiling for arrays with small numbers of items (referred to as set size), and performance declines as set size increases. Capacity is estimated from this task by combining performance across change and no-change trials, with corrections for guessing, across set sizes (see formula in Chapter 3). Adults' capacity is typically estimated to be approximately three to five simple items (e.g., colored squares or oriented bars) in the change detection task (see Cowan, 2010, for review). Although the change detection task may seem more like a simple task than the complex tasks described above, Cowan, Fristoe, et al. (2006) and Rose et al. (2012) have shown correlations between

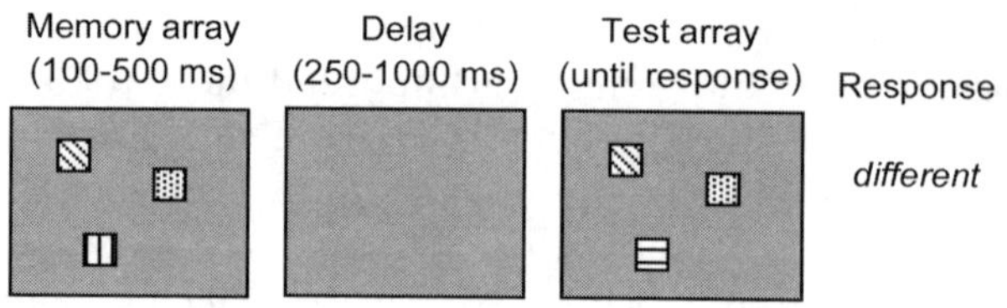

FIGURE 1.—Sample trial of the change detection task in set size three (not drawn to scale). Different patterns represent different colors.

this task and higher cognition, suggesting that it could tap the processes of interest when trying to explain fundamental cognitive skills.

To assess developmental changes in visual working memory capacity, the change detection task has been modified for use with children between the ages of 3 and 12 years by reducing the number of trials and extending the duration of the memory array (Cowan et al., 2005; Cowan, Fristoe, et al., 2006; Riggs, McTaggart, Simpson, & Freeman, 2006; Simmering, 2012). Figure 2 shows results across these studies, with estimates increasing from about two to five items during childhood. As this figure shows, capacity increases steadily across this age range (see Simmering, 2012, for discussion of differing estimates in 5-year-olds). Of the theories described in the working memory section above, only Cowan's embedded process model has been applied specifically to change detection performance. According to that perspective, the controlled nature of the change detection task leaves only increases in capacity (i.e., the scope of attention) to account for developmental improvements (Cowan et al., 2005; see also, Cowan, AuBuchon, Gilchrist, Ricker, & Saults, 2011). However, as noted above, this model does not include a specific mechanism by which capacity increases (Cowan, 2013). Riggs, Simpson, and Potts (2006) proposed that developmental changes in neural synchrony could account for this capacity increase (discussed further in Chapter 2).

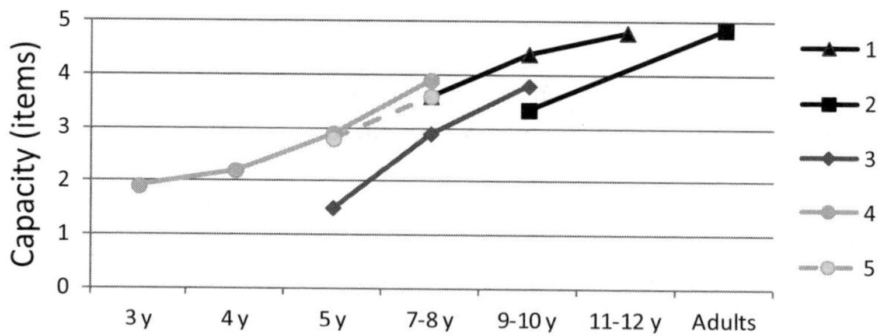

FIGURE 2.—Capacity estimates from the change detection task with children. References: 1 = Cowan et al. (2005), these estimates were approximated from figures, precise values were not reported in text; 2 = Cowan, Fristoe, et al. (2006); 3 = Riggs et al. (2006); 4 = Simmering (2012) "card" task; 5 = Simmering (2012) standard task.

20

To explore capacity changes during infancy, Ross-Sheehy, Oakes, and Luck (2003) combined features of the change detection task with the visual paired comparison task to develop the change-preference task. In this paradigm, arrays of colored squares, like those used in change detection tasks, were presented on two side-by-side displays and blinked on and off over the course of the trial. A schematic of this task is shown in Figure 3; in one display (determined randomly across trials), a single color within the array changed following each delay, approximating the change trials from the change detection task. The other display held the same set of colors following each delay, as in no-change trials from change detection.

Rather than requiring explicit "same"/"different" judgments as in the change detection task, the change-preference task relied on infants' general novelty bias, under the assumption that a novelty preference indicates memory for the items within the displays. By extension, if the number of items was beyond the infant's capacity, the infant would not be able to detect the difference across displays and should show no preference. As such, the amount of time the infant looked to each display was tabulated on each trial and change-preference scores were calculated as the proportion of time the infant looked at the change display. Mean change-preference scores were compared to chance (i.e., 0.5), and capacity was estimated as the highest set size in which mean change preference scores were above chance. Using this paradigm, Ross-Sheehy et al. (2003) found that 6-month-old infants only showed reliable change preferences for displays with one item each. By the age of 10 months, however, infants showed preferences when the set size (i.e.,

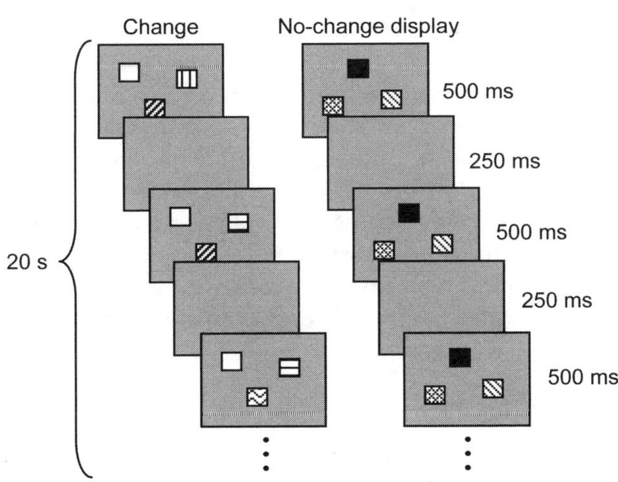

FIGURE 3.—Sample trial of the change-preference task in set size three (not drawn to scale). Different patterns represent different colors.

number of objects in each array) was as high as four items. These findings suggest that between the ages of 6 and 10 months, infants' visual working memory capacity increases rapidly to adult-like levels.

It is important to note that Ross-Sheehy et al. (2003) did not definitively argue that infants' preferences reflected changes in capacity as measured in the change detection task. They note that infants could use a variety of processes to support performance in this task, although they made efforts in the task design to isolate short-term memory (the term they preferred). Ross-Sheehy et al. suggested that even if the task does not measure "absolute" capacity, it shows increases in "relative" capacity, that is, in the context of the looking task. Although these authors were careful to avoid strong claims about exactly how capacity compared across tasks, this subtle distinction has not been preserved in the literature more generally (e.g., Blaser & Kaldy, 2010; Cowan, 2007; Cowan, Fristoe, et al., 2006; Feigenson, 2007; Oakes, Messenger, Ross-Sheehy, & Luck, 2009; Riggs et al., 2006). For the purposes of this monograph, the characterization of the change-preference and change detection tasks as both measuring capacity follows the general literature and should not be considered a representation of the view presented in the original study by Ross-Sheehy et al. Furthermore, even if the change-preference task is considered to measure "relative" capacity or more general properties of visual working memory, it is worth investigating how the mechanism underlying developmental improvements in this task related to performance and development in the change detection task.

Comparing studies with children (shown in Figure 2) to results from the infant task is not straightforward: why is there an apparent discrepancy in capacity estimates over development, with 10-month-olds' capacity estimated at four items in the change-preference task, but 3-year-olds showing capacity estimates of less than two items in change detection? Does this suggest the tasks are tapping different underlying cognitive systems and/or types of capacity, or could this pattern of results across tasks and development emerge through common processes? Addressing these questions requires under-standing both the real-time processes involved in performing these tasks, and the developmental processes that could explain capacity increases. To this end, Chapter 2 reviews these tasks and related theories in depth, then presents a new theoretical account of performance across tasks and development. The following section provides a brief overview of this new theory.

PROPOSING A NEW THEORY OF VISUAL WORKING MEMORY CAPACITY DEVELOPMENT

The theory put forth in this monograph builds on components of previous theories to strive toward a comprehensive explanation of performance across tasks and development. A central goal within this theoretical perspective is to understand the link between representations and behavior—what are the processes that operate in different lab tasks, and how do these relate to behavior beyond the lab? By establishing a specific account of the real-time processes by which visual working memory supports behavior, this theory can provide leverage on the questions of how visual working memory develops as well as how it relates to other cognitive skills. This monograph illustrates this theoretical account by bringing together the change-preference and change detection tasks within a single framework and showing how the same cognitive processes, as implemented in a processed-based model of visual working memory, can give rise to diverging capacity estimates across tasks.

As reviewed in the previous sections, a number of different explanations have been proposed to account separately for performance in complex tasks, infant looking paradigms, and assessments of visual working memory capacity. In particular, processing speed has been identified in both complex task performance and infant looking performance, although the sense of processing differs (i.e., performing operations vs. encoding, respectively). Increasing capacity was included in theories of both complex tasks and visual working memory capacity tasks. Within each of these domains, some theorists proposed that attention contributes to individual and/or developmental differences. Using a framework similar to Perone and colleagues' (Perone et al., 2011; Perone & Spencer, 2013b, 2014; Simmering & Perone, 2013), my theoretical perspective is designed to integrate these types of changes into a single account. In particular, within this computational framework, changes in the strength of connections between nodes lead to emergent consequences for encoding speed, looking behavior, capacity, and comparison between memory representations and perceptual inputs.

SUMMARY

Working memory is a vital cognitive skill that underlies performance in a broad range of everyday tasks. Working memory abilities correlate reliably with higher cognitive functions such as reasoning and intelligence, both concurrently and longitudinally. Understanding how working memory develops and relates to other cognitive skills requires bringing together research and theories across sub-domains that are currently evolving separately. Complex tasks that require both processing and storage are the standard assessment of working memory in older children and adults, and theories of developmental changes in working memory have been tailored to explaining these tasks. Infant studies cannot employ such complex tasks, resulting in a line of studies and theories that do not connect infants' developmental improvements in visual memory with the construct of working memory in later childhood and adults. As a bridge between these disconnected research areas, this monograph focuses on the change-preference and change detection tasks to develop a more general theory, with a goal of identifying common processes across tasks and development.

The next chapter presents the *cognitive dynamics* theory, implemented in a dynamic neural field model, to explain previous findings using these tasks and generate novel predictions for how these tasks relate within the same participants over development. Simulations illustrate how the model's performance can explain not only why capacity estimates differ, but also how performance relates across tasks and what developmental changes could explain improvements in both tasks. These model simulations led to a set of three specific behavioral predictions, tested empirically in Chapter 3 by comparing performance of the same participants across the change-preference and change detection tasks. In Chapter 4, I test a fourth prediction—that this modeling framework can quantitatively capture these differences in capacity estimates across tasks and development using an existing developmental mechanism, the strengthening of excitatory and inhibitory connections in the model. Chapter 5 outlines remaining challenges and questions raised by these results, and concludes by discussing these findings within the context of the broader literature on working memory development.

II. THE COGNITIVE DYNAMICS THEORY OF VISUAL WORKING MEMORY

Vanessa R. Simmering

This article is part of the issue "Working Memory Capacity in Context: Modeling Dynamic Processes of Behavior, Memory, and Development," Simmering, Vanessa (Issue Author). For a full listing of articles in this issue, see: http://onlinelibrary.wiley.com/doi/10.1111/mono.v81.3/issuetoc.

The goal of this monograph is to advance a theory of working memory development that brings together concepts from prior theories to provide a more comprehensive account of behavior across tasks and age groups. As reviewed in Chapter 1, research on working memory in children and adults is largely disconnected from research on working memory during infancy. The current monograph focuses on two tasks—the change detection and change-preference tasks—as a way to bridge these literatures. This chapter begins by describing the theoretical accounts of development in these two tasks, then presents a new theory that focuses on cognitive dynamics as a way to understand capacity limits and development. This chapter describes the theory in detail as it is implemented in a formal model.

Computational models provide an important tool in evaluating possible cognitive processes in common across tasks and developmental periods (Simmering et al., 2008). Implementing multiple tasks within a single computational framework imposes a level of specificity that can reveal gaps in conceptual theories of behavior and development. The current model is designed to test whether the different cognitive mechanisms that have been proposed to account for developmental changes in working memory across

Corresponding author: Vanessa R. Simmering, 1202 W. Johnson St., Madison, WI 53706; email: simmering@wisc.edu

DOI: 10.1111/mono.12250

domains might be explained through a common underlying source. Furthermore, the specific formalization presented here is based on models of neural population dynamics, which may provide a more direct link between behavioral, cognitive, and neural development in the future.

THEORIES OF DEVELOPMENT IN THE CHANGE DETECTION AND CHANGE-PREFERENCE TASKS

Chapter 1 introduced two methods for assessing visual working memory capacity: the change detection task, which has been used with children as young as 3 years through adults, and the change-preference task, which has been used with infants between 4 and 12 months of age. Studies using the change detection task have shown a gradual increase in capacity estimates from about two items at 3 years, up to four to five items by 12 years (Cowan et al., 2005; Cowan, Fristoe et al., 2006; Riggs et al., 2006; Simmering, 2012). As reviewed briefly in Chapter 1, most theories attribute this developmental improvement to an increase in the number of items that can be held in visual working memory at one time (Cowan et al., 2005, 2011; Riggs et al., 2006). However, Cowan (2013) noted that the mechanism by which capacity increases is still unknown.

Riggs, Simpson, and Potts (2011) proposed that capacity may increase through improvements in neural synchrony. In particular, they cite Vogel et al.'s (2001) description of the Raffone and Wolters (2001) model that attributes the limited number of items that can be held in memory to a limitation in the temporal resolution of synchronous neural firing. This model has been proposed to account for an object-based, rather than feature-based, capacity limit (e.g., adults can remember four multi-feature objects as robustly as they remember four single-feature objects, rather than features adding up across objects to exceed capacity; Luck & Vogel, 1997), but the same rationale can be applied to remembering single-feature objects. The speed of firing could increase developmentally, allowing more items to be represented simultaneously.

Although both of these developmental explanations focus on the number of items held in memory, theoretical accounts on the nature of capacity limits in the adult literature vary in the degree to which they emphasize the number of items (typically referred to as "slot" models) or the resolution of items in memory. From a resource perspective, Bays and Husain (2008) argued that adults can hold an unlimited number of items in memory, but as the number of representations increases their resolution decreases proportionally. As such, performance on high set size trials is limited due to the poor resolution of items, not a failure to encode some items. Two studies have shown that resolution improves developmentally during the same period that capacity increases (Burnett Heyes, Zokaei, van der Staaij, Bays, & Husain, 2012; Simmering & Patterson, 2012). Burnett Heyes et al. (2012) attribute this increase in resolution to "sharpening" neural representation; this is similar to the mechanism implemented in the current model (discussed further with respect to resolution in Chapter 5; see also Simmering & Miller, 2016; Simmering & Patterson, 2012).

The primary task used to assess capacity limits during infancy, the change-preference task, presents a seemingly inconsistent developmental trajectory. Results from this task suggest that capacity increases rapidly from one to four items between 6 and 10 months of age. In particular, capacity in 6-month-old infants was estimated to be only a single item, with no preference when tested in set size two or three (Oakes et al., 2009; Oakes, Ross-Sheehy, & Luck, 2006; Ross-Sheehy et al., 2003). When tested on variants of this task (described further below) 7.5-month-old infants' capacity was estimated to be at least three items (the highest set size tested with that age group; Oakes et al., 2006, 2009). In the original version of the task, 10-month-olds preferred the changing display in set size four but not six (Ross-Sheehy et al., 2003). Thus, across these studies, capacity increased from one to at least three items between 6 and 7.5 months, and to about four items at 10 months.

What could account for these seemingly inconsistent trajectories across tasks and development? Cowan and colleagues argued that we should assume developmental change in capacity is truly monotonic, and the discrepancy between infant and child results arose from underestimation of capacity in children and/or overestimation in infants (Cowan, Morey, Chen, Gilchrist, & Saults, 2008). Simmering (2012) tested whether the change detection task was underestimating capacity by modifying the task to be easier for young children. Even with these modifications, capacity estimates from change detection were lower for 3- to 7-year-olds than for infants in the change-preferences task (see Figure 2). Cowan et al. (2008 see also, Cowan, 2007) proposed that the infant task could overestimate capacity if memory for only a subset of items in the array was sufficient to drive a change preference. Further studies with infants, however, suggested this was unlikely. In particular, Oakes et al. (2009) tested 6-month-olds in the change-preference task, but replaced all three items in the change display with new colors after each delay. If memory for a single item within the array is sufficient to drive a change preference, young infants should reliably prefer this "all change" display. This was not the case: 6-month-olds showed no preference, suggesting that memory for a single item within the multi-item displays was not sufficient to drive a robust change preference (but see Perone et al., 2011, and discussion below for evidence that robust change-preferences do not require all items be held in memory).

Cowan (2007) also proposed that the discrepant estimates across tasks could be due to different attentional demands, with the change detection task being more demanding than the change-preference task. Support for this interpretation depends on how "attentional demands" are defined. In the change detection task, participants must attend to the display during specific windows of time within each trial to encode (during the memory array) and compare (during the test array) the items. By contrast, the change-preference task requires a participant to attend to two displays repeatedly across a 20-s test trial, with multiple opportunities to encode and compare items, then notice that items in one display change while items in the other display remain the same. Although these tasks arguably capture different notions of attention, it is not straightforward to determine a priori which would be more demanding.

As another explanation for the discrepancy between change detection and change-preference results, Riggs et al. (2006) suggested that the infant task either measures an aspect of visual working memory that does not scale with capacity, or measures a more passive type of memory. This suggestion is similar to competence-performance arguments proposed in other areas of cognitive development, suggesting that looking tasks reveal the underlying "competence," while other response types are more demanding and may limit performance (e.g., Baillargeon & Graber, 1988). Although this type of argument may be intuitively appealing, such arguments are essentially unfalsifiable (see Thelen & Smith, 1994, for further discussion), and may be explained through more specific accounts of how performance relates to underlying cognitive processes (e.g., Munakata et al., 1997; Samuelson, Schutte, & Horst, 2009).

Oakes and colleagues suggested that developmental changes in infants' performance in the change-preference task depends primarily on their ability to individuate items by binding the colors to locations in the task space (Oakes et al., 2006, 2009). In addition to the "all change" version described above (Oakes et al., 2009), 6-month-olds showed no preference in a condition in which the change display included the same three colors swapping positions within the display after each delay (Oakes et al., 2006). In both cases, however, 7.5-month-old infants exhibited reliable preferences for the change displays (Oakes et al., 2006, 2009). In these two conditions, the three items on the no-change display remained the same over delays, while all of the items on the change display change with each blink (either to new colors or to new color-location bindings). Oakes and colleagues argued that young infants failed to detect these changes because they cannot bind colors to locations— essentially, this lack of binding means that the three colors on the no-change display appeared to be changing because infants are unable to make the appropriate comparison to memory (i.e., without remembering which color was where, it is impossible to determine whether the colors are changing locations). Although this binding explanation could account for infants' performance across conditions in the change-preference task, Oakes and colleagues (2006, 2009) have not specified what developmental mechanism

28

underlies the emergence of color-location binding between 6 and 7.5 months, beyond noting that brain areas related to feature binding in adults undergo significant developmental change during this period.

Simulations by Perone et al. (2011) provided an alternative explanation for development in the change-preference task. Perone et al. argued that the processes of memory formation and comparison, combined with the dynamics of looking, could explain how preferences arise in the change-preference task (as well as other visual-paired comparison and habituation tasks; Perone & Spencer, 2013a,b, 2014). In this account, developmental improvements arose from changes in the robustness of these underlying processes (through strengthening connectivity within the model; described further below). Using this approach, Perone et al. simulated performance by younger (6 months) and older (7.5 to 10 months) infants to capture three empirical findings: (i) developmental increases in capacity in the standard task (cf. Ross-Sheehy et al., 2003, Experiments 1 and 3); (ii) young infants' preferences at higher set sizes in a non-memory version of the task (i.e., with no delays; cf. Ross-Sheehy et al., 2003, Experiment 4); and (iii) developmental change in the "all change" condition (cf. Oakes et al., 2009). These simulations suggested that young infants' lack of preference in both the standard and "all change" conditions arose through weak memory representations of the colors within the no-change display. In some ways, this is similar to Oakes and colleagues' explanation: both accounts attribute young infants' failure to inadequate memory of the no-change display. Oakes and colleagues suggest this is because young infants cannot individuate multiple items in memory due to inadequate color-location binding. By contrast, the Perone et al. model did not represent the locations of specific items within the displays (only which display they were on), indicating that color-location binding is not necessary for older infants to show a preference in the "all change" condition. Rather, changes in the robustness or stability of memory processes underlying the memory of multiple colors were sufficient to explain both younger and older infants' performance across conditions (Perone et al., 2011). Indeed, the young infant model could hold multiple items in memory, just not robustly enough to support a preference over the course of a trial. Furthermore, because the no-delay version did not require maintenance of items in the absence of input, younger infants could exhibit a robust preference in set sizes two and three, as the continued input provided more support for items in memory (discussed further in Chapter 5).

Could the developmental mechanism underlying improvements in infants' performance in the change-preference task also account for capacity increases in change detection? The current monograph uses two existing models as a starting point to test this possibility: the Perone et al. (2011) model that can explain development in the change-preference task, and a model using a similar architecture developed to explain adults' capacity limits in the change detection task (Johnson, Simmering, & Buss, 2014). As described in the section that follows, the Johnson et al. model provides an alternative to "slot" and "resource" explanations of capacity limits in adults. The current implementation of this model tests whether it can also account for developmental improvements in change detection using the type of mechanism in Perone et al.'s model. This developmental mechanism has successfully accounted for a number of phenomena in infant visual memory beyond capacity (e.g., Perone & Spencer, 2013b, 2014), and a similar modeling framework and developmental mechanism has accounted for spatial cognitive development from 2 to 6 years and into adulthood (e.g., Simmering et al., 2008).

The following section explains the current theoretical perspective, which emphasizes the importance of understanding cognitive dynamics, and the modeling framework in which this theory is implemented. Sample simulations demonstrate how the model performs both the change detection and change-preference tasks. Implementing a developmental change similar to Perone et al.'s (2011) in the model illustrates a collection of consequences referred to as real-time stability. Model simulations of both tasks with "child" and "adult" parameters lead to three specific empirical predictions, as well as a computational prediction, tested in the following chapters.

A NEW THEORY OF VISUAL WORKING MEMORY CAPACITY DEVELOPMENT: COGNITIVE DYNAMICS AND REAL-TIME STABILITY

In this section, I describe the model implementation of my theoretical perspective to illustrate key aspects of the theory. In particular, model simulations show how both the formation of memory representations and the influence of memory on behavior differs between the change detection and change-preference tasks due to the different task structures. These results illustrate the importance of *cognitive dynamics*, that is, how cognition functions within different task contexts (Simmering & Perone, 2013). Furthermore, simulations of development show that strengthening the connections that underlie these cognitive processes in the model increases the *real-time stability* of the memory system. In contrast to long-term notions of developmental stability in which early behavior predicts later behavior, real-time stability refers to how robustly the memory system functions in the moment of a behavioral task (see Simmering & Perone, 2013, for related discussion). The term real-time stability denotes a collection of consequences that arise from strengthening connectivity (described further in Chapters 4 and 5): faster encoding speeds; more accurate representation of stimuli; decreased interference and decay during maintenance; increased capacity; more reliable use of representation in service of different behaviors; and less influence of task context.

Before reviewing the model implementation in detail, it is important to note the specific formalization presented here is only a tool for testing the concepts embodied in the cognitive dynamics account. Other types of computational models could potentially produce the same patterns of performance by implementing similar characteristics. One goal in using any computational model is to achieve a level of specificity necessary to generate and test behavioral predictions. Chapter 5 includes discussions of the implications of this model implementation for other models and theories of working memory development.

Formalization of Cognitive Dynamics in a Computational Model

The cognitive dynamics theory and dynamic neural field model implementation (referred to as "the dynamic model" in the current monograph for simplicity) that are central to this monograph fall within the broader perspective of dynamic systems theory. A primary emphasis of dynamic systems theory is that behavior is not rigidly preprogramed; rather, behavior is emergent, organized in the moment in response to the demands of the task, the details of the environment, and the history of the organism (Thelen & Smith, 1994). Furthermore, theorists within this approach across domains have argued that knowledge cannot be dissociated from process (e.g., McMurray, Horst, & Samuelson, 2012; Schöner & Thelen, 2006; Smith, Colunga, & Yoshida, 2010; Smith, Thelen, Titzer, & McLin, 1999; Spencer, Clearfield, et al., 2006). A dynamic systems approach brings a new perspective to the question of the development of visual working memory because many previous theories have focused mostly on the whether and how information is represented (e.g., capacity, Cowan, 2013; Oakes et al., 2006, 2009; Riggs et al., 2006, 2011, or precision of memory, Burnett Heyes et al., 2012), not how that information is used to support behavior across multiple task contexts (see Simmering & Perone, 2013, for further discussion).

Within dynamic systems theory, the focus is on how behavior emerges from multiple underlying causes, encouraging researchers to explore the various contributions to behavior, and to evaluate the robustness of behavior relative to the circumstances required to support them. This approach highlights the influence of task details, and seeks to specify the processes and mechanisms by which such details should affect behavior (e.g., Schutte, Simmering, & Ortmann, 2011). Consistent with this dynamic systems view, a primary goal of the cognitive dynamics theory presented here is to reunite cognition and behavior by explicitly modeling the connection between underlying memory processes and the overt behavioral responses generated in specific memory tasks. The current project focuses on two tasks designed to assess visual working memory capacity, but ultimately this approach can be expanded to incorporate more tasks and domains (as discussed in Chapter 5).

The dynamic model presented here was derived from the Dynamic Field Theory framework (see Schöner, Spencer, & the DFT Research Group, 2015, for review).[i] Amari (1977) first proposed the class of dynamic neural field models to capture the real-time dynamics of neural activation in visual cortex.[ii] Specific values along metric dimensions are represented as localized peaks of activation (also called "bumps" in biophysical models; see, e.g., Edin et al., 2009; Wei, Wang, & Wang, 2012) within dynamic neural fields. Figure 4 shows a simple two-layer model architecture for illustration. In this architecture, the top layer consists of a single field of excitatory nodes, which are reciprocally coupled to the bottom layer of inhibitory nodes. Along the *x*-dimension in this figure is the continuous dimension to which both fields of nodes are "tuned" (e.g., color or space). Specifically, nodes that respond preferentially to similar values along this dimension in the excitatory field engage in locally excitatory connections (see solid-curved arrow in Figure 4), as well as projecting excitation to similarly tuned nodes in the inhibitory field. These inhibitory nodes, in turn, project broad lateral inhibition back to the excitatory field (see dashed arrows in Figure 4). Critically, the spread of inhibitory connections is wider than the spread of excitatory connections, which keeps excitation from propagating throughout the excitatory field.

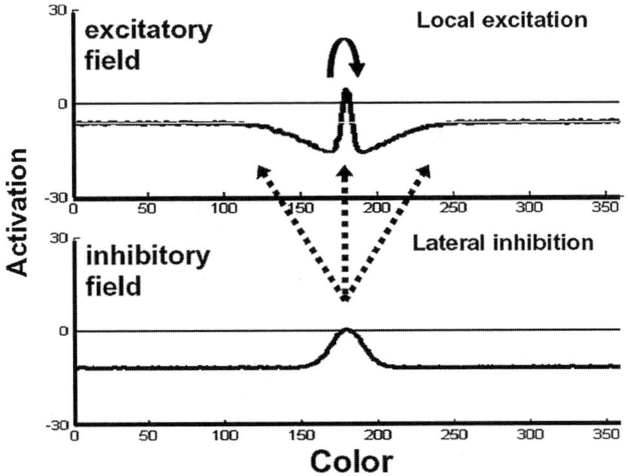

FIGURE 4.—A two-layer dynamic neural field model consisting of a single layer of color-selective excitatory nodes (top layer) reciprocally coupled to a similarly tuned layer of inhibitory nodes (bottom layer). Nodes coding for similar values along the metric dimension in the excitatory field engage in locally excitatory interactions (curved solid arrow), and transmit excitatory activation to the inhibitory layer (not shown). Nodes in the inhibitory layer transmit broad lateral inhibition back to the excitatory field (dashed arrows), which keeps activation localized within a "peak" in the excitatory field. Thick black lines within each field show the activation level across the metric color dimension, with thin black lines indicating the threshold (0) for interactions among nodes.

Through this local excitation-lateral inhibition profile of connectivity, activation in the excitatory field is able to form into localized peaks.

These peaks of activation have characteristics that can be specifically applied to model different cognitive processes. In particular, peaks may exist in an input-driven or *self-stabilizing* state, in which peaks remain active only as long as the input is present; once input is removed, however, activation falls back to the resting state (see Supplementary Video 1). This state can capture perceptual processes that serve to detect items in the environment, yet return to a resting state after the input is removed. Note that this state emerges when local excitatory connections are weak relative to lateral inhibitory connections. If local excitation is strengthened, fields operate in a *self-sustaining* state, in which peaks of activation remain above-threshold (i.e., above zero) even after input has been removed (see Supplementary Video 2). This self-sustaining state is the form of working memory that is central to the framework presented here.

This form of working memory—self-sustaining peaks of activation within a dynamic field—highlights a central characteristic of the cognitive dynamics theory: an emphasis on *stability*. Stability is necessary for memory representations to be used in service of behavior or other cognitive tasks. At its most basic level, stability means resistance to change. In the context of behavior, stability refers to the ability to repeatedly produce approximately the same behavior at different times. Reliably repeated behavioral forms are not static: for example, the ways in which one's hand moves to sign one's name are not identical across repetitions. However, stability in the organization of the muscles in the hand produces signatures that are similar enough across repetitions to differentiate the true signature from a forgery.

In the context of cognition, this notion of stability can be applied to the repeated use of a cognitive process to support behavior. For example, in spatial recall, participants show variability in their memory for the same location when it is tested throughout an experimental session (e.g., Spencer & Hund, 2002)—the same memory processes produce approximately the same outcome over repetitions (recall of the location), but this memory is not static (rather, it varies across trials). This notion of stability is referred to here as *real-time stability* to emphasize the organization of behavior in the moment of the task; as discussed further below and in Chapter 4, changes in real-time stability play an important role in the cognitive dynamics account of development.

The two-layer model shown in Figure 4 can operate in a perceptual state (with the formation of self-stabilizing peaks as shown in Supplementary Video 1) or a working memory state (with the formation and maintenance of self-sustaining peaks as shown in Supplementary Video 2). Taken separately, these states capture important components of visual working memory tasks: detecting inputs in the environment and maintaining specific information over the course of brief delays. To perform the change detection and change-preference tasks, however, these processes must be integrated. Such integration is achieved by combining two of these two-layer architectures—one with connectivity tuned to a perceptual state and one tuned to a working memory state—into a single three-layer architecture by pairing two excitatory fields with a single, shared inhibitory field, shown in Figure 5 (see Johnson & Simmering, 2015, for full description). This three-layer architecture combines perceptual and working memory processes to perform a third critical process in visual working memory: comparison.

The simulation shown in Figure 5 illustrates this comparison process in the three-layer architecture (see Appendix for details on the architecture and parameters). In this simulation, three items have been encoded in the working memory field (see peaks in bottom layer of Figure 5). Excitation associated with these peaks projects from the working memory field to similarly tuned nodes in the inhibitory field (see bumps in the middle layer of Figure 5). These nodes, in turn, project inhibition to similarly tuned nodes in both excitatory fields; local excitation in the working memory field is strong enough for the three peaks to sustain, but this inhibition suppresses further perceptual processing of the specific items that are held in memory (see top layer of Figure 5). Through this shared inhibition, detection of new items is driven by above-threshold activation in the perceptual field: input corresponding to a new color (i.e., one not held in memory) produces a self-stabilized peak in the perceptual field (see circle in Figure 5). As described

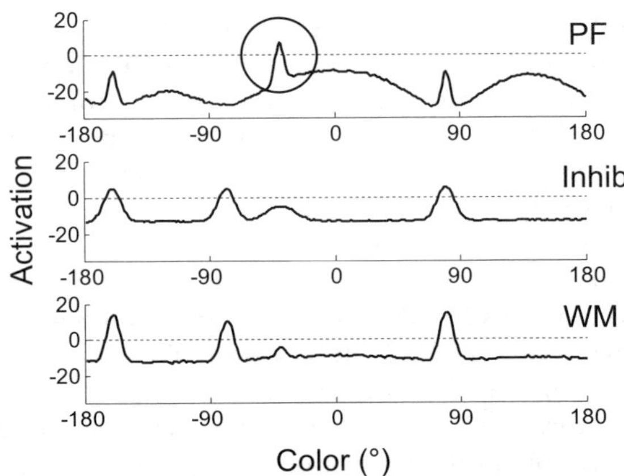

Figure 5.—The three-layer dynamic neural field architecture that forms the foundation of visual working memory processes in the cognitive dynamics theory. As in Figure 4, each layer is comprised of nodes selectively tuned to represent a continuous color dimension. Two excitatory layers perform perceptual (top layer; PF, perceptual field) and working memory (bottom layer; WM, working memory field) processes, while activation is mediated by a shared inhibitory field (middle layer; Inhib). This figure shows three self-sustaining peaks of activation within the working memory field, and a self-stabilized peak in the perceptual field. Axes for each field are as in Figure 4. See text for further details and interpretation.

further in the sections below, this activation in the perceptual field guides task-relevant behavior.

According to the cognitive dynamics account, performance in both change detection and change-preference tasks depends on the same basic processes of encoding, maintenance, and comparison embodied in the three-layer architecture. However, these processes are not sufficient to perform these tasks. The change detection task requires an explicit "same" or "different" judgment on each trial, and the change-preference task requires looking back and forth between displays. Furthermore, trials in the change-preference task are relatively extended in time (20 s compared to the 1–2 s trials in change detection), which brings long-term memory processes to bear on performance. Thus, in addition to the three-layer architecture, the dynamic model includes two Hebbian fields (to incorporate long-term memory) as well as a fixation system and a "same"/"different" response system.

The full model architecture used for this monograph is shown in Figure 6 (see Appendix for equations). The model consists of an excitatory perceptual

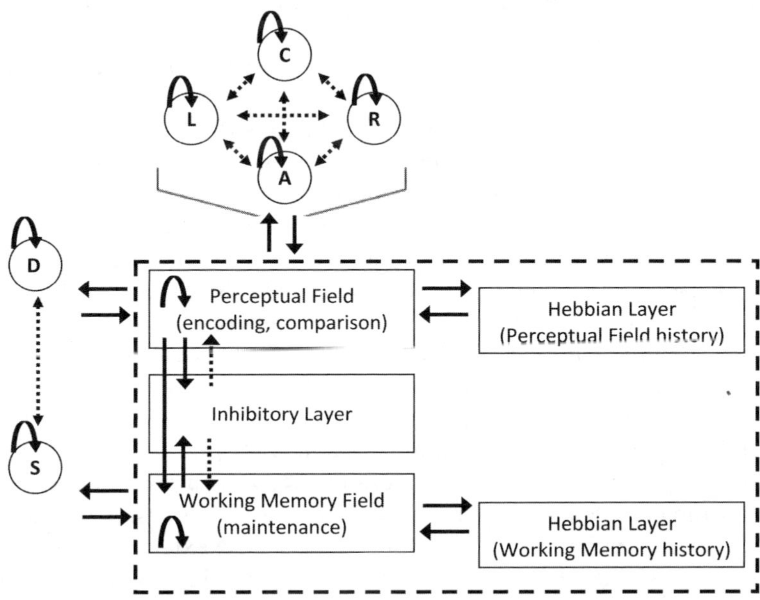

FIGURE 6.—The dynamic model used to simulate performance in the change detection and change-preference tasks. Shown within the dashed box, the five-layer dynamic neural field architecture consists of an excitatory perceptual field, an inhibitory layer, and an excitatory working memory field, with Hebbian layers connected to both excitatory fields. This architecture is connected to a fixation system (top) with nodes corresponding to looks to center (C), left (L), right (R), and away (A) locations within the task space, as well as a response system (left) with nodes corresponding to different (D) and same (S) decisions. Arrows indicate excitatory (solid) and inhibitory (dotted) projections between layers or nodes.

field, an inhibitory field, and an excitatory working memory field; the two excitatory fields are also reciprocally coupled to Hebbian fields. Each field consists of a collection of nodes tuned to represent a 360° color space. These fields pass excitation and inhibition as indicated by solid and dashed arrows, respectively, to capture the local excitation and lateral inhibitory connections described above. As activation builds in the perceptual or working memory field, traces of activation are laid down at associated sites in the respective Hebbian fields. These traces feed back onto the perceptual and working memory field, biasing the model to build peaks of activation at feature values that were activated before, leading to a form of long-term memory. Together, these five fields provide the perceptual, working memory, and long-term memory processes necessary to encode, maintain, and compare items presented over time in visual working memory tasks. To generate the behaviors relevant to the change detection and change-preference tasks, two simple behavioral systems are coupled to this system: a "same"/"different" responses system sends and receives activation from the perceptual and working memory fields; and a fixation system sends and receives activation from the perceptual field. How these systems function is described below in the context of the specific tasks.

Using this model as a formalization of the concepts in the cognitive dynamics theory, I address two key questions raised in Chapter 1: what *real-time processes* support performance in the change detection and change-preference tasks, and what *developmental processes* underlie visual working memory capacity increases? Similar models within the Dynamic Field Theory framework have been used to account for developmental changes in spatial cognition with a simple developmental mechanism, the spatial precision hypothesis (see Simmering & Schutte, 2015, for review).[iii] According to this hypothesis, connections within and between layers of the model strengthen over development. The current goal is to explore whether similar changes in visual working memory processes could account for capacity increases in both the change detection and change-preference tasks through increases in real-time stability. Testing this real-time stability hypothesis first requires understanding the processes that operate within each trial in the change detection and change-preference tasks. To this end, the following two sections explain how this dynamic model performs each task. Next, the final section of this chapter describes the consequences of strengthening connectivity within the model in the context of these tasks, leading to four specific predictions regarding how performance relates across tasks over development.

Change Detection Performance

To model performance in the change detection task, the necessary cognitive processes must first be identified. Recall the task design from

Chapter 1: each trial in the change detection task begins with a brief presentation (100–500 ms) of a memory array that includes a small number of colored squares to be *encoded*. After a short delay (250–1000 ms) during which colors must be *maintained* in memory, a test array is presented in which either all of the colors match the memory array (no-change trials) or one color has changed to a new color value (change trials). The participant's task is to *compare* the test array to the items held in memory and *respond* "same" or "different." Capacity is estimated from the number of correct responses on each trial type (using a formula described in Chapter 3).

The general processes of encoding, maintenance, and comparison were described above and illustrated in Figure 5, leaving only the response to be explained. As shown in Figure 6, nodes representing "same" and "different" responses are coupled to the working memory and perceptual fields, respectively. As such, activation from items (i.e., self-sustaining peaks) held in the working memory field supports a "same" response, while activation from the detection of new items (i.e., self-stabilized peaks) in the perceptual field drives a "different" response. Activation to these nodes is controlled by a "gating" node that autonomously controls the projection of activation from the excitatory fields to the response nodes; this prevents a response from being generated at the incorrect time in the trial (i.e., during presentation of the memory array). Once activation reaches the response nodes, they compete in a "winner-take-all" fashion such that only one node achieves above-threshold activation, thereby generating a discrete response on each trial.

Figure 7 shows activation within the three-layer architecture of the dynamic model during critical points during two trials to illustrate these processes. Although these figure panels could be construed as separate "stages" in the task, patterns of activation in the dynamic model evolve continuously throughout the trial. The stage-like character of performance arises through the timing of task events, rather than from different processes across stages. First, at the end of the memory array presentation, the three colors from the memory array have been encoded into the working memory field (Figure 7A). Next, these peaks were maintained throughout the delay, with shared inhibition producing troughs in the perceptual field at the same color values (Figure 7B). For a no-change trial, the same three colors were presented in the test array, which produced a slight increase in activation within the working memory field, but no above-threshold activation in the perceptual field due to the inhibitory troughs (Figure 7C). As such, activation from the working memory field projected to the "same" response node, leading to a correct response (Figure 7D). For a change trial, one color in the test array was new, leading to above-threshold activation in the perceptual field at this color value (Figure 7E). This activation projected to the "different" response node, leading to a correct response (Figure 7F).

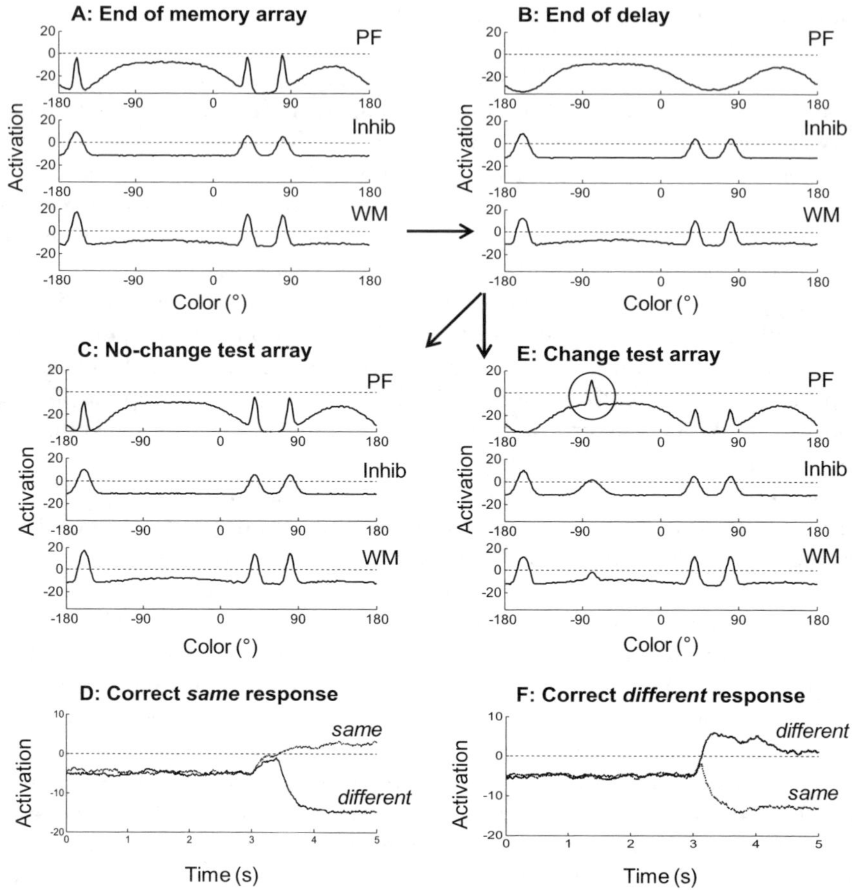

FIGURE 7.—Simulations of the dynamic neural field model performing set size three trials in the change detection task. Time-slices through the three-layer architecture are shown at the end of the memory array presentation (A), the end of the delay (B), and when the response is generated for a "correct rejection" trial (C) and "hit" trial (D), with corresponding activation of the response nodes (E and F). The threshold (zero) for interactions among nodes is shown with a dotted line in all panels. Axes for each field in are as in Figure 4; axes for response nodes show time within the trial on the *x*-axis and activation on the *y*-axis. PF, perceptual field; Inhib, inhibitory field; WM, working memory field.

How does this characterization of visual working memory compare to the "slot" and "resource" accounts that currently dominate the adult literature? As explained in depth by Johnson et al. (2014), this dynamic model encompasses components of these alternative accounts, but it is not a hybrid account. One of the key contrasts between these perspectives is in the proposed source of errors within the change detection task. From a slots perspective, errors primarily arise from items not being held in memory (i.e., capacity is lower than the number of items in the array), although a smaller number of errors may arise through guessing (e.g., Cowan, 2001; Luck & Vogel, 1997; Pashler, 1988) or attentional lapses (e.g., Rouder, Morey, Morey, & Cowan, 2011). From a resource perspective, on the other hand, errors are attributed to insufficient resolution only (e.g., Bays & Husain, 2008). By contrast, errors within the dynamic model can arise through any of the underlying processes: encoding, maintenance, comparison, or response (see Johnson et al., 2014, for further comparisons with slot and resource accounts).

Failures in encoding and maintenance are similar to the capacity limitations proposed by slot accounts, as the number of peaks that can be held in the working memory field at one time is limited. However, as illustrated by Johnson et al. (2014), two important contrasts with slots accounts arose through simulations of the dynamic model. First, the capacity limit in the dynamic model is not fixed: the number of peaks that were maintained across trials varied some due to noise, but also showed systematic influence of the stimuli that were presented. Their simulations showed that, at high set sizes, more similarity among the items within the memory array led to fewer peaks in the working memory field sustaining through the memory delay. The influence of similarity on memory illustrate why it is important to consider the dynamics of cognition—what is being remembered cannot be separated from the processes of remembering. In particular, the lateral inhibitory connections within the dynamic model produce a spread of inhibition surrounding each peak in the working memory field. When multiple peaks form near one another, their related inhibition combines, making it more difficult to form new peaks. Inhibition in the dynamic model also includes a global component that is independent of the peak locations; this global inhibition contributes to capacity limits by preventing new peaks from forming once activation has reached a certain point (see Johnson et al., 2014, for related simulations and behavioral analyses).

The second important contrast that arose through simulations of the dynamic model account of visual working memory is that the capacity estimate derived from behavioral responses was not equal to the number of peaks in the working memory field. Specifically, Johnson et al. (2014) calculated the mean number of peaks held on each trial in each set size for simulations of adults' performance in the change detection task. Their behavioral results showed a mean capacity estimate of 4.58 items, while their model simulations produced a mean capacity estimate of 4.64 items, providing a close fit to the behavioral data. Analysis of the peaks within the model, however, showed that, on average, 5.79 peaks were held in the working memory field during the delay on set size six trials. Johnson et al. also calculated the mean number of peaks separately for each response type (correct versus incorrect "same" and "different" responses) and found that the model nearly always held all of the items in the working memory field on "miss" trials (incorrect "same" responses) and sometimes had fewer peaks on "hit" trials (correct "different" responses), with the lowest number of peaks on "false alarm" trials (incorrect "different" responses). These simulation results highlight the importance of addressing more than just the nature of representations: how memory is used in service of behavior can produce errors even when all of the items are held in memory.

To illustrate capacity limits and potential sources of errors in the dynamic model, Figures 8 and 9 shows time slices through the three-layer architecture on incorrect trials. Figure 8 shows that all colors were represented in the working memory field at the end of the memory array (8A) and delay (8B). When the test array was presented (Figure 8C), though, the new color happened to be at a value that fell between two of the colors in memory (i.e., at 0° between −40° and 40°). Although activation pierced threshold in the perceptual field at this new color value, the lateral inhibition associated with the nearby peaks in the working memory field kept the overall level of activation too low to generate a correct "different" response (see Figure 8D). This "miss" error could be construed as a combined failure in

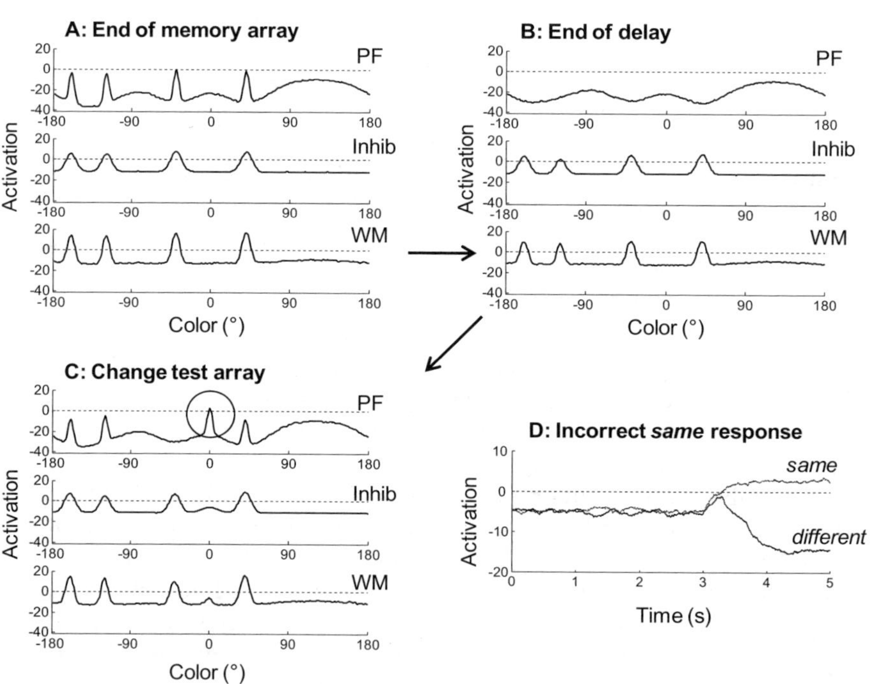

FIGURE 8.—A simulation of the dynamic neural field model performing a set size four "miss" trial in the change detection task. Panels and axes are as in Figure 7A–D.

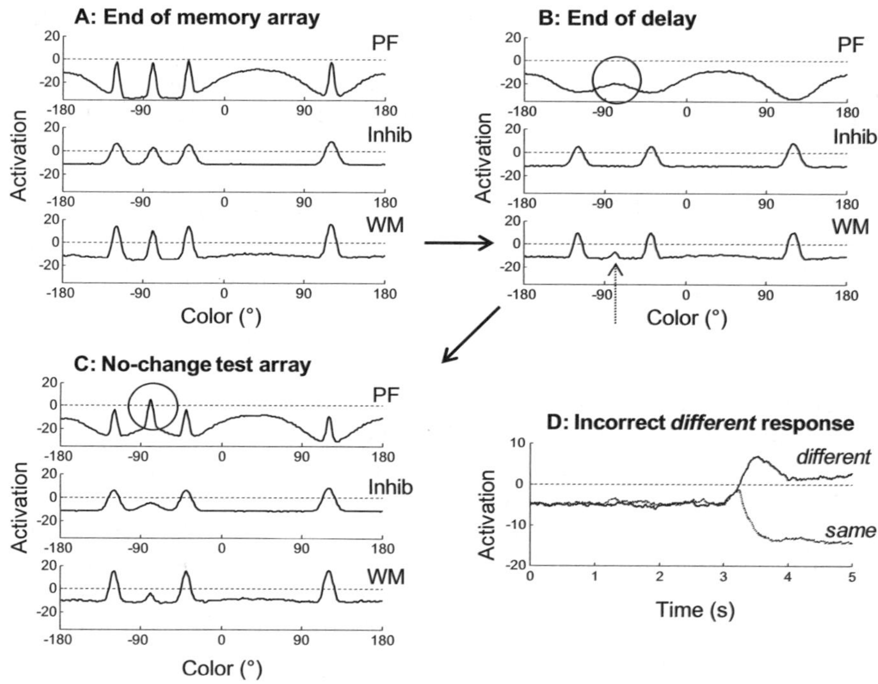

FIGURE 9.—A simulation of the dynamic neural field model performing a set size four "false alarm" trial in the change detection task. Panels and axes are as in Figure 7A–D.

comparison—the surrounding inhibition made it difficult for the new input to be detected—and response—a signal too weak to generate the correct response.

Figure 9 shows a simulation of the dynamic model producing a false alarm error on a set size four no-change trial. On this trial, the four items were initially encoded, with peaks forming in the working memory field (Figure 9A). However, during the delay, these peaks were not all maintained: the peak at 80° died out (dashed arrow in Figure 9B). Without this peak in the working memory field, there was no corresponding trough of inhibition in the perceptual field at this color value (circle in Figure 9B). When the test array was presented with the same four colors, an input-driven peak formed at −80° in the perceptual field (circle in Figure 9C), leading to a "different" response (Figure 9D). This false alarm error reflects a failure in maintenance of the items from the memory array, leading to a repeated item appearing novel at test.

As these simulations illustrate, formalizing the processes of encoding, maintenance, comparison, and response in a dynamic model can shed light onto capacity limits and errors in the change detection task. Through this formalization, Johnson et al. (2014) identified conceptual gaps in previous accounts of capacity limits, in that they did not address how representations were compared and how responses were generated in the task. This level of formalization also allows for testing whether and how the same processes could support performance in the change-preference task, how performance relates across tasks, and what developmental changes in these processes might capture the seemingly discrepant capacity estimates from the literature. The following sections consider these questions in turn.

Change-Preference Performance

The same general processes of encoding, maintenance, and comparison that were described above and illustrated in Figure 5 also support performance in the change-preference task. Recall the task design from Chapter 1: infants are presented with two displays, each of which contains a small number of colored squares. The colors are presented simultaneously for 500 ms, followed by a 250-ms delay in which both displays show a blank gray background, then a new 500-ms presentation of colors. On the no-change display, all of the colors remain the same following each delay. On the change display, one randomly selected color changes to a new color (not already present within the change display). Over the course of a 20-s trial, infants' looking to each of the displays is recorded, and a change preference score is calculated from the proportion of time spent looking at the change display (out of the total time looking to either display). For infants to show a preference they must *encode* the colors on a given display, *maintain* them in memory through the delay(s), then *compare* them to the new display to determine if any colors have changed. If no colors have changed, the familiarity of the display leads to *decreased looking* to the current display; if a color has changed, the novelty supports *continued looking* to the current display.

This characterization of the relation between memory formation, recognition, and looking is formalized in the dynamic model. In addition to the processes of encoding, maintenance, and comparison shown in Figure 5, the fixation system (shown in Figure 6) allows the model to use these processes to generate looking behavior. This system consists of four self-excitatory and mutually competitive nodes: one associated with the left (no-change) display, one for the right (change) display, one for the center (attention-getter) light, and one for looks away from the testing apparatus. Activation to this system comes from two sources. First, input to the left and right nodes represents the presence of stimuli on those displays, with weaker inputs to the center and away nodes, where no task-relevant information is presented. With this input, activation builds in parallel for all four nodes until

42

one of the nodes "wins" this mutual competition by entering a stable "on" state (i.e., above zero activation). Above-threshold activation of a fixation node represents the related fixation within the task (i.e., the left display, right display, center, or away). Fixating one of the displays in the task allows task-relevant input (i.e., the colors within that display) to enter the five-layer memory architecture.

Once activation enters the five-layer memory architecture, the encoding, maintenance, and comparison processes are engaged. These processes provide the second source of input to the fixation nodes: when activation is above-threshold within the perceptual field, it projects back to the fixation nodes (see bi-directional arrow in Figure 6), increasing the likelihood that the current fixation will continue. Thus, activation in the perceptual field—which corresponds to perceptual processing of new inputs—is fundamentally linked to fixation. Within the dynamic model, perceptual processing is suppressed for familiar items, which ultimately produces a novelty preference in the model.

Figure 10 illustrates how these processes operate in the context of a set size four trial of the change-preference task. Figure 10A shows activation of the fixation nodes over the 20-s trial. As this figure shows, the model primarily fixated the two displays, with some "away" fixations. Over the course of the trial, as the items were encoded in the working memory field and associated Hebbian field, the model fixated the change display (blue line) more than the no-change display (red line), resulting in a robust change preference. To illustrate the model's performance, time-slices through the perceptual and working memory fields are shown during the dynamic model's fixations of the no-change display (Figure 10C), the change display (Figure 10D and E), and back to the no-change display (Figure 10F). The stimuli presented at these points in the trial are shown in Figure 10B.

During the first fixation of the no-change display (Figure 10C) the four colors are encoded, forming peaks in the working memory field. The inhibition associated with these peaks suppresses activation at these values in the perceptual field, which reduces the activation sent back to the fixation system. This reduction in support for fixation, combined with the dynamics of the fixation system (see Appendix for description), leads the model to look away from the no-change display (see decrease in the node's activation in Figure 10A). Through the dynamics of the fixation system, the activation of the node corresponding to the change display rises above threshold next, leading the model to fixate this display and receive those four color inputs. Note that, through random selection, one of the colors in the change display matched one from the no-change display (cyan, localized at 80°; see Figure 10B). Because this input matched an item in memory, there was no above-threshold activation in the perceptual field for this color (Figure 10D). Similarly, the input at −160° did not pierce threshold due to surrounding

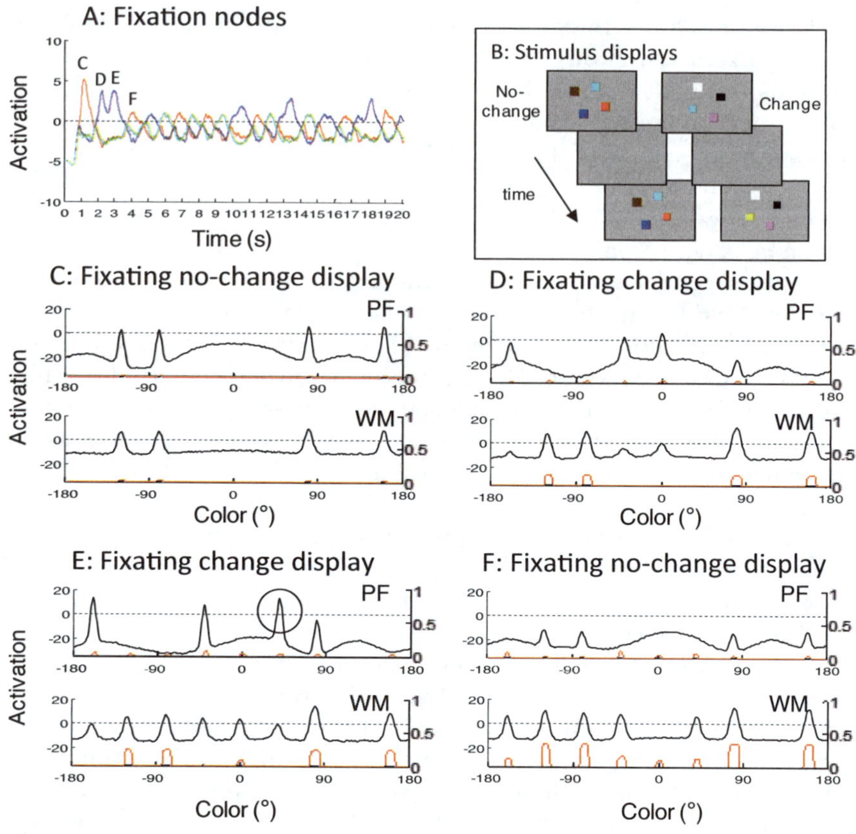

FIGURE 10.—A simulation of the dynamic model performing a set size four change-preference trial. (A) Activation of the fixation neurons over the course of the trial (red, no-change; blue, change; green, away). (B) Schematic of the stimulus display for a portion of the trial. Time slices through CF and WM show activation during (C) the first fixation of the no-change display, (D) the first fixation of the change display, (E) the second fixation of the change display, and (F) the second fixation of the no-change display.

inhibition from nearby colors held in the working memory field (at $-120°$ and $160°$; note that the color space "wraps" from -180 to $180°$). Thus, even though there were four colors in this display, only two produced peaks in the perceptual field.

Because fixation is supported by above-threshold activation in the perceptual field, there was less support to the right/change node during this fixation than in the previous fixation. As a result, the activation of this fixation node began to fall (see Figure 10A). Before the fixation ended, however, one item in the display changes (cyan to yellow), which led to a peak in the perceptual field (circle in Figure 10E). Note that the repetition of the other colors in the display allowed the peak at $-160°$ to pierce threshold in the perceptual field (Figure 10E). With more activation in the perceptual field, this maintained the models' fixation of the change display (see D and E in Figure 10A). As the peaks built more strongly in the working memory field during this display presentation, more inhibition projected to the perceptual field and eventually drove activation below threshold, releasing fixation. Next, the model fixated the no-change display again. The model had maintained all of these colors in the working memory field during the fixations to the change display (see peaks at -120, -80, 80, and $160°$ in Figure 10D and E). As a result, activation at these values did not pierce threshold in the perceptual field, and fixation quickly released (see F in Figure 10A).

The dynamic model's performance in this simulation highlights how the same visual working memory processes that support change detection performance contribute to looking behavior in the change-preference task: if peaks that correspond to the colors in the no-change display build quickly in the working memory field (with support from the associated Hebbian field), this inhibits activation in the perceptual field and removes support of the active fixation node. Essentially, the model tends not to fixate items that are held in memory—rather, it looks to items that are new. Over the course of many fixations and stimulus presentations within a change-preference trail, a preference for the change display emerges.

These two sections have illustrated my formalization of the processes of encoding, maintenance, and comparison in visual working memory, as well as how these processes interact with the response required in the change detection task and looking behavior in the change-preference task. This formalization of both tasks within a single computational framework provides the opportunity to bridge between infancy and later childhood to advance a more general theory of working memory development that can span multiple tasks and developmental periods. The next question addressed in this chapter is whether a single developmental mechanism within this unified computational framework could account for behavioral changes in both tasks. These simulations also address the discrepancy in capacity estimates across tasks and development, leading to empirical predictions described in the final section.

Predictions Across Tasks Over Development

As described briefly above, Perone et al. (2011) simulated developmental changes in infants' performance in the change-preference task using a similar dynamic model architecture. They implemented development following the spatial precision hypothesis, which has been used extensively in the Dynamic Field Theory framework, especially with models of spatial cognition (see Simmering & Schutte, 2015, for review). In particular, to capture developmental improvements in visual working memory, Perone et al. increased the strength of excitatory connections within the perceptual and working memory field, as well as the inhibitory connections from the inhibitory field to these two fields. By strengthening these connections the encoding, maintenance, and comparison functions within the dynamic model became more stable and robust for the "older" infant parameters. Their simulations showed that stronger connectivity led to a range of consequences: peaks in the working memory field formed more quickly and sustained more reliably (i.e., better encoding and maintenance), activation in the perceptual field was suppressed more effectively through shared inhibition (i.e., better comparison), and a closer correspondence between fixations and the contents of memory (i.e., better mapping of memory to behavior). These consequences are components of the notion of real-time stability introduced above. Put simply, with stronger connections, the dynamic model *forms and uses memories more reliably* in the context of the change-preference task.

The current monograph tests the hypothesis that increasing real-time stability can account for improvements in both the change-preference and change detection tasks through early childhood into adulthood. How would changes in real-time stability affect performance in the change detection task? This question can be answered through sample model simulations that scale connectivity over development. Because only adults' performance has been fit before, this requires modeling development "backward" by decreasing the strength of connections to simulate earlier development. I conducted exploratory simulations with the parameters used to generate Figures 7–10 scaled to approximate children's performance (see Appendix for details). Because these simulations are qualitative rather than quantitative in nature, I simply scaled the strength of local excitatory and lateral inhibitory connections by 0.5 (i.e., making these "child" parameters half the strength of the "adult" parameters), as well as scaling the input to be weaker and broader (multiplying the strength by 0.5 and width by 1.5; cf. Simmering et al., 2008).

Figure 11 shows a sample simulation of the dynamic model, using these "child" parameters, performing a set size four change detection trial. When the four items were presented, four peaks initially formed in the working memory field (Figure 11A). In comparison to Figures 7–9 with the adult parameters, the peaks formed by the child parameters are notably weaker and the inhibition that projects back to the perceptual field is quite weak; in Figure 7, inhibitory troughs are apparent in the perceptual field, whereas almost no inhibition is seen in the perceptual field in Figure 11. These differences are due to the relatively weak connections within and between fields with the child parameters. Another consequence of these weaker connections is shown in Figure 11B when two peaks "die out" during the memory delay (circle in Figure 11B). Essentially, reduced real-time stability

46

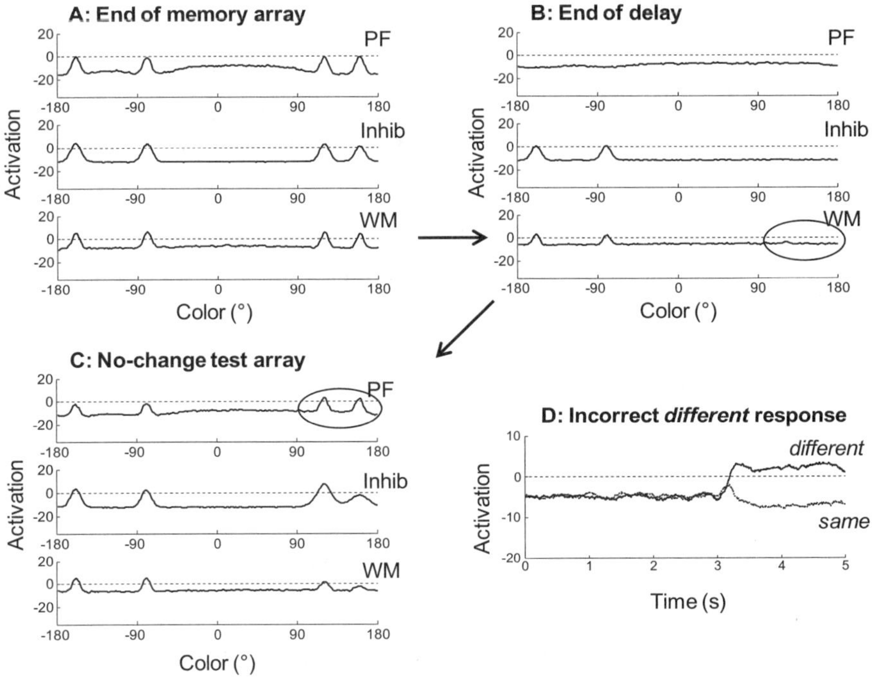

FIGURE 11.—A simulation of the dynamic model performing a set size four "miss" change detection trial with parameters scaled to approximate children's performance. Panels and axes are as in Figure 7A–D.

led to a failure in maintenance for these items. As such, when the same four items were presented at test, the model made a false alarm error, indicating that these two items were new (see peaks in the perceptual field, circled in Figure 11C). This sample simulation suggests that increasing real-time stability through strengthening connectivity within the dynamic model could capture developmental improvements in change detection performance.

Figure 12 shows the same "child" parameters in the context of a set size four change-preference trial, as Figure 10 showed with the adult parameters. Figure 12A shows activation of the fixation nodes over the course of the trial, with the stimuli from the first two presentations in Figure 12B. The model first fixated the no-change display (Figure 12C), and the four inputs formed peaks in the perceptual and working memory fields, although relative to the adult simulation (cf. Figure 10C) activation in these fields was lower and the inhibition projected into the perceptual field was much weaker. After the release of fixation to the no-change display, the model fixated the change display. As in the prior simulation (Figure 10), one color overlapped between the two displays (black, localized at −160°; see Figure 12B), which supported

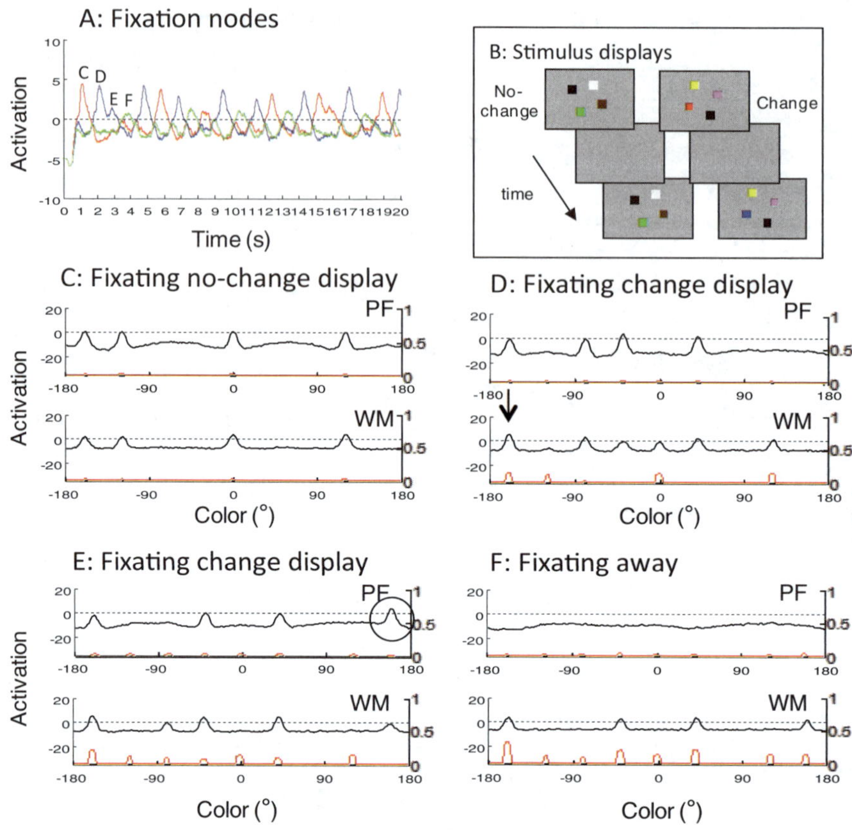

FIGURE 12.—A simulation of the dynamic model performing a set size four change-preference trial with parameters scaled to approximate children's performance. Panels and axes are as in Figure 10.

the continued maintenance of this peak in the working memory field (see arrow in Figure 12D) and suppression of the related peak in the perceptual field. Activation corresponding to the other colors was again near threshold in the perceptual field, which led to a rapid decline in fixation (see blue line in Figure 12A). Just before the model looked away from the change display, however, one color changed (red to blue, localized at $-120°$ and $160°$, respectively), which produced a peak in the perceptual field at the new color value (circled in Figure 12E). This activation was relatively weak, however, and activation of the fixation node dropped below threshold (labeled E in Figure 12A). Next, the model fixated away, but the four peaks in the working memory field corresponding to the previous input remained above-threshold (Figure 12F).

This simulation with the child parameters illustrates the consequences of decreased real-time stability. Relative to the simulation with adult parameters, fewer peaks were maintained in the working memory field at one time, and the peaks were more likely to die out without support from input (i.e., without a repeated presentation of the item). However, over the course of a complete trial, items repeat regularly (due to the relatively small number of colors available) and Hebbian learning increases the support for peaks in the working memory field. Thus, although performance with the child parameters differed notably from that with the adult parameters in the moment-by-moment interactions, over the course of the entire task, performance may be more similar across parameter sets.

To test the consequences of these changes more concretely in the change-preference task, I conducted 40 simulations each with the child versus adult parameters (80 simulations total) in this task. In particular, I used the details from Ross-Sheehy et al.'s (2003) Experiment 3 (see Chapter 4 for details of the implementation in the model), in which they tested infants in two trials each in set sizes two, four, and six. The results of these simulations revealed change-preference scores that were significantly above chance (0.5) at all three set sizes for both parameter sets ($M_{SS2\text{-child}} = 0.55$, 95% CI [0.53, 0.56]; $M_{SS4\text{-child}} = 0.54$, 95% CI [0.52, 0.55]; $M_{SS6\text{-child}} = 0.55$, 95% CI [0.52, 0.56]; $M_{SS2\text{-adult}} = 0.57$, 95% CI [0.55, 0.59]; $M_{SS4\text{-adult}} = 0.55$, 95% CI [0.53, 0.57]; $M_{SS6\text{-adult}} = 0.56$, 95% CI [0.53, 0.59]). Thus, the dynamic model's capacity as estimated from the change-preference task would be at least six items for the child and adult parameters.

These simulation results illustrate my first behavioral prediction: capacity estimates in the change-preference task should continue to increase over development, with both children and adults showing capacity estimates above the four items estimated at 10 months. According to the cognitive dynamics account, this increase in capacity relative to infants arises through continued increases in real-time stability: the processes that Perone et al. (2011) simulated through infancy continue to improve through early childhood into adulthood. It is not clear whether this prediction would be unique to the cognitive dynamics account and dynamic model presented here. The binding account put forth by Oakes et al. (2006, 2009) clearly explains the increase in capacity from one to two or more items, but it is less clear whether it would predict that capacity should increase from two to three to four items gradually during infancy, or beyond four items later in development. Rather, it might predict different developmental processes underlying the transition in memory from one item to more during infancy versus increases in capacity later in development.

The next question addressed by these simulations is how performance should compare across tasks when tested within the same individuals. Answering this question requires enumerating the differences between the tasks contexts. First is the number of stimulus presentations: a trial in the change detection task includes colors in only two arrays (memory and test) separated in time; many trials are presented to the participant over the course of a session, but the colors are only meant to be maintained and compared within a single trial (indeed, failing to update memory from one trial to another would lead to errors). By contrast, a trial in the change-preference task includes two arrays presented simultaneously across displays 27 times throughout the trial, with ongoing comparisons that can occur within a single display across presentations, or between displays within a single presentation and/or across presentations. Second, the delays in the change detection task (1 s) are longer than in the change-preference task (250 ms), which could tax maintenance processes more, especially early in development when memory representations are relatively unstable.

The structure of the change-preference task allows for more items to be held in memory, even by the same memory system: the field parameters that could sustain a maximum of six peaks in the change detection task, as shown by Johnson et al. (2014), were used to generate Figure 10, which shows seven peaks sustaining in the working memory field. This difference in the dynamic model's performance across tasks comes from both the long-term memory contribution (through the Hebbian field) as well as the repeated presentation of some of the same stimuli. Together, these two sources of activation support more items in the working memory field. Thus, the different task structures lead to memory for more items in the change-preference task than the change detection task.

The third important contrast between tasks is in the behavioral response. The change detection task requires a discrete "same" or "different" response on each trial, whereas preference scores in the change-preference task are calculated from the accumulation of looking to the two displays over the course of each 20-s trial (see Chapter 5 for discussion of a new "one-shot" version of the infant looking task by Oakes, Baumgartner, Barrett, Messenger, & Luck, 2013). The all-or-none response for change detection requires a robust signal from the corresponding component of the visual working memory system: activation in the perceptual field for a "different" response and activation in the working memory field for a "same" response. This mechanism of producing responses biases the dynamic model toward responding "same" (i.e., there is virtually always at least one peak in the working memory field to send activation to the "same" node), but it fits adults' pattern of responses across trial types and set sizes well (Johnson et al., 2014). As shown in Figure 8, however, the response system is not error-proof, as activation in the perceptual field may be too weak to generate a response.

Looking behavior, in contrast to the "same"/"different" responses, can play out in a number of ways over a trial and still lead to a preference for the change display. As Figure 10A illustrated, fixations of both displays continued

50

throughout the 20-s trial. A robust preference could arise through multiple differences between looks to the change versus no-change displays—more fixations, longer duration of fixations, or both. The preference magnitudes reported by Ross-Sheehy et al. (2003) were around 0.55–0.58, with infants looking to both displays for about 10 s total per trial. This translates to infants looking, on average, about 1–1.5 s longer to the change display than the no-change display within a trial. This more graded measure of the underlying visual working memory system allows for a weaker—or less stable—memory system supporting preferences (see Chapter 4 for further discussion and illustration with model simulations).

A related point becomes apparent when comparing quantitative simulations across the change-preference (Perone et al., 2011) and change detection (Johnson et al., 2014) tasks: the mapping from peaks in the working memory field to capacity estimates is not direct in either task. Perone et al. found that a robust preference could be supported without representing all of the items from either display. In particular, they showed that the dynamic model could exhibit a significant change preference even when only half of the items from either display were held in the working memory field at any given time. This suggests that change-preference scores may overestimate the number of items held in memory. By contrast, Johnson et al. found that capacity calculations were lower than the number of peaks in memory (as reported above: a mean of 5.79 peaks yielded a mean capacity estimate of 4.64).

To summarize, these simulations suggest that the structure of the tasks allows more items to be encoded during the change-preference task than the change detection task. Furthermore, capacity estimates may be higher than the number of items in memory for the change-preference task, but lower than the number of items in memory for the change detection task. Together, these differences across tasks lead to a second empirical prediction: capacity estimates should differ across tasks even when tested in the same individuals. Is this prediction unique to the cognitive dynamics account? The most likely answer is "no," although other theories have not specifically addressed this question. Cowan's (2007) proposal that the change detection task could be more attentionally demanding than the change-preference task suggests he would predict this difference within individuals. Furthermore, the suggestion by Riggs et al. (2006) that the change-preference and change detection tasks tap different memory processes could also lead to a predicted discrepancy across estimates within individuals.

Although other theories may converge with the cognitive dynamics account on the predicted difference in capacity estimates across tasks, the dynamic model simulations specify that the *same memory processes* support performance across tasks. This leads to my third empirical prediction: performance should be correlated across tasks. Put differently, if the predicted difference in capacity estimates across tasks is supported empirically, does performance in the change-preference task provide any index of capacity estimates in change detection? Based on prior empirical work, two possibilities arise. First, as reviewed in Chapter 1, Rose et al. (2012) found that novelty preferences during infancy predicted later cognitive functions, including working memory. Because the processes that support novelty preferences in infant visual-paired comparison tasks lead to preferences for the change display in the change-preference task, it is possible that preference scores could relate to capacity from change detection. Second, Rose et al. (2012) have suggested that switch rates are an important individual difference, as they also predict later cognitive functions; from their perspective, switch rates provide an index of attention.

Beyond these empirical results, however, the dynamic model simulations can provide further insight into potential relations in performance across task. In particular, the formalization of cognitive processes into a computational model allows for the assessment of the underlying processes that give rise to the variables suggested by prior research—change preference scores and switch rates—to predict whether and how they might relate to change detection performance. These two variables are affected most prominently by different factors within the dynamic model: excitation supporting fixation for change preference scores and inhibition releasing fixation for switch rates. This suggests that these factors could provide separable contributions to performance in the change detection task (discussed further in Chapter 4).

Consider change preference scores first. Because maintaining fixation of a given display in the dynamic model is driven by continued activation in the perceptual field (see Figures 10 and 12), change preference scores can be interpreted as the representation of new items from the change display. These representations are realized as self-stabilized peaks piercing threshold driven by excitation in the perceptual field. In the context of the change detection task, better representation of new items would correspond to higher hit rates (i.e., better performance on change trials) and therefore higher capacity estimates.

In contrast to change preference scores, switch rates in the dynamic model depend more on inhibition. In particular, fixation switches when activation projecting from the perceptual field decreases to the point that one of the competing fixation nodes can pierce threshold. As demonstrated in Figures 10 and 12, activation in the perceptual field is suppressed through inhibition corresponding to the peaks held in the working memory field. Thus, the more quickly peaks form in the working memory field, the more quickly inhibition suppresses activation in the perceptual field, and the more quickly fixation switches. In the context of the change detection task, this formation of peaks and suppression of activation is important for recognition of items already in memory, which should contribute most prominently to correct rejection rates (i.e., better performance on change trials) and therefore higher capacity estimates in change detection.

These analyses of the dynamic model's performance reveal the potentially separable contributions of excitatory and inhibitory connections to produce higher change preference scores and switch rates, respectively. Both excitatory and inhibitory processes are fundamental to how the dynamic model performs the change detection task, suggesting that preference scores and switch rates could both relate to capacity estimates from the change detection task. Although these predicted correlations may seem intuitive given some evidence for these looking measures' predictive power, only through the level of specificity achieved in the dynamic model formalization can these predictions be attributed to the specific underlying processes (i.e., detecting novelty vs. familiarity, realized through excitatory vs. inhibitory connections). Prior explanations for performance and development in the change detection and change-preference tasks have not addressed the processes of comparison for detecting novelty versus familiarity in either task, but rather have focused on the nature of representations (mostly through slot-like characterizations). Through the simulations and predictions described here, the cognitive dynamics account provides both more specificity—detailing the processes of encoding, maintenance, comparison, and response—and more generality—predicting how these processes operate across tasks—than previous explanations of visual working memory development.

These first three predictions test key components of the cognitive dynamics account of performance in the change-preference and change detection tasks. The final prediction tested in this monograph focuses on the implementation of this theory in the dynamic model. Specifically, I present quantitative simulations to test whether developmental changes in both of these tasks could arise through the same underlying mechanism, namely, strengthening excitatory and inhibitory connections that support increasing real-time stability. Prior theories have put forth different explanations for the capacity increases in each task. If the same underlying mechanism could explain performance improvements in both tasks, however, this would provide a critical step toward identifying a more general source of developmental change in visual working memory. As outlined in Chapter 1, performance on working memory tasks in infancy and childhood predict more general cognitive skills, but to date the nature of these relationships is poorly understood. Most critically, it is currently unknown whether the processes that drive these correlations with general cognitive skills are the same between infant working memory tasks and tasks assessing working memory during childhood. If the dynamic model implementation provides evidence that a common developmental mechanism can span these two tasks from infancy through later childhood, this provides an important first step toward establishing a more general theoretical account of working memory development.

SUMMARY

The goal of this chapter was to put forth a specific theory of performance in the change-preference and change detection tasks over development. This account focuses on cognitive dynamics, that is, the processes that support encoding, maintenance, comparison, and responses within various behavioral contexts. This approach brings a new perspective to the study of developmental changes in capacity limits, as most prior theories have focused on the nature of representations (i.e., capacity vs. resolution, whether colors are bound to locations) rather than how representations support different behaviors across task contexts. A central goal of the cognitive dynamics account is to use a computational implementation to illustrate the connections between cognition and behavior in the real-time context of laboratory tasks. By specifying these processes, this theory can provide an entry point to understanding how behavioral improvements over development relate to underlying cognitive changes.

Simulations of the change-preference and change detection tasks within the dynamic model led to four specific predictions to be tested with behavioral experiments and simulations in the subsequent chapters. A series of experiments tested children's (ages 3, 4, and 5 years) and adults' performance in both change-preference and change detection tasks. These experiments tested three specific predictions. First, when tested in the change-preference task, children and adults should show capacity estimates higher than infants—at least six items. Second, estimates of capacity measured from the same individuals in the change detection task should be lower than estimates from the change-preference task. Third, despite divergent capacity estimates, performance should be correlated across these tasks because they rely on the same underlying visual working memory system. In particular, model simulations suggest that both change preference scores and switch rates could provide potentially separable indexes of detection of novelty versus familiarity, which support performance on change and no-change trials, respectively, in the change detection task.

In Chapter 4, I use these empirical data to test my fourth prediction, that strengthening connectivity within the dynamic model can quantitatively fit developmental changes in visual working memory capacity across both tasks. Results supporting these four predictions demonstrate the utility of a computational implementation of the cognitive dynamics theory to explain how performance relates across tasks and development. Moreover, this project provides a test of the real-time stability hypothesis as an explanation of developmental increases in visual working memory capacity from infancy through early childhood and into adulthood.

NOTES

i. I use the term "Dynamic Field Theory framework" to refer to a collection of theoretical and computational principles that have been implemented in dynamic neural field models. Although the model used for the current monograph is similar to other implementations within Dynamic Field Theory framework, the different theoretical context leads me to refer to the model separately from the larger framework.

ii. Although the original formulation by Amari (1977) was developed to model recordings of neural activation, the model presented here is abstracted away from this level of detail. Rather than focusing on neural dynamics directly, this type of model builds upon principles derived from neural data without specifying precise neural analogs (see Schneegans, Lins, & Schöner, 2015; Schoner, Reimann, & Lins, 2015, for further discussion). For this reason, the terminology conventionally used to describe neurons within fields and neural interactions within the model is not used in the current monograph.

iii. The term "spatial precision hypothesis" has been used extensively within the Dynamic Field Theory framework to refer to similar changes in connectivity within and between layers in dynamic neural field models (Perone et al., 2011; Perone & Spencer, 2013b, 2014; Schutte & Spencer, 2009, 2010; Simmering & Patterson, 2012; Simmering et al., 2008; Spencer & Hund, 2003; Spencer, Simmering, & Schutte, 2006; Spencer, Simmering, Schutte, & Schöner, 2007). Earlier implementations of the spatial precision hypothesis also included changes in the spread of connections (i.e., how broadly connections spread along the spatial dimension; Schutte, Spencer, & Schöner, 2003; see also Schutte & Spencer, 2009, Experiment 1). The current monograph includes slightly different implementation of these changes than has been used previously (see Appendix for details) and therefore uses the terminology "real-time stability" to describe the cognitive consequences of these types of changes in connectivity in order to keep the focus at the conceptual level rather than the specific model implementation.

SUPPORTING INFORMATION

Additional supporting information may be found in the online version of this article at the publisher's website.

III. EMPIRICAL TESTS OF PREDICTIONS COMPARING CAPACITY ESTIMATES ACROSS TASKS AND DEVELOPMENT

Vanessa R. Simmering

This article is part of the issue "Working Memory Capacity in Context: Modeling Dynamic Processes of Behavior, Memory, and Development," Simmering, Vanessa (Issue Author). For a full listing of articles in this issue, see: http://onlinelibrary.wiley.com/doi/ 10.1111/mono.v81.3/issuetoc.

The experiments in this chapter test three behavioral predictions of the cognitive dynamics account, generated by implementing both change detection and change-preference tasks in a dynamic neural field model. First, capacity estimates for children and adults should be greater than four items in the change-preference task. Second, capacity estimates for the same participants should be lower in the change detection than change-preference task. Third, despite these divergent capacity estimates, performance should be correlated across tasks over development because both depend upon the same visual working memory system. Experiment 1 includes a large sample of 3-, 4-, and 5-year-olds and adults in the change-preference task. A subset of these participants also participated in Experiment 2 or 3, which tested color and shape versions of the change detection task, respectively (using modifications described in Simmering, 2012). Note that all participants completed the change-preference task first to prevent potentially introducing a bias to look for changes in the displays based on experience in the change detection task (where attention to change is explicitly instructed). Both tasks were completed within a single experimental session. To alleviate potential

Corresponding author: Vanessa R. Simmering, 1202 W. Johnson St., Madison, WI 53706; email: simmering@wisc.edu

DOI: 10.1111/mono.12251

concern that the order of tasks impacted performance, I compared the current Experiment 3 in a replication of this method with 3- and 5-year-olds that did not follow the change-preference task (Simmering, Miller, & Bohache, 2015); an ANOVA with Age Group (3 years, 5 years) and Change-Preference Task (with, without) comparing capacity estimates (K_{max}, described in Experiment 3 Results) showed no difference associated with completing the change-preference task (Task main effect $p = .63$, interaction $p = .62$). This suggests that the task order did not systematically affect children's change detection performance.

EXPERIMENT 1: CHANGE-PREFERENCE TASK

Method

Participants

A total of 154 children participated in this study: 56 three-year-olds (M age $= 3$ years, 4.46 months; $SD = 2.52$ months; 26 girls, 30 boys), 44 four-year-olds (M age $= 4$ years, 2.87; $SD = 1.93$ months; 22 girls, 22 boys), and 54 five-year-olds (M age $= 5$ years, 0.83 months; $SD = 1.75$ months; 28 girls, 26 boys). An additional eight children participated but were not included in analyses for the following reasons: incomplete data (1 five-year-old; see below for details), a visual abnormality (1 five-year-old), equipment failure (1 five-year-old), or experimenter error (1 three-year-old, 2 four-year-olds, 2 five-year-olds). Forty adults also participated in this study (M age $= 21$ years, 5.35 months; $SD = 3.53$ years; 22 women, 18 men). An additional three adults participated but were not included in analyses because they wore glasses; the glare from the two displays made it impossible to code their looking direction.

Potential child participants were identified from a database of birth records maintained at a large Midwestern university. Parents of these children were contacted by mail and phone to schedule participation. Children received a small gift after participating. Adult participants were recruited through an introductory psychology course and received research participation credit, or were volunteers from the community. Adult participants and parents of child participants all reported normal or corrected-to-normal vision and no history of color-blindness.

Apparatus

The apparatus and stimuli were identical to those used in the infant study described previously (Ross-Sheehy et al., 2003, Experiment 3). Stimuli were presented on two 17-inch ViewSonic monitors using a Macintosh G3 computer. The monitors were positioned side by side with a 22 cm gap between them. Participants were seated approximately 100 cm from the displays; viewing distance and angle differed across participants due to variations in height. From this distance, each monitor subsumed approximately 18.26° (w) by 13.50° (h) of visual angle. The total eccentricity of the displays was 88 cm (approximately 47.5° of visual angle).

As shown in Figure 3, a solid gray background was continuously present on both monitors, with arrays of colored squares blinking on and off together in time; one monitor contained the change display and the other monitor contained the no-change display. Each display contained two, four, or six colored squares that measured approximately 5 cm by 5 cm each. The set size (i.e., the number of squares on each monitor) matched across the two displays and remained constant throughout a trial. The initial square colors on each trial were selected at random from a set of nine colors: green, brown, black, violet, cyan, yellow, blue, red, and white. RGB values for the colored squares and background were black (0, 0, 0), blue (0, 0, 255), cyan (0, 255, 255), green (0, 255, 0), gray (150, 150, 150), red (255, 0, 0), violet (238, 130, 238), white (255, 255, 255), yellow (255, 255, 0). See Vogel et al. (2001) for approximate CIE values. Following Ross-Sheehy et al. (2003), the colors always differed from others within the same display, but could be repeated across the two displays.

The squares on both monitors appeared simultaneously for 500 ms, disappeared for 250 ms, and continued appearing and disappearing at these intervals for a total of 20 s per trial. For the no-change display, the colors remained unchanged throughout the 20-s trial. For the change display, one color would change to a new color at each onset; the location of this square was selected at random for each presentation, and the new color was selected at random from the set of colors that was not currently included in that display.

Procedure and Experimental Design

The procedure for this task was adapted from infant studies (Ross-Sheehy et al., 2003, Experiment 3) for use with older children. After completing the consent form, the participant was taken into the testing room; a parent sometimes accompanied child participants, but most children completed the task alone. The participant sat on a chair (or, for some of the younger children, in a parent's lap) facing the two computer monitors. If a parent sat with the child in the testing room, she or he wore occluding glasses during the session. A large black curtain hung from ceiling to floor with openings to display the two monitors, as well as a small black box used as an attention-getter. The black box produced a red light and tone to draw the participant's attention at the beginning of each trial.

In contrast to the infant version of this task, participants were given brief instructions to ensure that they would attend to the stimuli during the task. Specifically, they were told that they were going to watch six short videos, and that the experimenter would ask them questions about the videos at the end. No further instructions were provided to prevent potential bias in looking behavior. After the task, the experimenter asked the participant whether he or she noticed any difference between the two displays in the videos. Most children's responses referred to changes in the numbers, positions, and colors of the items across trials; only one child (a 5-year-old) correctly reported that the colors would change on one screen while the colors on the other screen did not change. Approximately, 70% of adults reported this difference across displays.

Each session included two trials in each of the three set sizes—one with the change display on the left, and one with the change display on the right—for a total of six trials. The order of trials, as well as which side the change display was on, was determined randomly for each participant. The experimenter was seated behind the curtain to initiate each trial. For most sessions, a trained observer recorded the duration of participants' looking to each of the two monitors online using a program developed for the Macintosh computer (Habit; Cohen, Atkinson, & Chaput, 2000); when she was not available, however, she coded sessions offline using the video recording. In all cases, the coder could not see the images being presented on the monitors.

Each trial began with the attention-getter (the black box with a flashing red light and synchronous beeping); once the participant attended to the light, the experimenter pressed a key to begin presentation of the displays. For the duration of the 20-s trial, she then coded the participant's gaze as looking to the left or right monitor. If the participant looked away from the displays, no look was recorded. Upon completion of each trial, the attention-getter was reactivated, beginning the same sequence for the next trial. This sequence was repeated across all six trials. The entire task took less than 5 min to complete.

Results

Because the same trained observer coded every behavioral session, typical calculation of interrater reliability is not possible. However, to ensure that this observer was sufficiently trained, a set of trained observers recoded approximately 25% of the sessions (49 of 195); the Pearson's correlation between these coders' results and the original coder were $r = 0.93$ for total looking time, $r = 0.92$ for change-preference scores, and $r = 0.90$ for switches. These interrater correlations are slightly lower than those typically reported in infant studies because coding children's and adults' looking is more challenging due to their more subtle eye movements; however, these values are similar to those reported in studies with participants from a comparable age range (e.g., $r = 0.91$ reported by Overman, Bachevalier, Sewell, & Drew, 1993).

Before analyzing the results, I inspected the data for trials on which the participant fixated only one display for the entire duration of the trial.

I excluded these trials because it was impossible for the participant to detect a difference between the two displays if only one display had been fixated. This led to the exclusion of 16 trials from 12 children's data; these trials were roughly evenly distributed across set sizes. Half of these trials were fixations of only the change display, while the other half were fixations of only the no-change display. Five of these sixteen trials were from one 5-year-old child's data, leading to only one trial of usable data from this participant; as a result, this participant was excluded from analyses (as listed Participants section above). Following Ross-Sheehy et al. (2003), the data were analyzed by comparing the total duration of looking per trial across age groups and set sizes, as well as computing change-preferences scores for comparison across age groups and set sizes. Additionally, I included a third analysis of switch rates across age groups and set sizes. As described in Chapter 2, switching may provide an index of how quickly and robustly memory representations are formed (Perone & Spencer, 2014).

Total looking time was computed automatically by Habit as the time the participant looked at either display on each trial. Scores were then averaged across the two trials to the same set size. Mean total looking times are shown in Figure 13A. Total looking time varied little across set size and age group, although adults' looking time was slightly longer than children's. Ross-Sheehy et al. (2003) reported that 10-month-old infants in Experiment 3 looked just under 10 s per trial on average for each set size ($M_{SS2} = 9.82$ s, $M_{SS4} = 9.48$ s, $M_{SS6} = 9.22$ s); children and adults in the present study looked considerably longer overall, but showed a similar pattern across set sizes.

I analyzed these data in a two-way ANOVA with Set Size (2, 4, 6) as a within-subjects factor and Age Group (3 years, 4 years, 5 years, adult) as a between-subjects factor. This analysis revealed only a significant main effect of Age Group ($F_{3, 190} = 15.62$, $p < .001$ $\eta_p^2 = 0.20$). Follow-up Tukey HSD tests ($p < .05$) showed that adults' total looking time ($M = 16.57$ s) was greater than children's total looking time for all three age groups, with no differences across the child age groups ($M_{3y} = 14.54$ s, $M_{4y} = 14.44$ s, $M_{5y} = 14.63$ s).

Change-preference scores were computed as the time each participant looked to the change display divided by total looking time to both displays for each trial. Scores were averaged across the two trials to the same set size. Mean change-preference scores for each age group are shown in Figure 13B. As this figure shows, change-preference scores were generally higher for set size two (SS2), with little change across age groups. Compared to the 10-month-old infants' scores reported by Ross-Sheehy et al. (2003) in Experiment 3 ($M_{SS2} = 0.56$, $M_{SS4} = 0.58$, $M_{SS6} = 0.52$), children and adults showed similar preference scores (means reported below).

These scores were analyzed in an ANOVA with Set Size as a within-subjects factor and Age Group as a between-subjects factor. This analysis revealed only a significant main effect of Set Size ($F_{2, 380} = 6.04$, $p = .003$, $\eta_p^2 = .03$).

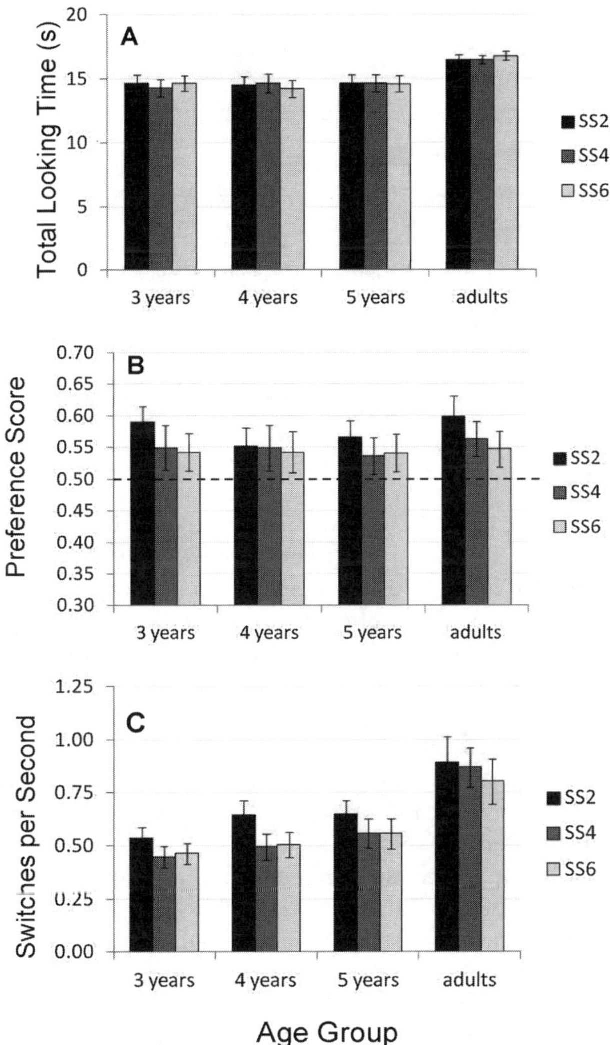

FIGURE 13.—Experiment 1 results across set sizes (SS) and age groups: (A) mean total looking time, (B) mean change preference scores, and (C) mean switch rates. Error bars show 95% confidence intervals. Dashed line in (B) indicates chance performance.

Follow-up Tukey HSD tests ($p < .05$) showed that change-preference scores in SS2 ($M = 0.58$) were significantly higher than in SS4 ($M = 0.55$) and SS6 ($M = 0.54$); change-preference scores did not differ between SS4 and SS6. To estimate capacity, I also compared mean change-preference scores to chance (0.50) using two-tailed t-tests (see Table 1). As indicated by the confidence

TABLE 1

RESULTS OF *T*-TESTS COMPARING CHANGE-PREFERENCE SCORES TO CHANCE (0.50)

Age Group	df	Set Size		
		2	4	6
3 years	55	$M = 0.59$, $SD = .09$	$M = 0.55$, $SD = 0.14$	$M = 0.54$, $SD = 0.11$
		$t = 7.26^{***}$, $d = 1.96$	$t = 2.74^{**}$, $d = 0.74$	$t = 2.80^{**}$, $d = 0.76$
4 years	43	$M = 0.55$, $SD = 0.10$	$M = 0.55$, $SD = 0.12$	$M = 0.54$, $SD = 0.11$
		$t = 3.46^{**}$, $d = 1.06$	$t = 2.63^{*}$, $d = 0.80$	$t = 2.57^{*}$, $d = 0.78$
5 years	53	$M = 0.57$, $SD = 0.10$	$M = 0.54$, $SD = 0.11$	$M = 0.54$, $SD = 0.11$
		$t = 5.14^{***}$, $d = 1.41$	$t = 2.45^{*}$, $d = 0.67$	$t = 2.71^{**}$, $d = 0.74$
Adults	39	$M = 0.60$, $SD = 0.11$	$M = 0.56$, $SD = .09$	$M = 0.55$, $SD = .09$
		$t = 5.77^{***}$, $d = 1.85$	$t = 4.54^{***}$, $d = 1.45$	$t = 3.29^{**}$, $d = 1.05$

$^{*}p < .05$, $^{**}p < .01$, $^{***}p < .001$ (two-tailed).

intervals shown in Figure 13B, change-preference scores were significantly above chance for all set sizes for all age groups. These analyses yielded a capacity estimate of at least six items for all age groups; capacity estimates may have been higher if trials with higher set sizes had been included (discussed further below). The capacity estimates from this task showed an increase relative to 10-month-olds, but also suggest a higher capacity than the typical three to four items estimated in change detection studies with adults (e.g., Vogel et al., 2001), confirming my first prediction.

For the final analysis, switches between displays were tabulated as the number of times the participant looked from one display to the other during each of the six trials. Because there was a significant difference in total looking time between children and adults, I normalized these values by dividing the number of switches by the looking time on each trial to arrive at a switch rate. Switch rates were then averaged across the two trials to the same set size. Mean switch rates are shown in Figure 13C. As this figure shows, adults switched more frequently than children; in addition, children switched more frequently in SS2 than SS4 and SS6, whereas adults switched more frequently in SS2 and SS4 than in SS6.

I analyzed these data in an ANOVA with Set Size as a within-subjects factor and Age Group as a between-subjects factor. This analysis revealed significant main effects of Set Size ($F_{2, 380} = 20.13$, $p < .001$, $\eta_p^2 = 0.10$) and Age Group ($F_{3, 190} = 44.66$, $p < .001$, $\eta_p^2 = 0.41$). Follow-up Tukey HSD tests ($p < .05$) showed that switch rates were higher in SS2 ($M = 0.67$) than in SS4 ($M = 0.58$) and SS6 ($M = 0.57$), which did not differ. As can be seen in Figure 13C, this difference across set sizes is driven primarily by children's pattern of performance, although the interaction did not approach significance ($p = .278$). Additional Tukey HSD tests showed that adults ($M = 0.86$)

switched more frequently than children did, and switch rates did not differ significantly across the child age groups ($M_{3y} = 0.48$, $M_{4y} = 0.55$, $M_{5y} = 0.59$).

Discussion

Children and adults showed change-preference scores significantly above chance for all set sizes tested, leading to an estimated capacity of at least six items for all age groups. Analyses showed no developmental differences in preference scores; both total looking time and rates of switching between displays were higher for adults than for children. Interestingly, the only significant differences found across set sizes in any measure were between set sizes two and four—roughly equivalent to expected capacity in change detection (cf. Figure 2). Both change-preference scores and switch rates were significantly higher in set size two, suggesting a possible link between capacity in change detection and performance in this task. I return to this question when comparing performance across tasks.

One important finding from this experiment is the comparison between children and infants tested by Ross-Sheehy et al. (2003). In their study, 10-month-old infants showed a significant change preference in set size four but not six, suggesting an adult-like capacity of four items. In the current experiment, children and adults' change preference scores in set size six were significantly above chance, implying a higher capacity of at least six items. This suggests that capacity—as estimated in the change-preference task—continues to increase beyond infancy. It remains for future studies to explore this developmental transition further, mapping how performance changes across intermediate ages, as well as testing the upper limits of capacity in this task with older children and adults. The current study could not yield capacity estimates higher than six items because larger set sizes were not tested.

Set sizes larger than six were not tested in this experiment for two reasons. First, only nine colors have been included as stimuli in this task when used with infants; if set size was increased to, for example, eight items, each presentation would include at least seven colors that matched across the two displays. That amount of similarity across displays would likely alter results relative to the smaller set sizes that have been tested. Although more colors could be included, it is possible that memory performance would differ for a larger range of colors: multiple studies with adults have shown that change detection performance is affected by similarity between colors (Johnson, Spencer, Luck, & Schöner, 2009; Lin & Luck, 2009; Makovski, Watson, Koutstaal, & Jiang, 2010), and initial evidence with children suggests this effect could change developmentally (Grahn, Cooper, Miller, & Simmering, 2015; Simmering, Andrews, & Cooper, 2016). Second, increasing the number of items in each display would require altering the sizes and/or proximity of the stimuli. The effect of shrinking the stimuli is untested, and it is unclear whether this would affect performance in this task differentially over development. Increasing the spatial distribution of the stimuli would require more fixations per display in order to encode all of the stimuli. Although this would probably not affect adults' performance, it is possible that infants and/or children could have a harder time integrating across fixations and associating the stimuli within the correct display. These questions are important to consider in future research, and suggest possibly adapting new methods for testing the upper limits of performance in looking tasks over development.

EXPERIMENT 2: COLOR CHANGE DETECTION

To allow for comparisons across tasks, a subset of the participants from Experiment 1 also participated in the color change detection task that has been modified for use with young children (Simmering, 2012). By testing the same participants in both tasks, I can directly compare capacity estimates across the change-preference and change detection tasks to test the prediction that performance should be correlated across tasks.

Method

Participants

A subset of the participants from Experiment 1 also participated in this experiment: 14 three-year-olds (M age $= 3$ years, 4.68 months; $SD = 2.35$ months; nine girls, five boys), 14 four-year-olds (M age $= 4$ years, 2.56 months; $SD = 1.77$ months; six girls, eight boys), 14 five-year-olds (M age $= 5$ years, 0.36 months; $SD = 0.78$ months; five girls, nine boys). An additional 19 children were excluded from analyses for the following reasons: eight children did not understand the task (7 three-year-olds, 1 five-year-old); nine chose to end early (4 three-year-olds, 5 five-year-olds); one experimenter error (3-year-old); and one equipment failure (3-year-old). Fourteen adults from Experiment 1 also participated in this experiment (M age $= 24$ years, 0.91 months; $SD = 4.67$ years; eight women, six men).

Percentage correct and capacity estimates from these children were described previously (Simmering, 2012). The current monograph presents a more complete description of the data, including analyses of accuracy (A'), statistical comparisons to adults' performance, and correlations with performance in the change-preference task. Simmering (2012) also included data from 7-year-olds, as well as comparison between this task and a control condition replicating the exact method used by Riggs et al. (2006) with 5- and 7-year-olds.

Apparatus

The apparatus and procedure were identical to Simmering (2012), and differed slightly for children versus adults, as described below when relevant. Children were familiarized with the change detection task using flashcards (3″ × 3″) that showed SS1, SS2, and SS3; adults were given a verbal description of the task with sample trials illustrated on a sheet of paper. The task was completed on an 18″ Macintosh computer monitor, which a female experimenter controlled with a keyboard and mouse that were kept out of the child's view. The experimenter entered responses for child participants on the keyboard following their verbal responses, and adult participants entered their own responses while holding the keyboard in their lap. All participants were seated in an adjustable-height chair at a viewing distance of approximately 24–28″ from the screen.

In contrast with the standard version of this task (shown in Figure 1), the items were presented within a rectangular frame to facilitate the description as a card-matching game (see Figure 14). The background of the computer screen was black, and the frame was a 5.75″ tall × 4.75″ wide gray rectangle. The position of the "cards" alternated between the left to right halves of the screen across trials. This helped reduce interference across trials. Stimuli were 1″ × 1″ colored squares as used by Simmering (2012), drawing from the set of colors used in Experiment 1: red, green, blue, yellow, cyan, violet, black, and

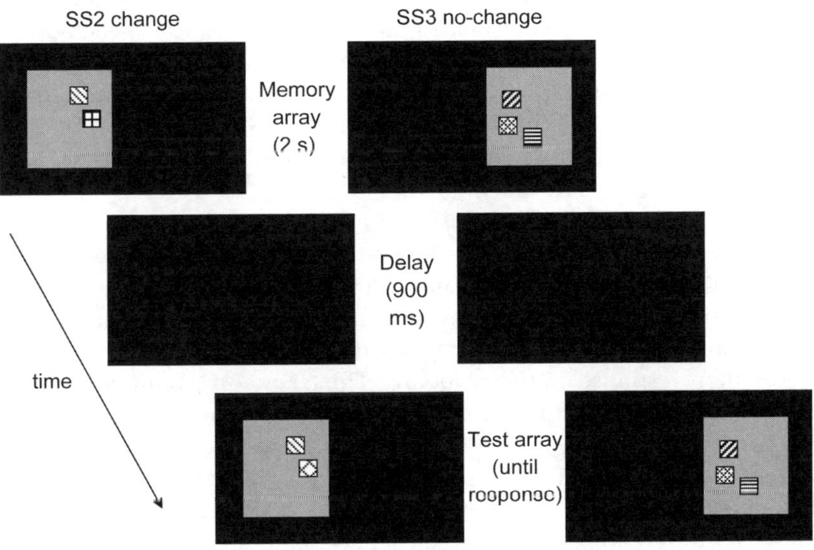

Figure 14.—Sample change detection trials from Experiment 2 (not drawn to scale). Different patterns represent different colors.

white. Colors were selected randomly on each trial without replacement (i.e., a color could not appear twice within an array). Stimuli could appear at any of five equally spaced positions in a 3″ diameter invisible circle around the center of the frame. For SS2–SS4, the stimuli appeared in neighboring positions; all five positions were filled for SS5. For each set size, the positions were chosen randomly for the first trial, but remained constant across the 12 trials in that set size.

Procedure

After completing the change-preference task, child participants took a short break before starting the change detection task to ensure that fatigue would not impair performance. Adult participants were also offered a break, though none chose to take one. Once the participant was seated in the testing room, the task was explained and the necessary training completed. For adults, sample trials were shown on a sheet of paper while the experimenter described the task. For children, the task was described as a matching game in which they had to help a teddy bear find cards that matched. The experimenter then demonstrated the task using flashcards for training. Flashcards were placed on the right or left side of a large sheet of cardstock in the experimenter's lap, alternating across trials. The first (memory array) card was shown for approximately 2 s, and the child was instructed to "Look at the picture and remember the colors." The card was then removed and after a brief delay, the second (test array) card was shown in the same location. The experimenter then asked the child if the two cards matched. After the child responded, the experimenter placed the cards face up next to each other on the cardstock and praised or corrected the child as needed. Flashcard trials were presented in the following order for all child participants: SS1 no-change, SS1 change, SS2 change, SS2 no-change, SS3 change, SS3 no-change. If the experimenter felt the child still did not understand the task, flashcard trials were repeated as needed.

Once the participant understood the task, the experimenter began the computerized version of the task. The first block of trials were practice, with a 2 s duration of the memory array and a 900 ms delay. After the delay, the test array remained visible until a response was entered. Children responded verbally, and the experimenter entered the response on a keyboard; adults entered their response on the keyboard. The *a* key corresponded to a "same" response and the *l* key to a "different" response, with stickers marking the keys to help participants remember the correspondence. After a response was entered, a chime played if the response was correct. This positive feedback was included to help children stay motivated. If children seemed fatigued, they were offered a break in between set size blocks.

The practice block included eight trials in random order: four trials in SS1 and four trials in SS2 (two trials in each set size were change trials, two were no-change trials). Within all blocks, a key press was required to initiate each trial; this allowed the experimenter to pace the task to each child's attention, and reduced the likelihood that errors came from children not attending to the stimuli. Between each block of trials, the child was offered a short break. The order of test blocks was semi-randomly assigned, such that the first two blocks were either SS1 or SS2; for 3- and 4-year-olds, the third block was always SS3; for 5-year-olds and adults, SS3–SS5 were randomly ordered across the third, fourth, and fifth blocks. A different order was used for younger children because they often chose not to complete SS4 and SS5; these high set size blocks were difficult for all children, and young children tended to become discouraged as their performance declined. Each block of test trials included six change and six no-change trials in random order. For 5-year-olds, the duration of the memory array on test trials was shortened to 500 ms, to be comparable with previous studies (Riggs et al., 2006, see Simmering, 2012, for direct comparison); the longer duration was used for younger children to ensure adequate time for encoding, as young children tended to look away from the screen more frequently during stimulus presentation. The total duration of the task was approximately 20–30 min.

One additional feature of the task differed for adult participants relative to child participants. Because this design includes a longer memory array, which may encourage verbal recoding and/or rehearsal in adults, adults were given a verbal load to rehearse. At the beginning of each block, a three-digit number appeared on the computer screen, and adults were instructed to repeat this number throughout all of the trials for that block. The verbal load was not included for children because previous research suggests that children this young do not spontaneously verbally recode or rehearse visual stimuli (e.g., Hitch, Woodin, & Baker, 1989; Miles, Morgan, Milne, & Morris, 1996, see Pickering, 2001, for review).

Results

Participants' responses were classified as correct rejections, hits, misses, and false alarms, as described in Chapter 2. Figure 15 shows the distributions of these response types for each age group separately. Note that correct rejections and false alarms sum to 1.0 (all no-change trials) and hits and misses sum to 1.0 (all change trials); overall percent correct can be estimated as the average of correct rejections and hits for each age group. As this figure shows, these two classes (i.e., correct responses) were the most common responses across ages and set sizes. In addition, performance generally decreased (i.e., errors increased) as set size increased, especially for children.

For each set size, two measures were computed from participants' responses: accuracy (A') and capacity estimates (K). Although most 5-year-olds and all adults completed SS4 and SS5, many 3- and 4-year-olds did not due

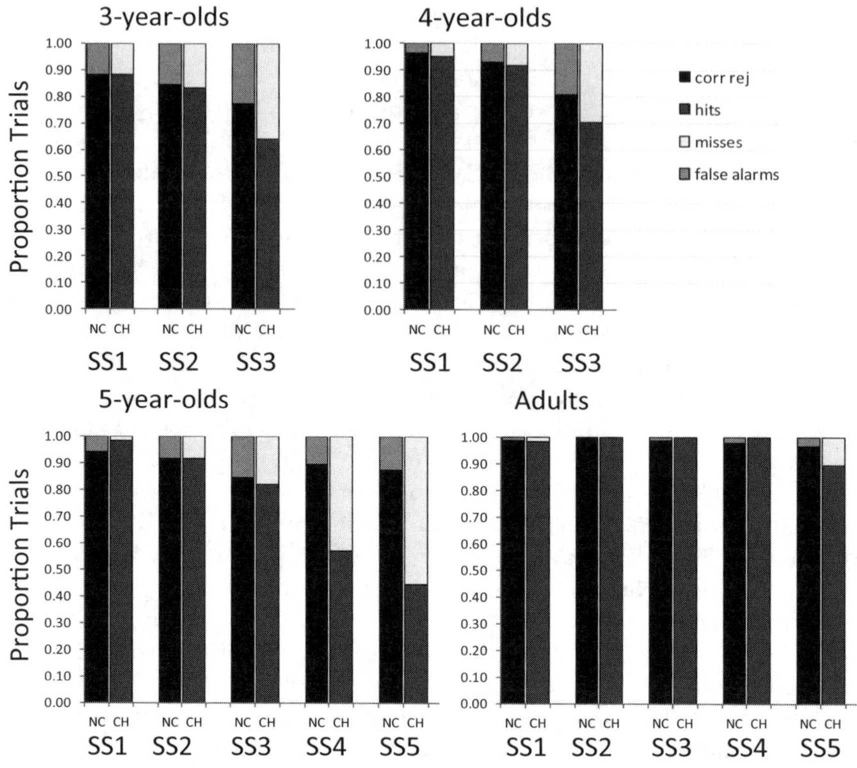

FIGURE 15.—Response distributions across set sizes (SS) and trial types for each age group in Experiment 2. Note that $n = 12$ for 5-year-olds in SS4 and SS5; in all other cases, $n = 14$. NC, no-change; CH, change.

to difficulty keeping children motivated to complete blocks with harder trials. Therefore, I analyzed accuracy across all age groups for SS1–SS3 only, but across all set sizes for 5-year-olds and adults. For each participant, however, I included data from all completed set sizes to compute the maximum capacity estimate (described below).

Accuracy (A')

Accuracy was calculated based on rates of hits (H) and false alarms (FA), using Grier's (1971) formula, updated by Aaronson and Watts (1987) to accommodate below-chance performance:

$$\text{If } H \geq FA : A' = 1/2 + \{[(H - FA)*(1 + H - FA)]/[4*H*(1 - FA)]\}$$

$$\text{If } H < FA : A' = 1/2 - \{[(FA - H)*(1 + FA - H)]/[4*FA*(1 - H)]\}$$

An accuracy score of 1 indicates perfect performance, and a score of 0.5 indicates chance performance. This measure was chosen because, like d', it is affected differentially by errors on change versus no-change trials, but unlike d' it allows for cases in which the false alarm rate exceeds the hit rate (as was the case for some children) and follows a more intuitive range (similar to percent correct). One limitation of this approach is that this equation is invalid when H and FA are equal to each other and 0 or 1, producing 0 as the denominator. In these rare cases (only 2 of the 56 A' scores calculated here), I set A' to 0.50 (chance) because they reflect participants repeating a single response across all trials within that set size.

Accuracy scores were computed separately for each set size block for each participant. Mean accuracy scores across set sizes for each age group are shown in Figure 16. As this figure shows, accuracy was highest for adults and lowest for 3-year-olds, and decreased across set size for all age groups. Error bars showing 95% confidence intervals indicate that, even at their lowest accuracy, children were still performing above chance (0.50); also, adults' performance was not distinguishable from ceiling (1.0) across SS1–SS4.

An ANOVA with Set Size (1, 2, 3) as a within-subjects factor and Age Group (3 years, 4 years, 5 years, adult) as a between-subjects factor revealed significant main effects of Set Size ($F_{2,\ 104} = 41.35$, $p < .001$, $\eta_p^2 = 0.44$) and Age Group ($F_{3,\ 52} = 17.71$, $p < .001$, $\eta_p^2 = 0.51$), which were subsumed by a significant Set Size × Age Group interaction ($F_{6,\ 104} = 5.75$, $p < .001$, $\eta_p^2 = 0.25$). Tests of simple effects for each age group separately revealed significant set size main effects for 3-, 4-, and 5-year-olds ($F_{2,\ 26} = 12.43$, 21.59, 14.69, respectively; all $p < .001$; $\eta_p^2 = 0.49$, 0.62, 0.53, respectively), but not for adults ($p = .55$). For each group of children, follow-up Tukey HSD tests ($p < .05$) showed that accuracy was lower in SS3 than in SS1 and SS2, although SS1 and SS2 did not differ from each other (see Figure 16). Thus, the Set Size by Age Group interaction was driven by a different pattern across set sizes for

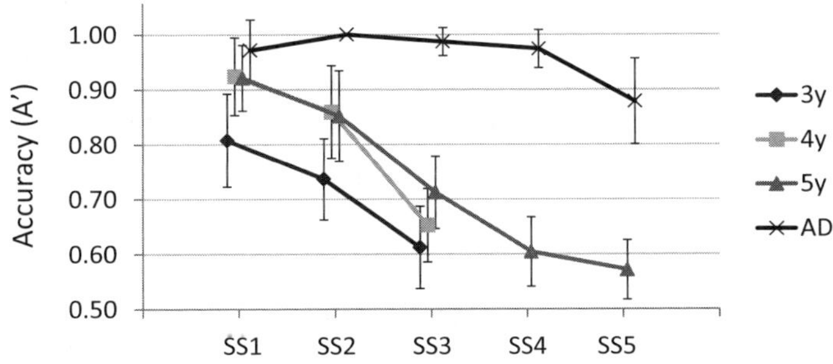

FIGURE 16.—Mean accuracy scores (A') in Experiment 2 across set sizes (SS), separately for each age group; note that chance equals 0.5. Points are offset horizontally to improve visibility. Error bars show 95% confidence intervals.

children than adults, with children's performance declining significantly in SS3.

Because most 5-year-olds ($n = 12$) completed all set sizes, I was also able to compare their performance and adults' in an ANOVA with Set Size (1, 2, 3, 4, 5) as a within-subjects factor and Age Group (5 years, adults) as a between-subjects factor. As with the analysis of smaller set sizes and all age groups, this ANOVA showed significant main effects of Set Size ($F_{4, 96} = 18.37$, $p < .001$, $\eta_p^2 = 0.43$) and Age Group ($F_{1, 24} = 107.70$, $p < .001$, $\eta_p^2 = 0.82$), which were subsumed by a significant Set Size $\times$ Age Group interaction ($F_{4, 96} = 9.69$, $p < .001$, $\eta_p^2 = 0.29$). Tests of simple effects revealed significant set size effects for both 5-year-olds ($F_{4, 44} = 20.63$, $p < .001$, $\eta_p^2 = 0.65$) and adults ($F_{4, 52} = 3.76$, $p = .009$, $\eta_p^2 = 0.22$). Follow-up Tukey HSD tests ($p < .05$) showed that 5-year-olds' accuracy in SS4 and SS5 was significantly lower than in SS1 and SS2; all other differences were not significant. For adults, accuracy in SS5 was lower than only SS2 and SS3 (see Figure 16). Again, the Set Size by Age interaction is driven by a different pattern over set sizes for 5-year-olds than adults, with the latter group not showing a decline in performance until SS5.

Capacity Estimates (K)

Capacity estimates were calculated using Pashler's (1988) formula, separately for each set size (SS): $K = SS^* (H - FA)/(1 - FA)$; note that capacity can, at maximum, equal the set size in each block. Because of this limit on capacity estimates, it is not sensible to analyze these data across set sizes. Moreover, calculating an average capacity estimate across blocks would result in an artificially low number by including set sizes below capacity. To avoid this limitation, I chose to use each participant's highest estimate across set size blocks, K_{max} (for further discussion, see Simmering, 2012; see also Olsson & Poom, 2005; Todd & Marois, 2005). Mean K_{max} estimates were, respectively, across age groups, 1.90 (95%CI [1.55, 2.25]), 2.20 (95%CI [1.92, 2.48]), 2.90 (95%CI [2.51, 3.28]), and 4.62 (95%CI [4.38, 4.86]) items. I analyzed mean K_{max} estimates in a one-way ANOVA with Age Group as a between-subjects factor, revealing a significant main effect ($F_{3, 52} = 55.76$, $p < .001$, $\eta^2 = 0.76$). Follow-up Tukey HSD tests ($p < .05$) showed that K_{max} estimates did not differ between 3- and 4-year-olds, but all other differences were significant.

Discussion

Results from the color change detection task were analyzed using accuracy and capacity estimates. Accuracy (A') showed that adults performed at ceiling for all set sizes except five, and children's performance was below ceiling and above chance for all set sizes. For all groups of children, accuracy decreased significantly from set size two to three; for 5-year-olds, accuracy also decreased to set sizes four and five. Adults' performance in set size five was only significantly lower than set sizes two and three. These decreases in accuracy relate to capacity estimates, with significant decreases in accuracy near each age group's estimated capacity. The key result from this experiment was the increase in maximum capacity estimates over development: children's capacity increased significantly from approximately two items for 3- to 4-year-olds, to approximately three items for 5-year-olds, and again to between four and five items for adults. In all of these cases, capacity estimates from change detection were lower than the six items estimated from the change-preference task, supporting the difference across tasks predicted by the cognitive dynamics account and model simulations.

EXPERIMENT 3: SHAPE CHANGE DETECTION

A second subset of the participants from Experiment 1 participated in a shape change detection task. The goal of this experiment was to provide a second test of the predicted differences across change-preference and change detection tasks, and to see if the capacity limits found in Experiment 2 are specific to color, or if similar patterns occur in memory for other visual features. Research with adults has shown small but reliable differences across stimulus dimensions; in particular, capacity tends to be slightly lower for shapes than for colors (e.g., Wheeler & Treisman, 2002). Thus, results may be lower in this experiment than in Experiment 2.

Method

Participants
Forty-two children from Experiment 1 also participated in this experiment: 14 three-year-olds (M age $= 3$ years, 6.39 months; $SD = 1.22$ months; eight girls, six boys), 14 four-year-olds (M age $= 4$ years, 3.93 months; $SD = 0.61$ months; nine girls, five boys), 14 five-year-olds (M age $= 5$ years, 2.21 months; $SD = 2.09$ months; nine girls, five boys). An additional 10 children were excluded from analyses for the following reasons: seven children did not understand the task (4 three-year-olds, 3 four-year-olds); two chose to end early (3-year-olds); and one experimenter error (3-year-old). Fifteen adults from Experiment 1 also participated in this experiment (M age $= 21$ years, 4.30 months; $SD = 2.90$ years; 10 women, 5 men).

Apparatus
The apparatus was identical to that used in Experiment 2 with one exception: rather than colored squares, the stimulus set comprised eight white shapes from Wheeler and Treisman (2002), shown in Figure 17.

FIGURE 17.—Shape stimuli from Experiment 3.

Procedure

The procedure was identical to Experiment 2 with two exceptions. First, the memory array was presented for 2 s for all children (rather than only 500 ms for 5-year-olds). Second, all participants completed set size blocks in the same order: SS2, SS1, SS3, SS4, SS5.

Results

As in Experiment 2, participants' responses were classified as correct rejections, hits, misses, and false alarms. Figure 18 shows the distributions of these response types for each age group separately. As this figure shows, correct responses were most common across ages and set sizes. In addition, performance generally declined as set size increased, especially for children. Relative to Experiment 2, performance is slightly lower, consistent with adult studies comparing memory for shapes and colors (e.g., Wheeler & Treisman, 2002).

For each set size, two measures were computed from participants' responses: accuracy (A') and capacity estimates (K). As in Experiment 2, many 3- and 4-year-olds did not complete SS4 and SS5 due to difficulty keeping children motivated to complete blocks with harder trials. Therefore, I analyzed accuracy across all age groups for SS1–SS3 only, but across all set sizes for 5-year-olds and adults. Again, data from all completed set sizes were used to compute capacity estimates.

Accuracy (A')

Accuracy was computed as in Experiment 2. Figure 19 shows mean accuracy scores across set sizes separately for each age group. As can be seen, accuracy was highest for adults and lowest for 3-year-olds, and generally decreased across set size for all age groups. Error bars showing 95% confidence intervals suggest that, even at their lowest accuracy, children were still performing above chance (0.50); adults' performance was not distinguishable from ceiling (1.0) in SS1 and SS2.

An ANOVA with Set Size (1, 2, 3) as a within-subjects factor and Age Group (3 years, 4 years, 5 years, adult) as a between-subjects factor revealed

72

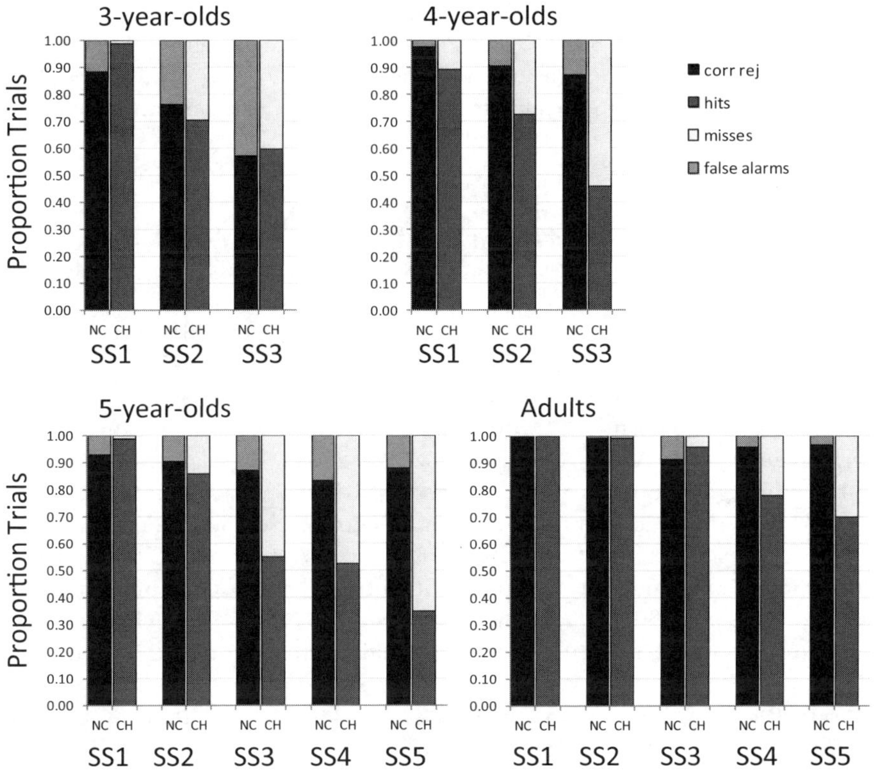

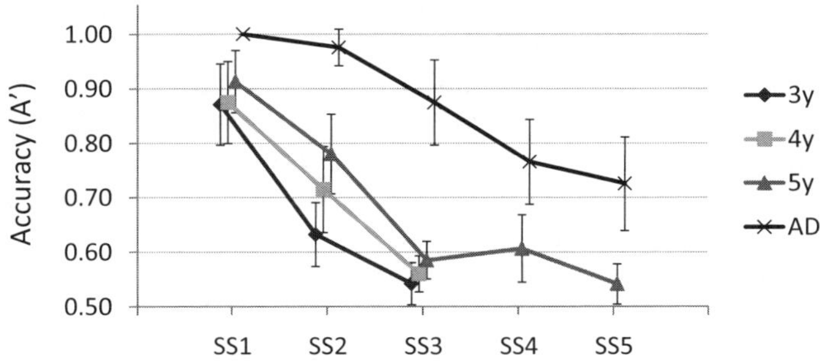

FIGURE 18.—Response distributions across set sizes (SS) and trial types for each age group in Experiment 3. Note that $n = 10$ for 5-year-olds in SS5; in all other cases, $n = 14$. Corr rej, correct rejections; NC, no-change; CH, change.

FIGURE 19.—Mean accuracy scores (A') in Experiment 3 across set sizes (SS), separately for each age group; note that chance equals 0.5. Points are offset horizontally to improve visibility. Error bars show 95% confidence intervals.

significant main effects of Set Size ($F_{2, 106} = 91.27$, $p < .001$, $\eta_p^2 = 0.63$) and Age Group ($F_{3, 53} = 46.80$, $p < .001$, $\eta_p^2 = 0.73$), which were subsumed by a significant Set Size $\times$ Age Group interaction ($F_{6, 106} = 4.31$, $p = .001$, $\eta_p^2 = 0.20$). Tests of simple effects for each age group separately showed significant set size main effects for all age groups ($F_{2, 26} = 31.62$, 24.16, 33.26, 8.48, respectively; all $p < .001$; $\eta_p^2 = 0.71$, 0.65, 0.72, 0.38, respectively). Follow-up Tukey HSD tests ($p < .05$) revealed different patterns across the age groups (see Figure 19). For 3-year-olds, accuracy in SS1 was higher than in SS2 and SS3, but did not differ between SS2 and SS3. For 4-year-olds, accuracy decreased significantly from SS1 to SS2 and from SS2 to SS3. For 5-year-olds and adults, accuracy did not differ between SS1 and SS2, but both were higher than SS3. Thus, the Set Size by Age interaction was driven by different patterns of Set Size effects across the different age groups.

Next, as in Experiment 2, I compared 5-year-olds' ($n = 10$) and adults' performance in an ANOVA with Set Size (1, 2, 3, 4, 5) as a within-subjects factor and Age Group (5 years, adults) as a between-subjects factor. This ANOVA also showed significant main effects of Set Size ($F_{4, 92} = 36.18$, $p < .001$, $\eta_p^2 = 0.61$) and Age Group ($F_{1, 23} = 77.46$, $p < .001$, $\eta_p^2 = 0.77$), which were subsumed by a significant Set Size $\times$ Age Group interaction ($F_{4, 92} = 2.63$, $p = .039$, $\eta_p^2 = 0.10$). Tests of simple effects for each age group separately revealed significant set size main effects for both 5-year-olds ($F_{4, 36} = 32.08$, $p < .001$, $\eta_p^2 = 0.78$) and adults ($F_{4, 56} = 14.27$, $p < .001$, $\eta_p^2 = 0.50$). Follow-up Tukey HSD tests ($p < .05$) showed that 5-year-olds' accuracy in SS4 and SS5 was lower than in SS1 and SS2, but did not differ from SS3; for adults, accuracy in SS4 and SS5 was lower than all others and did not differ from each other (see Figure 19). Again, the Set Size by Age Group interaction is driven by a different pattern over set sizes for 5-year-olds than adults.

Capacity Estimates (K)

Capacity estimates were calculated as in Experiment 3 in each set size for each participant. Mean K_{max} estimates were, respectively, across age groups, 1.75 (95%CI [1.45, 2.06]), 2.61 (95%CI [1.88, 3.33]), 2.26 (95%CI [1.92, 2.61]), and 3.92 (95%CI [3.57, 4.28]) items. I analyzed mean K_{max} estimates in a one-way ANOVA with Age Group as a between-subjects factor, revealing a significant main effect ($F_{3, 53} = 16.10$, $p < .001$). Follow-up Tukey HSD tests ($p < .05$) showed K_{max} estimates differed among all age groups except 5-year-olds did not differ from 3- and 4-year-olds.

Discussion

As in Experiment 2, accuracy scores (A') showed that change detection performance improved over development, although K_{max} estimates did not reflect this improvement statistically during childhood. This is likely due to the fact that performance on change trials (i.e., hits) was considerably lower than in Experiment 2. A key finding from this experiment was again the K_{max} estimates: children's capacity was estimated around two items between 3 and 5 years, with adults showing significantly higher capacity of approximately four items. In all of these cases, capacity estimates from change detection were lower than the six items estimated from change-preference, supporting the difference across tasks predicted by the cognitive dynamics account.

COMPARISONS ACROSS TASKS

Experiments 1–3 confirmed the first two predictions of the cognitive dynamics account of visual working memory capacity: children and adults showed capacity estimates of six items in change-preference, which is higher than infants show in this task, as well as the commonly accepted adult-like capacity of three to four items; these capacity estimates were also higher than the capacity estimates derived from the change detection task for the same individuals (approximately two to three items for children, between four and five items for adults). The third prediction of the cognitive dynamics account is that performance in both tasks depends on the same underlying visual working memory system, which should be evident in correlated performance across tasks.

This prediction was tested in a multiple regression analysis across tasks for all child participants who completed both the change-preference and color change detection tasks. I chose to include only the color version of the change detection task because it is not clear how separable memory is for colors versus shapes. As noted previously, in adults capacity for shapes is often slightly lower than capacity for colors (e.g., Wheeler & Treisman, 2002); the results from Experiments 2 and 3 show this pattern extends into childhood as well (see also Simmering et al., 2015). Thus, for the cleanest comparison across tasks, it seems best to focus only on comparison within a single feature dimension to begin with.

I also chose to exclude adults' data from these analyses for two reasons. First, there were clear differences between children's and adults' performance in Experiments 1 and 2. These relatively large developmental differences may mask more subtle developmental and/or individual differences within the child age groups. Second, 7 of the 12 adults who completed both tasks had K_{max} estimates at ceiling (i.e., five items), presenting the possibility that this measure was artificially limited for these participants and therefore would not present a complete picture of how performance relates across tasks.

Participants

The 51 children who participated in the change-preference task and successfully completed the color change detection task were included in these analyses: 14 three-year-olds (as reported in Experiment 2), 14 four-year-olds (as reported in Experiment 2), and 23 five-year-olds (13 from Experiment 2 plus 10 from a condition reported in Simmering, 2012, which replicated the method from Riggs et al., 2006 M age $= 5$ years, 0.37 months, $SD = 0.69$ months; 11 girls, 13 boys). An additional 20 children participated in these tasks but were excluded from analyses: 19 (13 three-year-olds and 7 five-year-olds) for reasons described in Experiment 2, and 1 five-year-old whose K_{max} estimate was five items. Because it was not possible for K estimates to exceed five in this task, this child's K_{max} estimate may have been artificially limited by the task design, leading me to exclude his data from this analysis.

Before considering the results of this analysis, it is important to note potential limitations of the current sample. First, the inclusion of only children who successfully completed both change-preference and change detection tasks was not random. Inclusion in the analysis of Experiment 1 but not here resulted from random assignment for most children (i.e., they were assigned to Experiment 3 or a change detection condition not reported here; $n = 49$ and 34, respectively). Of the 19 children who completed Experiment 1 but were assigned to Experiment 2 and then excluded from analyses of the change detection task, 17 either did not understand the task ($n = 8$) or did not complete enough trials for a capacity estimate to be calculated ($n = 9$). This could result in the current sample including only high-performing children, especially for 3-year-olds. Second, the final sample size for this cross-task comparison is relatively small for addressing individual differences. This is an unfortunate limitation that arises in studies recruiting populations that are not easily accessed (i.e., young children). Both of these limitations make the current analyses more likely to produce a null effect, however, suggesting that any significant findings are worth pursuing for replication with larger, more representative samples.

Variable Selection

The primary measure of interest from change detection is capacity; as such, the K_{max} estimate for each individual was the dependent measure used in these analyses. In the change-preference task, however, there is no direct calculation of capacity per participant. As described in Chapter 2, simulations of the dynamic model revealed how looking behavior relates to the underlying cognitive processes. Of particular relevance for this analysis are change preference scores, which reflect the detection of novelty, and switch rates, which reflect the detection of familiarity. Because these two measures each have three scores, one derived from each set size, all six scores were included in these analyses. Finally, because capacity in change detection was significantly higher for 5-year-olds in Experiment 2, I included age (as a continuous variable) as well. Thus, in this analysis I tested which of the following variables predicted change detection capacity: age; change preference scores in SS2, SS4, and SS6; and switch rates in SS2, SS4, and SS6.

Results

Simple correlations among these factors (Pearson's r) are shown above the diagonal in Table 2 (note that correlations with K_{max}, which are of most interest, are in bold). As expected, K_{max} estimates from change detection were most strongly positively correlated with age, although age did not correlate significantly with any of the measures from the change-preference task. In addition, positive correlations between K_{max} and change preference scores from SS2 and switch rate in SS6, were significant, as well a trend toward a correlation with SS4 switch rate. Table 2 also includes partial correlations (below the diagonal; correlations with K_{max} in bold) controlling for age. Notably, the only effect that changed significance was the correlation with SS4 switch rate, which reached significance with age partialled out.

To test the robustness of the relations among these variables further, I conducted a hierarchical regression analyses with three models including Age, Change Preference Scores, Switch Rates to predict K_{max}. Table 3 shows these three models for comparison. Model 1 included only Age; as expected, it accounted for a significant proportion of the variance in K_{max} (see Table 3). Next, for Model 2, I entered Change Preference Scores from SS2, SS4, and SS6 to test whether the scores used to estimate capacity correlated across tasks. Similar to the simple correlations shown in Table 2, in this model only SS2

TABLE 2

SIMPLE CORRELATIONS COMPARING CHANGE-PREFERENCE AND COLOR CHANGE DETECTION TASKS

Variable		1	2	3	4	5	6	7
Age		**.58*****	−.08	.02	−.05	.04	−.01	−.06
1.	**Capacity (K_{max})**		**.29****	**−.05**	**−.03**	**.15**	**.20**†	**.31****
2.	SS2 change pref.	**.40*****		−.25*	−.07	−.16	−.02	.13
3.	SS4 change pref.	**−.08**	−.25*		.20†	.05	−.07	−.13
4.	SS6 change pref.	**.00**	−.07	.21†		.09	−.04	−.16
5.	SS2 switch rate	**.15**	.17	.04	.09		.44***	.35**
6.	SS4 switch rate	**.25***	−.02	−.07	−.04	.44***		.54***
7.	SS6 switch rate	**.43*****	.13	−.13	−.16	.35**	.54***	

Note. $N = 51$. Values above the diagonal indicate bivariate correlations (Pearson's r); values below the diagonal indicate partial correlations corrected for age. Correlations with K_{max} (the dependent variable of primary interest) are in bold. SS2, set size two; SS4, set size four; SS6, set size six.
†$p < .10$, *$p < .05$, **$p < .01$, ***$p < .001$ (one-tailed).

TABLE 3

REGRESSION MODEL PREDICTING CHANGE DETECTION CAPACITY ESTIMATES

Predictor	Model 1	Model 2	Model 3
Age (β)	.58***	.60***	.62***
SS2 preference scores (β)		.33**	.32**
SS4 preference scores (β)		.03	.05
SS6 preference scores (β)		.00	.07
SS2 switch rates (β)			−.08
SS4 switch rates (β)			.08
SS6 switch rates (β)			.31*
R^2	.33***	.40***	.48***
ΔR^2		.07	.08
F change (df)		2.92* (3, 47)	3.24* (3, 42)

Note. Parameter estimates are standardized (β) and R^2 adjusted. F change results are in comparison to the prior model.
*$p < .05$, **$p < .01$, ***$p < .001$.

Change Preference Scores accounted for additional variance beyond Age alone (see Table 3). Further, this model provided a significantly better fit than Model 1. Finally, for Model 3, I added Switch Rates in SS2, SS4, and SS6. In this model, only SS6 Switch Rates accounted for a significant additional proportion of the variance (see Table 3). This model also provided a significantly better fit than the previous models.

These results provide initial evidence that performance is related across the change-preference and change detection tasks, even though the capacity estimates differed across tasks. As an exploratory follow-up analysis, I also tested whether these measures from the change-preference task relate differentially to hits versus correct rejections in the change detection task. As described in Chapter 2, the dynamic model simulations suggest that change preference scores should relate more strongly to hits (i.e., detecting novelty) and switch rates should relate more strongly to correct rejections (i.e., detecting familiarity). However, the standard implementation of the change detection task is not ideal for addressing this question: unlike K_{max} estimates, which can be calculated for each individual regardless of the number of set sizes completed, rates of hits, and correct rejections are linked to set size (see Figure 15). Furthermore, children completed a relatively small number of trials per trial type in each set size, which could artificially reduce variability across participants. As such, this analysis is a limited approach to testing this question, but results consistent with the cognitive dynamics account would be encouraging for further investigation into how these measures and processes relate across tasks.

For this analysis, I chose to compare children's performance on highest set size they completed in the change detection task[i] with the significant change-preference measures from the regression analysis above. As a first step, I tested whether hit rates and correct rejection rates from the highest set size completed were related to the K_{max} estimates used in the hierarchical regression analysis. They were not significantly correlated ($r_{49} = 0.10$, $p = .23$, for both measures), indicating that these analyses could reveal different relations to the change-preference task than the regression on K_{max} estimates. Next, I tested the predictions laid out in Chapter 2: SS2 change preference scores were significantly correlated with hit rates ($r_{49} = 0.23$, $p = .048$) and SS6 switch rates were marginally correlated with correct rejection rates ($r_{49} = 0.22$, $p = .065$). These exploratory correlations suggest that both the change-preference and change detection tasks can provide separable measures of the processes that support detection of novelty versus familiarity, and that these same processes operate across tasks.

Discussion

Using hierarchical regression, I tested whether capacity estimates from the color change detection task were predicted by change preference scores and/or switch rates from the change-preference task. After controlling for age, both set size two change preference scores and set size six switch rates accounted for significant variance in capacity estimates. As predicted by the dynamic model simulations in Chapter 2, these contributions to performance were separable, as set size two change preference scores did not correlate with set size six switch rates (see Table 2) and they explained unique variance in the regression model. Exploratory analyses comparing these measures separately to hit versus correct rejection rates suggest that change preference scores could provide an index of novelty detection (correlated with hit rates) and switch rates could provide an index of familiarity detection (correlated with correct rejection rates). However, a more stringent test of this predicted relation between tasks is needed to determine whether these effects are reliable.

An important remaining question is why the predictive factors in the regression model were limited to only set size two for change preference scores and set size six for switch rates. Model simulations can provide some insight into this question: in the following chapter, I show how the formation and use of memory representations differs across set sizes in the change-preference task, which could lead to behavioral differences that contribute to these correlations. Together these two measures can be considered components of the real-time stability of the memory system, with more stable memory processes supporting better performance in the change detection task.

As noted above, these results should be interpreted with some caution due to limitations in the sample. However, further investigation of the relation between looking measures and working memory seems warranted based on these findings. The capacity estimates derived across Experiments 1–3 alone would not suggest that such correlations would exist; there were no developmental differences in change preference scores (and therefore capacity estimates) in Experiment 1, even between children and adults. This could have been interpreted as evidence that this task measures a different type of memory than change detection (as had been proposed by Riggs et al., 2006). Instead, by implementing both tasks within a formal model, the cognitive dynamics theory explained how the different patterns of performance across tasks could result from the same underlying system, and that capacity in change detection could be predicted by change-preference performance. Moreover, this comparison across tasks in preschool-aged children suggests that looking tasks may still be a viable method for identifying individual differences beyond infancy.

SUMMARY

The experiments presented in this chapter supported the first three predictions of the cognitive dynamics account that were outlined in Chapters 1 and 2. First, Experiment 1 showed that capacity as estimated by the change-preference task continues to develop beyond infancy: 3- to 5-year-old children and adults all demonstrated significant change preferences in set size six. Second, the same participants showed higher capacity estimates in the change-preference versus change detection task, specifically estimated to be at least six items for all age groups in the change-preference task, but only two to three items for children and between four and five items for adults in the change detection tasks. Third, and most critically for the cognitive dynamics account and dynamic neural field model implementation, even though capacity estimates differed across tasks, performance was positively correlated, with set size two change preference scores and set size six switch rates in the change-preference task predicting capacity estimates in color change detection task, even after controlling for age-related increases. These results provide an answer for the question of why previous results seemed inconsistent across these two visual working memory tasks over development, and whether they rely on the same underlying memory system. Furthermore, they align with the cautious interpretation put forth by Ross-Sheehy et al. (2003), in that capacity estimates were not isomorphic across tasks. The next, deeper question to address is what mechanism underlies developmental change in these tasks. The following chapter tests my fourth prediction: whether implementing a variant of the spatial precision hypothesis—strengthening connectivity within the model—can capture the pattern of behavioral results described here.

NOTE

i. One participant (a 5-year-old) responded "same" on every trial in set size five, leading to a hit rate of 0 and a correct rejection rate of 1. For this participant, set size five was also the last set size tested within the random order, suggesting that fatigue may have contributed to this pattern of responding. Thus, I chose to use this participant's data from set size four in this analysis.

IV. MODEL SIMULATIONS TESTING THE REAL-TIME STABILITY HYPOTHESIS OF DEVELOPMENTAL CHANGES IN VISUAL WORKING MEMORY

Vanessa R. Simmering

> This article is part of the issue "Working Memory Capacity in Context: Modeling Dynamic Processes of Behavior, Memory, and Development," Simmering, Vanessa (Issue Author). For a full listing of articles in this issue, see: http://onlinelibrary.wiley.com/doi/10.1111/mono.v81.3/issuetoc.

The review of the literature in Chapter 1 identified the need for a general explanation of working memory development. Chapter 2 introduced the cognitive dynamics theory and real-time stability hypothesis as a way to synthesize findings across multiple tasks and developmental period. Implementing this theory in a computational model led to three empirical predictions that were supported by behavioral results in Chapter 3. The current chapter describes tests of the fourth prediction from the model implementation, specifically that developmental improvements in both change-preference and change detection performance could arise from a common underlying source. According to the real-time stability hypothesis, behavior improves developmentally through increasing stability in the underlying visual working memory system. In the type of model introduced in Chapter 2, increasing stability in infants' memory has been simulated through strengthening connections within and between layers of the model (Perone et al., 2011). Here, I test whether this implementation can be expanded to account for development through early childhood and into adulthood in the change-preference task, as well as the change detection task.

Corresponding author: Vanessa R. Simmering, 1202 W. Johnson St., Madison, WI 53706; email: simmering@wisc.edu

DOI: 10.1111/mono.12252

In the sections that follow, I first present quantitative simulations of the dynamic model showing that strengthening connections within the three-layer architecture, combined with changes to accumulation of long-term memory and the task-specific behavioral systems, can fit the pattern of data reported in Chapter 3. Next, I analyzed how the processes within the model differ as a function of this developmental change to provide a further explanation of changes in real-time stability. Then, I use the model's performance to explain the correlations in Chapter 3, with capacity estimates in color change detection predicted by change preference scores from only set size two and switch rates from only set size six. Finally, in the last section I discuss potential sources of this developmental change in connectivity as it relates to questions of maturation versus experience. This section also considers whether individual and developmental differences could arise from the same sources.

QUANTITATIVE SIMULATIONS OF EXPERIMENTS 1 AND 2 RESULTS

Experiments 1–3 showed that the change-preference and change detection tasks lead to different capacity estimates when testing the same individuals in both tasks. In particular, capacity estimates were higher in the change-preference task (at least six items) and did not change over development from 3 to 5 years or to adulthood. Capacity estimates in change detection ($K_{\max}$), on the other hand, were low for young children (about two items) and increased over development (to about three items for older children to between four and five items for adults). In addition, comparisons across tasks revealed that set size two change preference scores and set size six switch rates in the change-preference task independently and significantly predicted capacity in change detection, even after controlling for variance due to age.

These results support the first three predictions generated with the dynamic model implementation of the cognitive dynamics theory: capacity estimates for older children and adults were greater than four items in the preferential looking task; capacity estimates for the same participants were substantially lower in change detection; and performance was related across tasks despite divergent capacity estimates. This support for the model prediction suggests that these two tasks rely on the same underlying visual working memory system. But can the dynamic model produce this pattern of results across tasks and age groups with a single developmental mechanism? This is an important question because a common source of developmental change from infancy through childhood could shed light onto the processes that relate working memory at these different points in development to higher cognitive skills. This section includes quantitative simulations of both tasks testing the fourth prediction generated in Chapter 2: development in these tasks can be captured within the dynamic model through strengthening connectivity as an implementation of the real-time stability hypothesis.

Before considering the simulation results in detail, it is important to note that the precise implementation of the model architecture and the parameter values are not the ultimate goal of this exercise. Rather, these simulations are a demonstration proof that many of the cognitive concepts that have been invoked to account for developmental changes in memory, either independently or in opposition, could arise through a shared mechanism. Similar model implementations within the Dynamic Field Theory framework have led to novel behavioral predictions in visuospatial cognition over development (see Johnson & Simmering, 2015; Simmering & Schutte, 2015, for reviews), but such predictions do not depend on specific details of the simulations: there could be minor variations in architecture and/or parameters that still produce the same general outcome. Thus, rather than focusing on whether simulations like these capture behavior to the exclusion of other model implementations, the question of interest is whether the theoretical constructs of cognitive dynamics and real-time stability can explain performance and development in these tasks and, ultimately, whether it could be generalized more broadly (as discussed in Chapter 5). Using a formal model to test this theory provides a level of specificity not often achieved in developmental theories (see Schlesinger & McMurray, 2012; Simmering & Patterson, 2012; Simmering & Spencer, 2008, for further discussion).

Quantitative simulation of the behavioral data from Experiments 1 and 2 is a formidable task, given the different developmental trajectories across tasks (e.g., few differences between age groups in the change-preference task but many differences between age groups in the change detection task). Furthermore, the data set provides a large number of means to fit: in the change-preference task, I fit three behavioral measures (total looking times, change preference scores, switch rates) across three set sizes and four age groups, for a total of 36 means; in the change detection task, I fit percent correct on two trial types (change and no-change trials) in three set sizes for 3-year-olds, four set sizes for 4-year-olds, and five set sizes in 5-year-olds and adults, for a total of 34 means. Thus, varying a relatively small number of parameters in the model (described further below), I was able to fit the dynamic model to 70 behavioral means across tasks and development.

To test whether the dynamic model could fit this pattern of data through strengthening connectivity over development, I began with parameters tuned to fit adults' performance in other tasks (described further below; Johnson et al., 2014; Lipinski et al., 2010) and simulated adults' change detection performance. I chose to fit change detection performance first because there was more variance across data points, providing more constraints on the parameter space that could produce this developmental pattern. Because the dynamic model used by Johnson et al. to fit adults' performance did not include Hebbian fields, I first modified their parameters to fit the results with adults from the current Experiment 2. Next, I tested the effect of modifying the strength of connectivity over development by scaling a subset of the parameters to capture children's performance from Experiment 2. Lastly, I held the parameters in the five-layer architecture constant to simulate performance in the change-preference task, and modified a subset of the parameters in the fixation system relative to those reported by Perone et al. (2011) to fit the full data set from Experiment 1. In all cases, parameters were tuned "by hand," that is, by modifying the values based on previous implementations of the real-time stability hypothesis, then evaluating whether the means resulting from the simulations produced a satisfactory fit across behavioral measures, then iterating these parameters as needed (slightly stronger or slightly weaker) to approximate the behavioral data better. As a starting point, I defined a satisfactory fit as a mean absolute error (MAE) between the behavioral and simulation means, averaging across set sizes within each measure, less than 0.50; this corresponds to one-half of a unit of measure (i.e., trial for change detection, second in looking time, switch per second for switch rate). As results show, most fits surpassed this threshold and provided a closer fit to the behavioral data.

Simulation Method

Model Architecture and Parameters

The architecture consisted of the five-layer architecture described in Chapter 2 (shown in Figure 6) with the response nodes for the change detection task and the fixation system for the change-preference task (see Appendix for equations). Each of the five fields in the field model contained 361 nodes. Parameter values for the "adult" fits are shown in Table 4 and discussed within the simulation results sections below. Simulations were conducted in Matlab 2013 (Mathworks, Inc.) on a Dell Optiplex 330 with an Intel Core2 Duo 2660 MHz processor. The dynamic field equations were integrated using the Euler method with one time step = 2 ms. For these simulations, the model was presented with one to six inputs on each trial, depending on the set size, out of nine possible inputs that corresponded to different colors selected from a hypothetical continuous 360° color space (i.e., 1° in color space = one unit in the model), in which color stimuli were uniformly distributed with separations of 40°.

Change Detection Task Structure

Each simulation trial began with a 100-ms relaxation period that allowed the model to reach a stable resting state. This was followed by the 2-s

TABLE 4

Parameter Values Fitting Adults' Performance

Field/Nodes	τ	Resting Level	Self-Excitation	Excitatory Projection(s)	Inhibitory Projection(s)	Input	Noise
CF (u)	$\tau_u = 80$ $\tau_{qh} = 50^{a,c}$	$h_u = -6.75^a$	$c_{uu} = 2$ $\sigma_{uu} = 3$	$c_{uH} = 0.2^b$ $\sigma_{uH} = 6.4^b$ $c_{ud} = 1^d$ $c_{uf} = 1^d$	$c_{uv} = 1.85$ $\sigma_{uv} = 26$ $k_{uv} = 0.05^d$	$c_{ustim} = 30$ $\sigma_{ustim} = 3$	$q_u = 0.04^c$ $\sigma_q = 1^c$ $q_h = 6^{a,c}$
Inhib (v)	$\tau_v = 10$	$h_v = -12^a$		$c_{vu} = 2$ $\sigma_{vu} = 10$ $c_{vw} = 1.95$ $\sigma_{vw} = 5$			
WM (w)	$\tau_w = 80$	$h_w = -4.5^a$	$c_{ww} = 3.15$ $\sigma_{ww} = 3$	$c_{wu} = 1.6$ $\sigma_{wu} = 5$ $c_{wd} = 1^d$	$c_{wv} = 0.325$ $\sigma_{wv} = 42$ $k_{wv} = 0.08^d$	$c_{wstim} = 6$ $\sigma_{wstim} = 3$	
Hebb. (H)	$\tau_{Hbuild} = 3000^b$ $\tau_{Hdecay} = 100,000^b$						

Resp. (R)
  Diff. (d)
  Same (s)
	$\tau_R = 80$	$h_d = -5$
		$h_s = -4.75$
			$c_{RR} = 1.85$	$c_{Rg} = 4.25$
				$c_{du} = 1.4$
				$c_{sw} = 0.275$
					$c_{R-} = 14$		$q_R = .065$

Gate (g)	$\tau_g = 80$	$h_g = -4.92$	$c_{gg} = 4.8$	$c_{gw} = .03$		$c_{gstim} = .03$ $c_{gT} = 18$	$q_g = .025$
Fix. (F)	$\tau_F = 80$ $\tau_{hF} = 80$	$h_F = -5^e$ $h_{down} = -5.48^e$	$c_{FF} = 2.85$		$c_{F-} = 5$	$c_{FT} = 0.4$	$q_{FC} = 3^f$
Left (l)/right (r)			$q_{lu} = c_{ru} = 0.14$			$c_{lB} = c_{rB} = 1$ $q_{lC} = c_{rC} = 6.16$	
Away (a) Center (c)						$c_{aC} = 5.6$ $c_{cAG} = 5.5$	

Note. Following mathematical convention, parameter subscripts indicate the field receiving the projection followed by the field/node sending the projection (i.e., c_{wu} indicates the strength of a projection into w/WM from u/CF). Parameters shown in the Response (Resp.) row were identical for the Same and Different (Diff.) nodes; any parameters that differed between these nodes are shown in the following rows. Similarly, parameters shown in Fixation (Fix.) row were identical across Left, Right, Center, and Away nodes; any parameters that differed across fixation nodes are shown in the following rows.
[a]The resting levels of these three fields also included colored noise; the equation for these resting levels, which contains parameters q_h and τ_{qh}, is reported in the Appendix.
[b]Parameters were identical for both Hebbian (Hebb.) fields (i.e., $c_{uH} = c_{wH}$, $\sigma_{uH} = \sigma_{wH}$, $\tau_{uHbuild} = \tau_{wHbuild}$, $\tau_{uHdecay} = \tau_{wHdecay}$) and are shown only once for simplicity.
[c]These parameters were identical across all three fields, and are reported only once in the table for simplicity.
[d]These projections were applied uniformly across the fields, thus there are no corresponding σ values.
[e]The fixation node equations used dynamic resting levels; the equation for the resting level change, which contains the parameters h_F, h_{down}, and τ_{hF}, is reported in the Appendix.
[f]Noise for the fixation system was applied to the constant input strength to the Left and Right nodes (q_{lC}, c_{rC}) rather than the node activation at each time step; see Appendix for details.

presentation of the inputs corresponding to the memory array, then a 900-ms delay interval with no input, as in Experiment 2. Next, the inputs corresponding the test array were presented, in which either all items matched the memory array (a no-change trial) or one item changed to a new value (a change trial). As in Experiment 2, the new color value was chosen randomly from the remaining colors, and therefore could not match a color currently in the display. As shown in Table 4, inputs to the model projected strongly into the perceptual field, weakly into the working memory field (i.e., $c_{ustim} > c_{wstim}$), and to the gate node within the response system; the gate node also received a projection from the working memory field, with parameters tuned such that only the combination of items held in the working memory field and input (as occurs during presentation of the test array) were strong enough to drive activation of the gate node above threshold. Activation of the gate node was passed through a sigmoid function and multiplied by activation projecting from the perceptual and working memory fields to the response nodes (see Appendix for details); as a result, these nodes only received input from the respective fields if the gate node activation was above-threshold (>0). This gating mechanism served as an autonomous control that resulted in the model only generating a response once the test array was presented. Because the response nodes were coupled via strong inhibitory connections, only a single node surpassed threshold on each trial (with rare exceptions, as described in the Appendix).

In the behavioral task, the test array disappeared from the computer screen after a response key was pressed. This was approximated in the simulations by setting the end time of the test array presentation to be 250 time steps (500 ms) after the activation of one of the response nodes rose above threshold. To parallel the design of Experiment 2, each "session" for the model included 12 trials (six change, six no-change) in each of the five set sizes, presented in the following order: two, one, three, four, five. Note that 3-year-olds' performance was not fit for set sizes four and five because no children completed these blocks (as reported in Experiment 2). For 4-year-olds' performance, I included data from set size four to provide more constraints on the model's performance, although data from this block were not analyzed in Experiment 2 due to the small sample ($n = 3$). The model was then tested 20 times for each parameter set (comparable to running 20 participants per age group).

Change-Preference Task Structure

As with the change detection task, each simulation trial began with a 100-ms relaxation time that allowed the model to reach a stable resting state. This was followed by a 400-ms presentation of an attention-getter, which projected only to the center node. After the attention-getter ended, a 150-ms delay preceded the beginning of the 20-s trial. At the beginning of each trial, the illumination of the displays was modeled as a transient (250 ms) "attentional capture" input to the left and right fixation nodes. Through the entire duration of the trial, a constant input (with added white noise; see Table 4) was projected to the left, right, and away fixation nodes, indicating the presence of stimuli other than the attention-getter. Lastly, a transient "onset" input was projected to the left and right nodes for the first 250 ms of each stimulus presentation (i.e., 27 times throughout the trial), signaling the presence of the color stimuli on the displays. These inputs follow those used by Perone et al. (2011) and are described further in the Appendix.

When activation of either the left or right fixation node surpassed threshold (>0), the specific input from that display—that is, the colors that were presented on the corresponding display—was projected to the model (strongly into the perceptual field and weakly into the working memory field, as in the change detection task; see Table 4). Input streams for each display were constructed following the details of Experiment 1: each consisted of two, four, or six colors (depending on set size) that were on for 500 ms with 250 ms blank intervals in between. For the no-change display, the colors did not change over the course of the 20-s trial; for the change display, one of the colors, selected randomly, would be replaced with another color that was not currently present in that display. Note that, as in Experiment 1, it was possible for colors to be repeated across displays; because spatial location is not represented in this architecture, such colors would be represented with identical inputs to the fields. For each "session," the model was presented with six 20-s trials, two at each set size, in random order. The model was tested 40 times for each parameter set, reflecting the larger sample size from this experiment.

Simulation Results and Discussion

In this section, I describe the results of the simulations in the change detection task first, followed by the result in the change-preference task. Within each subsection, I discuss how I arrived at the parameter to capture adults' performance, then children's performance and report the closeness of the fit in MAE between the behavioral and computational means. This section concludes with an evaluation of the fits across tasks.

Change Detection Task Performance

To evaluate the fit of the model simulations to the behavioral data from Experiment 2 (plus data from ten 5-year-olds who completed a similar color change detection task reported by Simmering, 2012, and the cross-task comparison above), I chose to compare the number of correct trials, separately for no-change and change trials (i.e., correct rejections and hits); because the other measures of performance (accuracy and capacity estimates) are computed from these distributions, the fits would be similar across measures. Furthermore, considering the fit separately for each trial type provides more constraints than fitting a combined measure, such as accuracy, in which similar scores can result from different contributions of each trial type (e.g., an A' score of 0.60 would be derived from a hit rate of 0.67 and false alarm rate of 0.17, as well as a hit rate of 0.83 and false alarm rate of 0.33).

Figure 20 shows the mean number of correct trials for the change detection simulations for each parameter set (fitting the different age groups), with behavioral data for comparison. As this figure shows, the final simulations captured the relative rates of errors on each trial type. Moreover, the simulations yielded mean maximum capacity estimates similar to the behavioral estimates: 1.99 items with the 3-year parameters (1.90 in Experiment 2), 2.83 with the 4-year parameters (2.20), 2.93 with the 5-year parameters (2.87 combining Experiment 2 with the 5-year-olds from Simmering, 2012), and 4.50 with the adult parameters (4.62).

To arrive at these results, I began with the parameters from Johnson et al. (2014) for the three-layer architecture (i.e., the perceptual, inhibitory, and

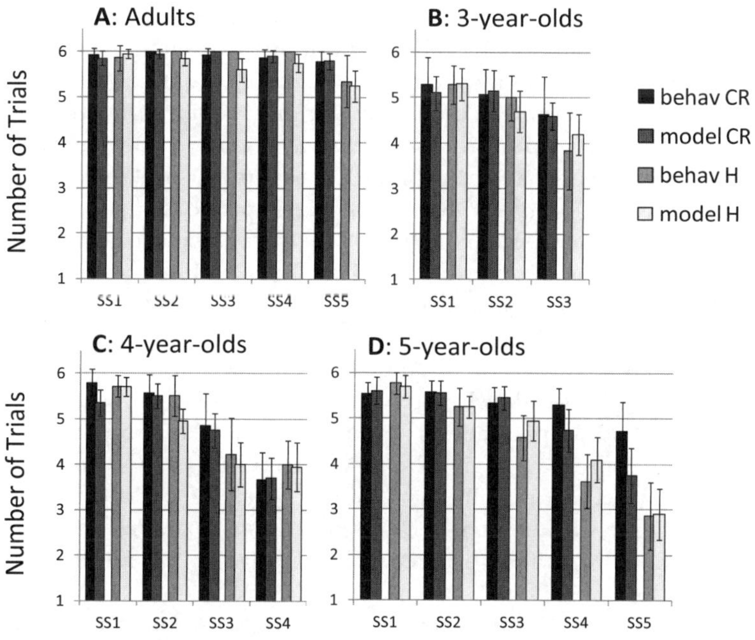

FIGURE 20.—Simulation fits to behavioral data (behav.) from Experiment 2 across set sizes (SS) separated by age group/parameter set: (A) adults, (B) 3-year-olds, (C) 4-year-olds, (D) 5-year-olds. Error bars show 95% confidence intervals. CR, correct rejections; H, hits; SS, set size.

working memory fields) and response nodes; for the Hebbian fields, I used parameters tuned for adults' spatial recall performance (Lipinski et al., 2010), as no previous fits of change detection performance have incorporated the Hebbian fields. These parameters provided a good fit to adults' performance on no-change trials across set sizes (MAE = 0.10 trials), but an inferior fit of adults' performance on change trials across set sizes (MAE = 0.67), with the model performing worse than adults at higher set sizes. This deficit in the model's performance can be characterized as a bias to respond "same" too often as more items were held in the working memory field. Within the full model architecture, there are multiple parameters that could be modified to decrease this bias; the simplest way was to adjust the response system to be less likely to respond "same." I did this by slightly decreasing the resting level of the "same" node (h_{is}) from -4.35 (the value from Johnson et al., 2014) to -4.75 (see Table 4). With this minor adjustment, the fit of the model's performance on no-change trials remained excellent (MAE = 0.05), and the fit on change trials improved to a satisfactory level (MAE = 0.20; overall MAE = 0.13). These fits are shown in Figure 20A, with the related parameters shown in Table 4.

The next step in my quantitative fits was to simulate the developmental improvements in change detection performance between 3 and 5 years and into adulthood. To this end, I modified the adult parameters according to the real-time stability hypothesis, specifically decreasing the strength of excitatory and inhibitory connections to capture children's poorer performance. Given the small difference in performance between 3 and 5 years (relative to the change between 5 years and adulthood), I began by simulating 3-year-olds' performance, then adjusted the parameters proportionally stronger as needed to approximate older children's performance. To achieve this fit, I made three types of changes to the three-layer architecture, two changes to the Hebbian fields, and five changes to the response system; the resulting parameter values are shown in Table 5. Parameters within the three-layer architecture were changed following previous fits of spatial recall performance over development (e.g., Schutte & Spencer, 2009). First, relative to the adult parameters, inputs were weaker and more diffuse (smaller c_{stim}, larger σ_{stim}) in the child parameters. Second, the local excitatory (c_{uu}, c_{ww}) and inhibitory (lateral, c_{uv} and c_{wv}, global k_{uv} and k_{wv}) connections were weaker (smaller) for the "child" parameters. Third, the child parameters included stronger noise relative to the adult parameters (larger $q_u / q_v / q_w$).

In addition to these established changes within the three-layer architecture, changes were needed in the Hebbian fields and response system to fit children's performance. The Hebbian fields were changed to build more quickly and decay more slowly (smaller τ_{build}, larger τ_{decay}) relative to the adult parameters, to reflect the greater influence of long-term memory

TABLE 5

Parameter Values Fitting Children's Performance

Field/Node	τ	Resting Level	Self-Excitation	Excitatory Projection(s)	Inhibitory Projection(s)	Input	Noise
CF (u)			$c_{uu} = 1.7$		$c_{uv} = .6475$ $k_{uv} = .0375$	$c_{ustim3} = 9$ $c_{ustim4} = 9.75$ $c_{ustim5} = 10.65$ $\sigma_{ustim} = 4.5$	$q_u = .05^a$
WM (w)			$c_{ww3} = 1.26$ $c_{ww4} = 1.4175$ $c_{ww5} = 1.6695$		$c_{wv3} = .1788$ $c_{wv4} = .1885$ $c_{wv5} = .2015$ $k_{wv} = .06$	$c_{wstim3} = 1.8$ $c_{wstim4} = 1.95$ $c_{wstim5} = 2.13$ $\sigma_{wstim} = 4.5$	
Hebb. (H)	$\tau_{Hbuild3} = 750^b$ $\tau_{Hbuild4} = 1{,}500^b$ $\tau_{Hbuild5} = 2{,}250^b$ $\tau_{Hdecay} = 150{,}000^b$						
Resp. (R)			$c_{RR} = 1.3875$		$c_{R-} = 10.5$		$q_R = .0813$
Diff. (d)				$c_{du3} = .75$ $c_{du4} = 1.05$ $c_{du5} = 1.246$			
Same (s)		$h_s = -4.5$		$c_{sw} = .01815$			
Gate (g)				$c_{gw} = .05$			
Fix. (F)		$h_{down3} = -4.4936$ $h_{down4} = -4.521$ $h_{down5} = -4.6032$			$c_{F-} = 4.5$		
Left (l)/right (r)				$q_{lu} = c_{ru} = .1596$		$q_{lC} = c_{rC} = 5.7288$	

Note. Only parameters that were changed relative to the adult values are shown in this table; all other values were identical to those reported in Table 4. Numbers at the end of each subscript indicate the corresponding age group in cases where the value changed between parameters tuned to 3 and 5 years. As in Table 4, parameters that were identical across Same and Different (Diff.) nodes are shown in the Response (Resp.) row; parameters that were identical across Left, Right, Center, and Away nodes are shown in the Fixation (Fix.) row.

[a]This parameter was identical across all three fields, and are reported only once in the table for simplicity.

[b]As in Table 4 parameters were identical for both Hebbian (Hebb.) fields (i.e., $\tau_{uHbuild} = \tau_{wHbuild}$, $\tau_{uHdecay} = \tau_{wHdecay}$) and are shown only once for simplicity.

on children's performance (indicated by reports from experimenters, e.g., that children sometimes tried to compare a new memory array to the previous test array). The response system was modified in parallel to the three-layer architecture, with weaker inputs (smaller c_{du}, c_{sw}), weaker self-excitation (smaller c_{rr}) and competition (smaller $c_{r\text{-}}$), and stronger noise (larger q_r) relative to adult parameters. Two additional changes to the response system were driven by evaluation of simulation fits. First, to compensate for weaker excitation in the working memory field with the child parameters, I increased the strength of the projection from the working memory field to the gating node (larger c_{gw}) relative to the adult parameters. Second, the resting level of the "same" node was higher (smaller h_{is}; recall that resting levels are negative) for the child versus adult parameters, reflecting children's overall bias to respond "same" more often.

With these changes, the model provided an excellent fit of 3-year-olds' performance on both no-change and change trials (MAE $= 0.10$ and 0.22, respectively; overall MAE $= 0.16$). These fits are shown in Figure 20B, and provide the first demonstration that changes in real-time stability could account for developmental differences in change detection performance. Next, to fit the model to 4- and 5-year-olds' performance, I made four changes relative to the 3-year-old parameters. Specifically, I increased the strength of the local excitatory and lateral inhibitory connections for the working memory field (larger c_{ww} and c_{wv}), the input (larger c_{ustim} and c_{wstim}), and the projection to the "different" node (larger c_{du}); additionally, I decreased the build rate of the Hebbian fields (larger τ_{build}). The fits for 4- and 5-year-olds' performance, shown in Figure 20C and D, were also quite good (4 years: MAE $= 0.16$, 0.21, and 0.19, respectively, for no-change trials, change trials, and overall; 5 years: MAE $= 0.35$, 0.19, and 0.27, respectively).

Change-Preference Task Performance

To evaluate the fit of the model simulations to behavioral data from Experiment 1, I compared total looking times, change preference scores, and switch rates across set sizes two, four, and six for each age group. To fit the model's performance in the change-preference task, I began with the four parameter sets for the five-layer architecture that were tuned to fit change detection performance across the four age groups, then tested performance with the fixation system parameters tuned to capture infants' performance by Perone et al. (2011). With these "infant" fixation parameters (averaging across all set sizes and age groups), the model provided a good fit of change preference scores (MAE $= .024$; equivalent to a difference of $0.36\,\mathrm{s}$ looking to the change display), an acceptable fit of switch rates (MAE $= 0.45$ switches per second), but an inferior fit of total looking time (MAE $= 2.76\,\mathrm{s}$). For all parameter sets, the model produced less total looking than in the behavioral data. This poor fit suggest that the developmental changes in the fields were not enough to produce the changes in looking behavior; rather, the dynamics of fixation appear to change over development as well.

To achieve a better fit to the behavioral data from the change-preference task, I held the parameters within the fields constant (i.e., as tuned for change detection performance for each age group) and scaled the infant fixation parameters in three ways. First, in parallel to the changes within the fields, I increased the strength of self-excitation and mutual inhibition (c_{ff} and $c_{\mathrm{f-}}$) for all parameter sets relative to the infant parameters. Second, I changed the relative influences of inputs to the fixation nodes by increasing the strength of the constant input from the displays (c_{fC}) and decreasing the projection from the perceptual field (c_{fu}); conceptually, this made the fixation system more responsive to the task context and less driven by novelty compared to the infant parameters. Lastly, I modified the dynamic resting level to make each of the fixation nodes more likely to transition between "on" and "off" states (through a lower negative attractor value, h_{down}; see Appendix for description of these dynamics). Table 5 shows these parameter values. Note that local excitation was equivalent across the four parameter sets, whereas the other parameters were all lower for the child versus adult simulations; additionally, only the low attractor varied across the three child parameter sets.

With these changes, the fits improved for total looking (MAE = 0.64, 0.74, 0.57, and 0.32 across parameter sets, respectively), change preference scores (MAE = .017, .010, .011, and .026, respectively), and switch rates (MAE = .08, .05, .06, and .03, respectively). Figure 21 shows these behavioral measures and the model fits with parameter values tuned for each age group. As this figure shows, fits for mean total looking time (Figure 21A) were satisfactory, although the model showed slightly more of an increase in looking over set sizes than seen in the behavioral data. Change preference scores (Figure 21B) were also fit well by the model across set sizes and age groups, and all of the mean change preference scores from the simulations were significantly greater than chance (dotted line). Lastly, the pattern of switch rates across set sizes—more switching in set size two—was fit well by the model (Figure 21C).

Evaluation

This chapter presented quantitative simulations to test my fourth prediction, that implementing the real-time stability hypothesis in the unified model could capture developmental changes in both change detection and change-preference tasks. To test this hypothesis, I conducted a series of simulations to capture the full range of behaviors across tasks and development. Across the two tasks, I compared 70 means between the simulations and behavioral data (34 in change detection, 36 in change-preference) and achieved an excellent fit overall, with the model performing well within a single unit of measure of the behavioral data (i.e., averaging across age groups: MAE = 0.19 trials in change detection; in the

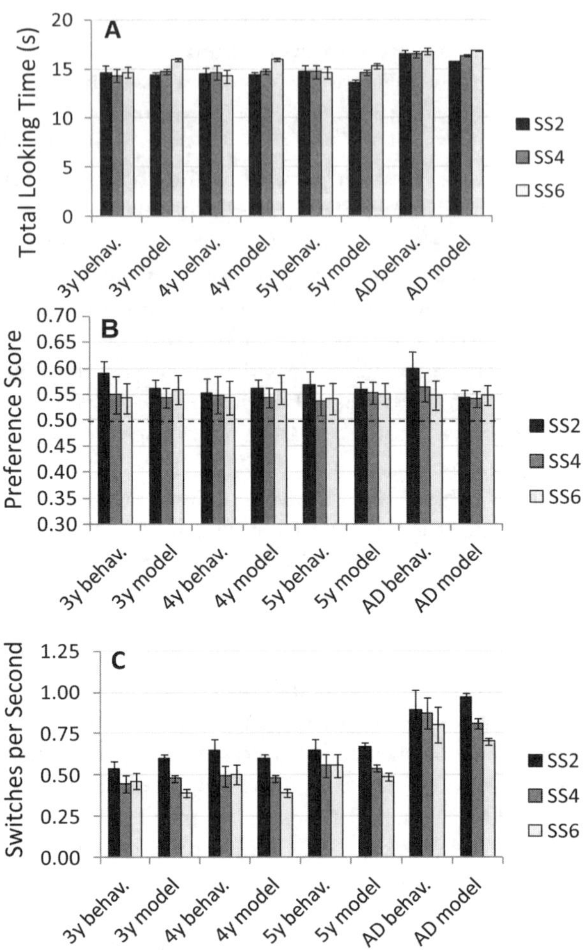

FIGURE 21.—Simulation fits to behavioral data (behav.) across set sizes (SS) from Experiment 1: (A) mean total looking time, (B) mean change preference scores, (C) mean switches between displays. Error bars show 95% confidence intervals. Dashed line in (B) indicates chance performance.

change-preference task, MAE = 0.57 s total looking, 0.016 preference score, and 0.06 switches per second).

These simulations provide support for the cognitive dynamics account of capacity estimates arising from both change detection and change-preference tasks, as well as the proposed developmental mechanism, increases in real-time stability through strengthening connectivity. The simulations presented here are a particularly stringent test for a computational model—few models are tested across multiple tasks, multiple measures within a task, and multiple points in development. As such, the simulations presented here move beyond many cognitive and developmental models in providing both specificity— producing a good fit to behavior on a trial-by-trial basis within each task—and generality—across tasks and development (see also Simmering & Spencer, 2008).

CONSEQUENCES OF STRENGTHENING CONNECTIVITY: INCREASES IN REAL-TIME STABILITY

One benefit of using formal models to evaluate theoretical constructs is the ability to "look inside" the model to understand the underlying causes of changes in the model's performance. In this section, I present an analysis of changes in the dynamic model's encoding and maintenance of items to illustrate how strengthening connectivity within the model gave rise to developmental improvements in performance through increases in real-time stability. In the following sub-sections, I consider developmental changes in seven components of real-time stability in turn: (i) strength of representations; (ii) encoding speed; (iii) resistance to interference and (iv) decay; (v) capacity limits; (vi) correspondence between memory and behavior across tasks; and (vii) effects of task context on memory.

Evaluating the formation and maintenance of memory representations requires considering how the representations change over time. To assess representations over time, I plotted the timecourse of above-threshold activation within the working memory field during the presentation of the memory array (encoding) and delay (maintenance) during the change detection task. I chose to limit this assessment to the context of the change detection task because the timing of events puts more of a demand on memory processes and can therefore reveal differences in real-time stability more clearly than the change-preference task (which also provides more support from long-term memory).

Figure 22 shows the timecourse of activation during encoding in the left column and during maintenance in the right column. Consider the encoding period first (recalling that the processes within the model do not differ between "stages" of the task; all that differentiates encoding from maintenance is the presence vs. absence of input). Figure 22A shows the rise time of activation for the adult parameters during encoding. As this figure shows, total activation generally increased with set size, but not linearly—that is, the amount of activation in set size three was not three times more than in set size one. As discussed by Johnson et al. (2014), this characteristic of the dynamic model contrasts with resource accounts of capacity limits: if activation is considered the resource that is shared among items, the amount allocated to each item does decrease as the number of items increases;

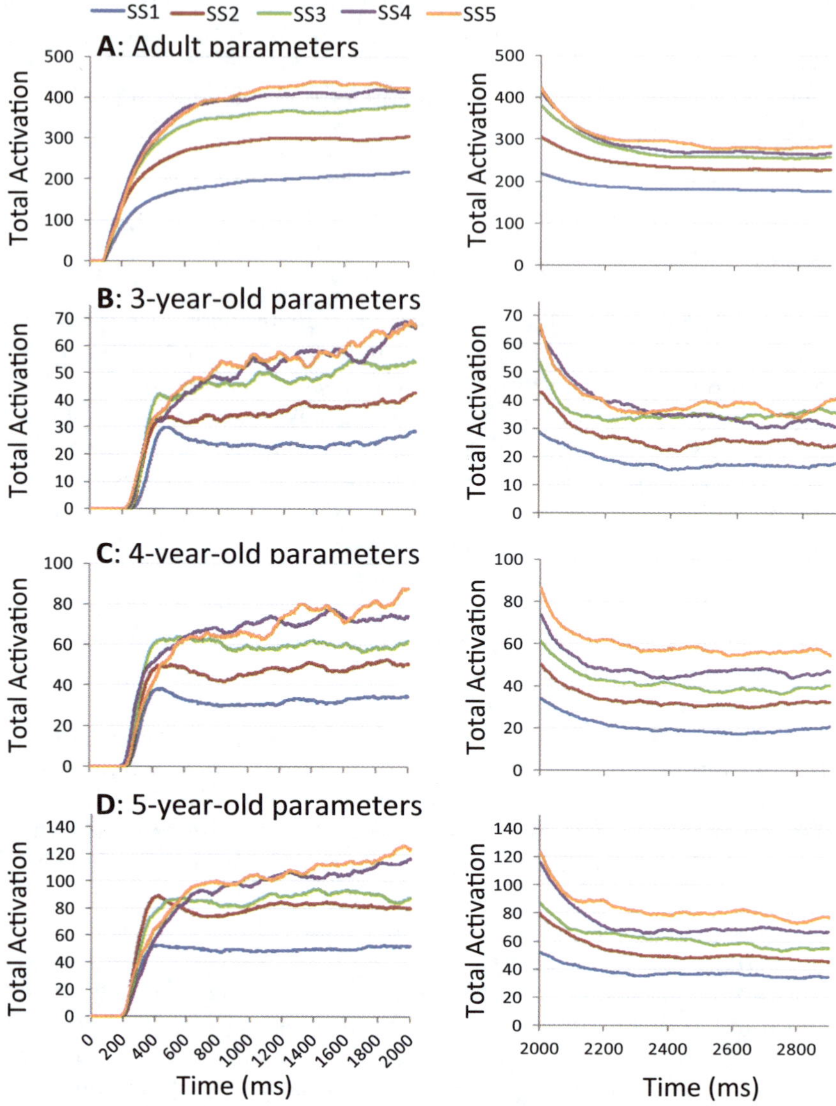

Figure 22.—Above-threshold activation over time in the working memory field during the change detection memory array presentation (left column) and delay period (right column), separately for each set size (SS) in simulations with (A) adult, (B) 3-year-old, (C) 4-year-old, and (D) 5-year-old parameter sets, averaged across trials within a run.

however, the total amount of resource (activation) across items is not fixed (i.e., total activation for set size five was twice that of set size one).

With weaker connectivity corresponding to earlier in development, four changes in the dynamic model's memory representations are evident. First, overall activation increased considerably over development, for all set sizes (see scaling of *y*-axes in Figure 22); note that this applies to both the encoding and maintenance phases of the trials. A second, related consequence is that the child parameters showed less of a difference in activation across set sizes. This is partly due to the lower number of peaks being formed (discussed below), but the mean activation per peak was also lower with the child parameters (see set size one in Figure 22). These differences are due to weaker individual representations (i.e., peaks) earlier in development. As such, total activation illustrates the first component of real-time stability, *stronger representations* over development, that arose through strengthening connectivity in the dynamic model.

A third notable difference across parameter sets is that, although the slope of the initial rise in activation appears comparable across parameter sets in Figure 22, the different amount of activation reached indicates that the child parameters built activation more slowly. For instance, consider the time to reach activation of 30 in set size one across parameter sets: 475 ms with the 3-year-old parameters, 360 ms with the 4-year-old parameters, 295 ms with the 5-year-old parameters, and 125 ms with the adult parameters. Thus, the adult parameters built activation nearly four times as quickly as the 3-year-old parameters, demonstrating a second component of real-time stability: developmental *increase in encoding speed* resulting from strengthening connectivity within the dynamic model.

Lastly, activation was less stable over time during the presentation of the memory array for the child parameters compared to the adult parameters. This is most strikingly demonstrated with the 3-year-old parameters (Figure 22B), which showed substantial fluctuation at the higher set sizes. The variation in activation can be attributed to the set size nearing the upper limit for the number of peaks that could build simultaneously with these parameters (discussed further below), even with continued input. This variation results from competition (or interference) between items being encoded in the working memory field: in set size one, activation was stable over time for all parameter sets; only when multiple items were being encoded at once did activation fluctuate notably over time. These simulations demonstrate a third component of real-time stability, *reduced interference among items* over development.

I next examined how above-threshold activation in the working memory field changed after the stimulus input was removed as peaks sustained through the memory delay, plotted in the right column of Figure 22. With the adult parameters (Figure 22A), activation decreased slightly after the removal of the input, then remained at a fairly constant rate as the self-sustaining peaks were maintained through the delay. Similar to the strength differences noted during encoding, the child parameters also resulted in less activation during the delay period relative to the adult parameters. Also, the variability in activation over time was greater with the child parameters, reflecting reduced real-time stability as peaks "die out" during the memory delay (cf. Figure 23B–D). Thus, the relatively small fluctuations over delay with increasingly strong connectivity illustrate *increased resistance to decay* over development.[i]

For the next assessment of the model's performance, I analyzed the number of peaks held in the working memory field at the end of the delay periods across tasks. I first calculated the mean number of peaks for each response type in the change detection task (i.e., correct rejections, hits, misses, false alarms) for each parameter set, shown in Figure 23. Note that the simulations with the 3- and 4-year-old parameters include set sizes four and five; even though there were no behavioral data for comparison at these set

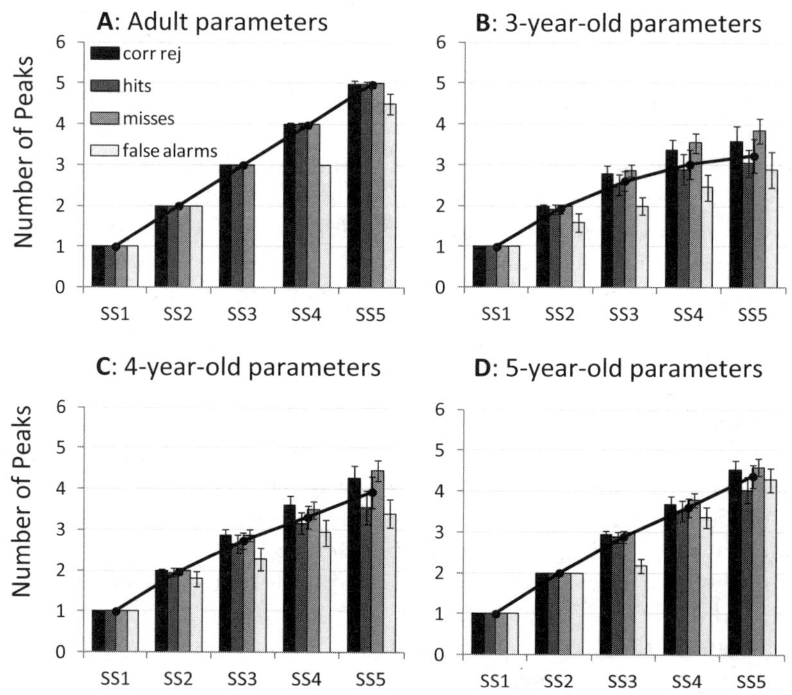

FIGURE 23.—Mean number of peaks sustaining in the working memory field at the end of the change detection delay period, separately for each parameter set (simulating different age groups). Lines show means across all trials, bars show means separated by response type. Error bars show 95% confidence intervals. SS, set size; corr rej, correct rejections.

sizes, it is useful to consider the model's performance on these trials to see the full effects of developmental changes in the parameters. As Figure 23 shows, the adult parameters maintained an average of 4.99 peaks in the working memory field on all set size five trials except the small number of trials that resulted in false alarms (on which the mean was 4.50; similar to results from Johnson et al., 2014). By contrast, fewer peaks were maintained in the working memory field with the child parameters, for example, reaching only 3.23 peaks on average across trials in set size five with the 3-year-old parameters. The number of peaks held in the working memory field at the lower set sizes also shows more variability with the child parameters relative to the adult parameters. This analysis demonstrates that *capacity increases* over development with increased real-time stability.

An important consideration for understanding the correspondence between memory and behavior in the change detection task is how the number of peaks in the working memory field differed across trial types. In particular, all parameter sets held fewer peaks on false alarm trials than on other trial types, suggesting that these errors result from "forgetting," that is, the loss of a peak in the working memory field (cf. Johnson et al., 2014). Sample simulations in Chapter 2 (Figures 9 and 11) demonstrated how this arises in the model. This type of error makes intuitive sense: a forgotten item would appear to be new, when presented in the test array.

Unlike the adult parameters, for the child parameters, the number of peaks in the working memory field was also lower on hit trials than miss trials, suggesting that correct "different" responses in the model sometimes arose when at least one item was forgotten during the delay, and miss errors could occur when all items were held in the working memory field (cf. Figure 8 in Chapter 2). Thus, although capacity was indeed lower with the child parameters—the model was able to hold fewer items in the working memory field than with the adult parameters—this difference is not the sole contribution to errors in the model (as discussed in Chapter 2; see also Johnson et al., 2014, for further discussion). Rather, more errors must arise through the processes of comparison and response within the child parameters. Consider, for example, that all parameter sets maintained the item presented in set size one on every trial (i.e., all means were 1.00 across response types). However, performance was below ceiling in this set size for the child parameters (cf. Figure 20). Thus, the same number of peaks in the working memory field did not produce the same level of performance, highlighting another component of real-time stability: *improved correspondence memory and behavior* over development.

For the last analysis of the model's representations, I calculated the number of peaks in the working memory field during each delay period in the change-preference task. Because there is not a single delay period for maintenance in this task, it is less straight forward to assess how many peaks

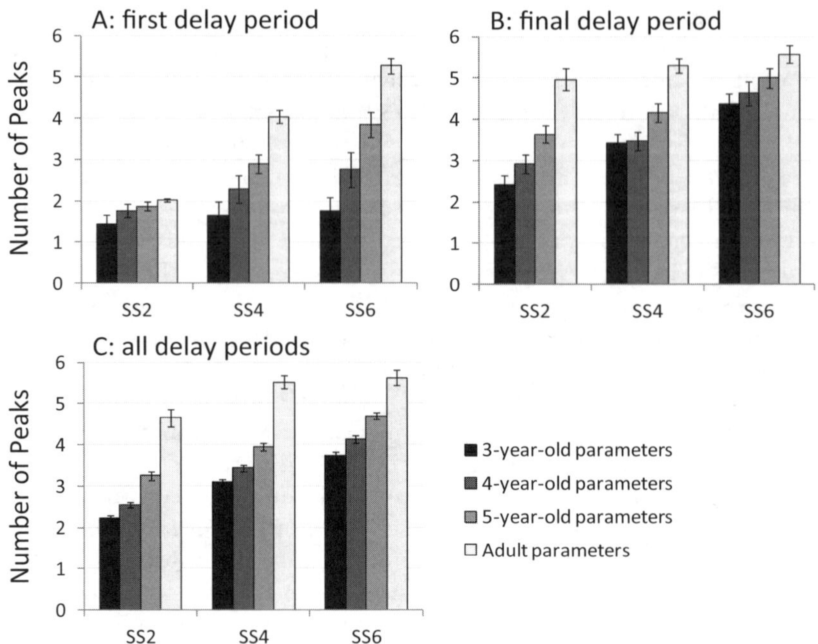

FIGURE 24.—Mean number of peaks sustaining in the working memory field in the change-preference task during (A) the first delay period, (B) the final delay period, and (C) averaged across all delay periods.

the model could hold within a trial. To address how capacity limits are realized in the change-preference task, I plotted the mean number of peaks held in the working memory field during the first delay period (Figure 24A), the final delay period (Figure 24B), and averaged across all delay periods (Figure 24C).

Figure 24A shows that the parameter sets varied little in the number of peaks maintained during the first delay period in set size two, but in set sizes four and six the "older" parameter sets held more peaks in the working memory field. This difference can be attributed not only to the faster encoding with stronger connectivity (cf. Figure 22), but also to the fixation dynamics: with stronger interactions within the fixation system, the model with the adult parameters was more likely to look at both displays during the first presentation. As a result, the model received more input with the adult parameters. The consequences of increased inputs can also be seen by comparing Figure 24A with B; during the final delay period, the model had received input across many stimulus presentations (27 per trial) and fixations (the "adult" model averaged 15.95 fixations per trial; cf. $M = 15.30$ fixations per trial in the behavioral data). As a result, the number of peaks in the working memory field was more similar across set sizes during the final delay period compared to the first delay period.

When comparing parameter sets, however, the capacity limits on the total number of peaks that can sustain in the working memory field are evident. Consider, for example, the adult parameters in set size six: although all nine stimulus colors were present across displays in each presentation (as described in Experiment 1), the model still maintained fewer than six peaks on average ($M = 5.58$) by the final delay period. This converges with simulations by Johnson et al. (2014) suggesting that a similar dynamic model has an upper capacity limit of six items, and shows that even the more supportive context of the change-preference task cannot infinitely increase the capacity of the working memory field in the model. By contrast, however, the peaks held in the working memory field with the 3-year-old parameters in set size six show a divergent pattern from the change detection simulations above. In change detection, these parameters averaged 3.23 peaks in set size five; the same parameters held an average of 4.38 peaks by the final delay period in the change-preference task. This demonstrates how the task context influenced the contents of the working memory field in the model: with repeated presentations and short delays, the child parameters could maintain, on average, 1.15 more peaks simultaneously during the change-preference task. By analogy to the behavioral task, this would imply that *children's capacity was actually higher*—remembering more items during the delay—in the change-preference task than the change detection task. The large difference in capacity limits across tasks early in development, combined with the relatively small difference in capacity limits later in development, point to another developmental change that is not often a focus of theories: the dynamic model's memory representations were *less affected by the task context* over development.

Lastly, note that the average number of peaks held across all delay periods (Figure 24C) was only at or above the number of items presented per display in some cases. Specifically, in set size two means ranged from 2.22 to 4.65 peaks over parameter sets, and in set size four the adult parameters held a mean of 5.52 peaks. In all other cases, the model was maintaining fewer items than the set size, but still showed a robust preference (Figure 21); these results converge with Perone et al.'s (2011) findings that a similar model with infant parameters held fewer peaks in the working memory field than suggested by capacity estimates (see McMurray et al., 2012, for simulations suggesting a similar divergence between vocabulary and fast mapping performance). This also contrasts with analyses of performance in the change detection task, which showed that the mean number of peaks in the working memory field was higher than the estimated capacity. These findings across tasks highlight the importance of linking representations to behavior when assessing constructs like capacity—even when similar numbers of items were held in the working memory field across tasks, the behavioral results yielded notably different estimates of capacity. The discrepancy across tasks decreased over development, however, providing a further example of improved correspondence between memory and behavior.

These simulations showed that the dynamic model can capture developmental improvements in change detection performance by implementing the real-time stability hypothesis as strengthening connectivity over development. Analyses of the processes underlying the model's performance provided evidence for the following consequences that comprise the notion of increasing real-time stability over development: stronger representations; faster encoding speed; reduced interference among items; increased resistance to decay; higher capacity; improved correspondence memory and behavior; and less effect of the task context on behavior. Thus, the real-time stability hypothesis not only provides a specific mechanism underlying developmental change—strengthening connections supporting encoding, maintenance, and comparison processes—but also specifies the process by which these changes influences performance in two different task contexts. As discussed further in Chapter 5, these characteristics of the real-time stability hypothesis converge with empirical findings and other theoretical accounts proposed to explain working memory development during infancy and developmental changes in complex tasks during childhood.

These results also provide an important qualification to the possibility Ross-Sheehy et al. (2003) raised, that the change-preference task might assess "relative" capacity while the change detection task assesses "absolute" capacity. One could conclude from the current behavioral results that the tasks indeed measure different types of capacity, as estimates differed notably across tasks. However, the correlations in Chapter 3 suggest shared underlying processes, and can be used to argue against dissociating the behavioral tasks. By taking a process-oriented approach and formalizing the theory of cognitive dynamics into a computational model, these simulations showed that *capacity differences emerged in the context of the tasks*; that is, the same cognitive system will be limited in different ways depending on the task context. Simulations showed that such differences arose simply through the stimulus timing, manner of presentation (i.e., on one vs. two displays), and behavioral responses required in the tasks. In the literature, these differences between tasks, as well as the different task instructions (i.e., no explicit instructions in the change-preference task vs. specifically reporting changes in change detection), have led theorists to propose that the tasks recruit different strategies or memory processes. For example, Riggs et al. (2006) suggested that looking tasks might rely on passive memory, and Oakes et al. (2013) questioned whether habituation or long-term memory contributed to preferences. The formalization presented here shows that invoking different processes to explain diverging results is not necessary; rather, such findings can be understood by considering representations in the context of the processes through which representations are created and used in the service of behavior (cf. McMurray et al., 2012; Schöner & Thelen, 2006; Smith et al., 2010, 1999; Spencer, Clearfield, et al., 2006).

RELATING PERFORMANCE ACROSS TASKS

The next important question to consider is whether these simulations can help explain the correlations across tasks described in Chapter 3. The rationale for the correspondence between change preference scores and hits in change detection (detecting novelty), and between switch rates and correct rejections in change detection (detecting familiarity), was laid out in Chapter 2. However, the sample simulations did not lead to a priori predictions for differences across set sizes. Recall the empirical findings from the cross-task comparison: capacity estimates in color change detection were predicted independently by (a) change preference scores from set size two and (b) switch rates from set size six (see Table 3). What would lead to these differences across set sizes in the cross-task relationships in children's performance? I consider these two measures in turn below.

As illustrated in Figure 24C, the child parameters maintained an average of 1.52 more peaks in set size six than set size two. How would the number of peaks in the working memory field affect change preference scores? As explained in Chapter 2, continued fixation of the change display depends on activation in the perceptual field. More peaks in the working memory field contribute to stronger inhibition projected into the perceptual field, resulting in lower activation. Thus, as more items are being maintained, the magnitude of the change preferences should be reduced. Restated conceptually, the more items that are being held in memory, the less novel the change display appears. This could explain why only change preference scores set size two—with the smallest number of peaks and therefore greatest activation (i.e., novelty) in the perceptual field—were predictive. This also could explain the main effect of set size from the change-preference task, in which change preference scores were significantly higher in set size two than four and six.

The effect of the number of peaks in the working memory field on switch rates would be opposite the effect on change preference scores because switching depends on a decrease of activation in the perceptual field. In particular, as more items are encoded in the working memory field, more inhibition projects to the perceptual field via the inhibitory field, and fixation is released more quickly. Thus, switch rates should increase as the number of items in memory increases over time. Although this would seem to imply that switch rates should be higher for set size six than two (opposite the empirical and computational results), it is important to note that the model's switch rates depend on the *rate of increase* in the number of peak over time within the trial, not just the overall number of peaks. The rate at which peaks increase is greater for set size two than six (cf. Figure 24A and B), leading to the higher switch rate in the lower set size.

Essentially, change preference scores and switch rates depend on more versus less activation in the perceptual field, which depends on inhibition projected into the perceptual field, which is stronger when more items are held in memory. This mechanism also explains why switch rates differed over development: the "adult" parameters held more peaks than the "child" parameters, and adults switched significantly more often than children. Why, then, did change preference scores not differ between age groups? In the context of this particular task, there were only nine possible colors that could be presented across both displays within the trial. As such, on a set size two trial the colors in the change display would begin to repeat after, at maximum, eight presentations (perhaps earlier—how soon the same color could re-appear was not constrained); on a set size six trial, the colors in the change display would begin to repeat after four presentations at most. Furthermore, duplication of colors across displays was not controlled, meaning a new item on the change display could be present within the no-change displays. Indeed, in set size six, a minimum of three colors had to be present in both displays, as the total number of colors presented across displays on a single set size six trial (12) was greater than the number of unique colors used (nine). Together, these details of the task limit how "new" a changed color can be; the accumulation of long-term memory of the colors within a trial, or even the sustained working memory for one or more presentations, would lead to a general suppression of the effect of novel colors on fixation of the change display. This could also explain why the effect of set size on change preference scores was relatively small ($\eta_{\mathrm{p}}^{2} = .03$).

The results of these simulations shed new light onto how memory representations form and influence behavior in the change-preference task. This level of formularization has revealed gaps in previous conceptual theories of performance in this task. In particular, Oakes et al. (2009) claimed that long-term memory could not easily be used to detect changes in the change-preference task due to the brief presentations and the frequent changes. However, as these simulations and those by Perone et al. (2011) showed, a robust memory for the *no-change* display is just as important for a change preference to emerge. Because the colors on this display remain the same over the duration of the 20-s trial, long-term memory can indirectly support a robust change-preference (but see Oakes et al., 2013, for a task that eliminates this characteristic, as discussed in Chapter 5). Furthermore, the original conceptualization of the task (Ross-Sheehy et al., 2003) focused on how items compared within a single display over time, but not across displays. These simulations suggest that duplications of colors across displays could help support memory representations and, by extension, a robust change preference. In the current formalization, however, there is no representation of which colors were on which display—it is possible that adding such information would change this characteristic of the model's performance.

POTENTIAL SOURCES OF DEVELOPMENTAL CHANGES IN CONNECTIVITY

The final question to consider in the context of these model simulations is what could cause the strengthening of connectivity that produces increases in real-time stability. Within the larger Dynamic Field Theory framework, most developmental simulations have included parameters modified "by hand" to capture different developmental levels (see Simmering & Schutte, 2015, for review), as was the case for the current simulations. However, in a recent series of simulation experiments, Perone and Spencer (2013a) showed how the accumulation of specific experiences over a sufficiently long timecourse approximated changes that have previously been implemented through strengthening connectivity. In particular, they exposed a number of "infant" models to multiple series of visual inputs to simulate real-world interactions with objects distributed through time (the equivalent of more than 500 hr of experience per "infant"). Importantly, these models included Hebbian layers similar to those in the current model, which allowed experience to build over these extended exposures.

Perone and Spencer (2013a) evaluated the effects of this accumulation of experience by testing the models in a processing speed task modeled after Rose, Feldman, and Jankowski (2002). They showed that allowing the model to develop autonomously through experience could produce the same types of outcomes as simulations in which development was implemented "by hand" (e.g., Perone & Spencer, 2013b). In particular, models with more experience exhibited a more mature pattern of performance, including stronger novelty preferences and more frequent gaze switching. Similar to the simulations presented here, models with more experience (i.e., "older" models) showed stronger representations and faster encoding speeds. Thus, Hebbian learning across a long range of specific experiences could result in general improvements in performance in a dynamic neural field model.

Perone and Spencer (2013a) also showed that this mechanism could address individual differences across "infant" models. They noted that individual differences across infants often parallel group level developmental differences (also discussed in Chapter 1). To test whether stable individual differences could emerge through the accumulation of experience, they conducted a second simulation experiment in which they assessed performance at three points during development for the individual models. Results showed that these models reproduced the same general pattern as in their first simulation experiment when tested as a group, and also revealed stable differences across models. Specifically, hierarchical regression showed that the models' performance on the processing speed task "early" in development (approximating 7 months of age) predicted their performance "later" in development (approximating 12 months of age). These simulations provided the first demonstration that models set to the same initial conditions could autonomously develop stable individual differences in visual memory performance.

How do the results from Perone and Spencer (2013a) relate to the empirical and computational results presented here? The simulations presented in this chapter included no sense of "individuals," in that each separate run of the model within a given age group had the same parameter values. Individual runs of the model varied slightly due to noise, and accumulated different experiences within the context of each task, but these would not be stable across tasks. Although the simulations by Perone and Spencer show a promising interpretation of individual differences, such an approach to the current empirical results is not practical due to the computational power required: Perone and Spencer reported that each individual model's development took more than 8 hr to simulate just to arrive at 12 months of experience. Simulating 3–5 years of experience for even only 10 individuals per age group, therefore, would require an unreasonable time commitment. Furthermore, this demonstration of how individual and developmental differences *could* arise through a common source does not necessarily imply that they *must* arise in this manner.

A more promising route to explore the possible explanatory power of such a mechanism conceptually is to test the effects of experience behaviorally. Perone and colleagues have shown one such application in the context of the dimensional change card sort task (Perone, Molitar, Buss, Spencer, & Samuelson, 2015). They tested 3-year-old children in the standard version of the task, in which sorting was tested first along a shape dimension, then a color dimension, and found typical rates of perseveration (i.e., many children continued to sort by shape on the color trials). They compared performance in this condition to a "memory" condition, in which children played a memory matching game with colored stimuli between the pre- and postswitch card sort trials. Given this extra experience along the color dimension, children in the memory condition were significantly less likely to sort perseveratively. That is, exposure to the colors in a memory game allowed children to show the more mature pattern of performance, correctly sorting by color on the postswitch trials. Perone et al. showed model simulations demonstrating how the accumulation of long-term memory of the colors supported performance in the card sorting task.

Even with these computational and behavioral demonstrations that relevant experiences can support more mature behavior, there remains the possibility of experience-general maturational improvements underlying behavior. These sources of change are not mutually exclusive and likely both play a role. Various studies have shown that there are changes in multiple brain regions over development that might produce effects similar to the changes in connectivity implemented in the dynamic model here. As an example, consider development of the prefrontal cortex, which plays a central role in a variety of working memory tasks (e.g., Crone, Wendelken, Donohue, van Leijenhorst, & Bunge, 2006; Diamond & Goldman-Rakic, 1989; Luciana, Lindeke, Georgieff, Mills, & Nelson, 1999). The prefrontal cortex continues to develop throughout childhood and adolescence (e.g., Huttenlocher, 1979, 1990, 1994; Jernigan, Trauner, Hesselink, & Tallal, 1991), suggesting that its development plays a likely role in developmental changes in working memory capacity. Myelination in the frontal lobe continues through early childhood (Sampaio & Truwit, 2001), and reductions in gray matter volume reflecting pruning of neural connections occurs though early childhood into the postadolescent years (Gogtay et al., 2004), in parallel with the developmental trajectory seen in the change detection task (Figure 2).

These types of neurophysiological changes during childhood relating to working memory improvements are consistent with changes in the dynamic model connectivity over development. For example, Edin and colleagues generated predictions for developmental changes in BOLD signal during a visuosptaial working memory task based on the consequences of synaptic pruning, synaptic strengthening, or myelination in a neural network model (Edin, Macoveanu, Olesen, Tegnér, & Klingberg, 2007). They compared the model's predicted BOLD activity to fMRI results from frontal and parietal regions with 13-year-olds and adults. The best correspondence between the model and neural data resulted from synaptic strengthening in the model—a mechanism likely to arise through experience similar to the implementation by Perone and Spencer (2013a).

The Representational Acuity Hypothesis proposed by Westermann and Mareschal (2004, 2012) also shows similar changes in processing and behavior. According to their hypothesis, developmental narrowing of receptive fields in visual cortex results in object representations that become more precise over development (i.e., fewer neurons respond to a given stimulus). This narrowing of receptive fields and resulting increase in precision is conceptually similar to increases in real-time stability described here (see also discussion of the resolution of visual working memory in Chapter 5). Their hypothesis has been implemented in a neural network model, which has captured developmental differences in infants' performance in categorization tasks (Westermann & Mareschal, 2004, 2012). These results converge with simulations within the Dynamic Field Theory framework across a range of tasks (described further in Chapter 5) to suggest that these types of neural changes could explain a wide range of behavioral phenomena over development.

Although evidence of these neural changes are promising for our understanding of development, this simply shifts the developmental question to another level of description, leaving the question open as to what drives the changes in cortex. These cortical changes likely arise through complex interactions among a host of factors from the genetic level to the level of large-scale interactions among populations of neurons in different cortical areas, which are probably experience-dependent. Given that the changes made to the dynamic model in these simulations involved primarily changes in the strength of excitatory and inhibitory connections, it is easy to imagine that such changes could arise from a simple Hebbian process that strengthens cortical connections as a function of experience (cf. Perone & Spencer, 2013a).

SUMMARY

This chapter included quantitative simulations of the dynamic model showing that strengthening connections within the three-layer architecture, combined with changes to accumulation of long-term memory and the task-specific behavioral systems, could fit the pattern of behavioral data reported in Chapter 3. Following these successful fits, I analyzed the processes within the model to show how changes in connectivity gave rise to seven characteristics of real-time stability, which contributed to changes in performance over development. Further analysis of the model's performance provided a potential explanation for the correlations reported in Chapter 3, with the number of items held in memory showing opposite effects on change preference scores versus switch rates across set sizes. Lastly, I described simulations in a similar architecture that suggest individual and developmental differences in performance could arise through a common source, namely extended experience with instances along a given dimension (i.e., color), and a recent empirical test that supports this possibility (see also Simmering et al., 2015 but see Cowan, Ricker, Clark, Hinrichs, & Glass, 2015, for evidence that specific knowledge cannot entirely explain developmental improvements).

NOTE

i. Note that the common sense of decay—a gradual loss of information over time—does not happen at the level of individual representations within the dynamic model. Rather, the "on" and "off" states of this type of bistable attractor network produce all-or-none representations: a peak is either held in the working memory field or not (see Zhang & Luck, 2009, for related behavioral evidence in visual working memory). The strength of the peak may decrease over time and the location of the peak may drift (i.e., change position within the field; see, e.g., Lipinski et al., 2010); these changes often arise due to interactions with other peaks and are therefore considered more to interference than decay.

V. NEW QUESTIONS AND REMAINING CHALLENGES TO ACCOUNT FOR DEVELOPMENTAL IMPROVEMENTS IN VISUAL WORKING MEMORY

Vanessa R. Simmering

This article is part of the issue "Working Memory Capacity in Context: Modeling Dynamic Processes of Behavior, Memory, and Development," Simmering, Vanessa (Issue Author). For a full listing of articles in this issue, see: http://onlinelibrary.wiley.com/doi/10.1111/mono.v81.3/issuetoc.

The goal of this monograph was to advance a process-oriented theory of visual working memory development that can span multiple tasks and developmental periods. As reviewed in Chapter 1, lab-based measures of working memory correlate both concurrently and longitudinally with measures of more general cognitive skills, highlighting the importance of understanding how working memory functions and develops. However, there currently exists a disconnect between research and theories of working memory during infancy and later childhood. As a bridge between these disconnected research areas, the current monograph focused on two tasks considered to measure visual working memory capacity, the change-preference task developed for infants, and the change detection task used with children and adults. Previous studies using these methods revealed seemingly inconsistent estimates of capacity over development, raising the questions of whether the tasks rely on the same underlying processes and whether a common developmental change could explain improvements in both tasks. Here I presented the cognitive dynamics theory, which emphasizes understanding the link between memory

Corresponding author: Vanessa R. Simmering, 1202 W. Johnson St., Madison, WI 53706; email: simmering@wisc.edu

DOI: 10.1111/mono.12253

representations to behavior across tasks contexts and development, as a way to reconcile previous behavioral results and theoretical accounts.

Chapter 2 introduced a modeling framework, the Dynamic Field Theory, to formalize the concepts embodied within the cognitive dynamics theory into a computational model. Using a dynamic neural field model implementation, I showed how these two behavioral tasks could be performed by the same cognitive system. Simulations of these tasks led to three specific behavioral predictions and one simulation prediction. First, simulations suggested that capacity estimates from the change-preference task should continue to increase over development beyond Ross-Sheehy et al.'s (2003) estimate of four items at 10 months. Second, the model's performance indicated that capacity estimates from the change-preference task should be higher than estimates from change detection within the same participants. Third, despite the predicted difference in capacity estimates across tasks, performance should be correlated across tasks because both tasks rely on the same underlying visual working memory system. In particular, model simulations demonstrated how change preference scores and switch rates in the change-preference task could provide indexes of the underlying memory processes, suggesting that both could relate to capacity estimates from change detection. Finally, I predicted that the full pattern of performance across tasks and development could be simulated using a single developmental mechanism—an increase in real-time stability—realized through strengthening connections in the dynamic model.

Chapter 3 presented three behavioral experiments confirming the first three predictions. In Experiment 1, 3- to 5-year-old children and adults completed the change-preference task from Ross-Sheehy et al. (2003) in set sizes two, four, and six. Change-preference scores were significantly above chance for all age groups at all set sizes, suggesting a capacity of at least six items by 3 years of age. Experiments 2 and 3 tested these same participants in the change detection task, in which capacity was estimated between two and three items for children and between four and five items for adults. Thus, as predicted, capacity estimates in the change-preference task increased beyond infancy, and were higher than estimates from change detection within the same group of participants. Furthermore, comparing performance across tasks revealed capacity estimates from change detection were significantly and independently predicted by change preference scores from set size two and switch rates from set size six in the change-preference task, even after controlling for age-related increases.

Chapter 4 presented a test of my fourth prediction, that the suite of behavioral effects across tasks and development could be quantitatively fit by the dynamic model using strengthening connectivity as the primary mechanism of change. These simulations provided a good fit to the empirical data, and analyses of the processes embodied in the model revealed seven consequences of strengthening connectivity, which comprise the notion of real-time stability in the cognitive dynamics account. Further analysis of the model's performance across set sizes revealed why the correlations in Chapter 3 were limited to the lowest set size for change preference scores, but the highest set size for switch rates. These simulations show the utility of formalizing theories with computational models, as they can provide insights into potential underlying mechanisms and reveal gaps in previous conceptual explanations of performance and development.

In this final chapter, I first describe remaining questions and challenges for this account of visual working memory. The next section includes discussion of possible generalizations of this perspective beyond visual working memory development, first to the theories and empirical findings reviewed in Chapter 1, and second across a broader range of domains.

REMAINING QUESTIONS AND CHALLENGES IN VISUAL WORKING MEMORY

The dynamic model implementation of the cognitive dynamics theory has answered some questions within visual working memory, addressing how capacity estimates relate to behavior in the change-preference and change detection tasks over development. In this section, I discuss four additional considerations from the literature on capacity limits: (i) a new eye-tracking measure of infants' capacity; (ii) the resolution of memory representations; (iii) the representation of multiple visual features in "bound" objects; and (iv) the role of attention in visual working memory performance.

A New Eye-Tracking Measure of Capacity in Infancy

Oakes and colleagues developed an infant "one-shot" change detection task to probe capacity without the extended trials used in the change-preference task. In the one-shot task, a single memory array of two colors was presented for 517 s, followed by a 317-ms delay, then a 3,000-ms test array in which one color remained the same and one color changed (Oakes et al., 2013). Oakes et al. (2013) tracked 6- and 8-month-old infants' eye movements during the presentation of the test array and found that 8-month-olds exhibited a preference for the changed color, while 6-month-olds looked equally to both colors. In a follow-up experiment, they presented memory arrays with two identical colors (essentially requiring the encoding of only a single item), and 6-month-olds exhibited a preference for the changed color at test. These findings converge with results from the change preference task, suggesting that capacity increases from one item at 6 months to two or three items at 8 months (Oakes et al., 2006, 2009; Ross-Sheehy et al., 2003).

How do these results align with the cognitive dynamics account of performance in the change-preference task? Although the dynamics of looking between two objects within a single display likely differ from the dynamics of looking between two displays that may contain multiple objects, the same notion of familiarity reducing fixation and novelty maintaining fixation would hold. Two phenomena from Oakes et al. (2013) need to be explained: the difference in performance between 6 and 8 months, and the difference in 6-month-olds' performance when the memory array contained one versus two colors. For the first finding, the mechanism from Perone et al. (2011) is applicable: the "older" infant parameters in their model formed memory representations more quickly, could hold more than one item in memory at once, and also used memory representations in service of behavior more stably.

Even if most 8-month-old infants were only able to stably encode a single item in memory, this may be sufficient to drive a preference for the new item at test. Assuming that infants would not be biased during encoding, about half of the infants would encode the item on the left, and half would encode the item on the right (for the sake of this example, presume the item on the right is the one that changed in the test display). At test, infants who encoded the left item would see one familiar item and one novel item; infants who encoded the right item would see two novel items. Presumably the left-encoding infants would prefer the novel item, but the right-encoding infants could prefer either (randomly) or show no preference. Depending on the strength of each infant's preference, these different patterns could average together as a significant preference for the changed item at the group level. The data presented by Oakes et al. (2013) were not intended to address individual differences, but this possibility could presumably be tested by analyzing individual infants' looking over time; fixations during the presentation of the memory array may also shed light onto which color(s) individual infants were likely to encode.

Understanding 6-month-olds' performance in the second experiment, with two identical colors in the memory array, follows directly from the previous example. In this version of the paradigm, only one color could be encoded during the memory array, and that memory was sufficient to drive a preference for the new color in the test array. In the context of the first experiment, though, which color each 6-month-old encoded would have presumably been random. Could the difference between 6 and 8 months still arise if each age group only encoded a single item in memory? Perhaps: as the simulations in Chapter 4 demonstrated, other changes within the visual working memory system could lead to different levels of performance even with the same memory representations. For example, if 8-month-old infants encode more quickly than 6-month-old infants, the younger infants may need more opportunities to encode a single color, which would occur as they looked between two identical items in the memory array from Experiment 2. This possibility could be tested by extending the duration of the memory array when it contained two different colors, to see if preferences then emerged in younger infants. Similar to the simulations presented in Chapters 2 and 4, this analysis of the one-shot task highlights the importance of considering not just what is remembered but the processes supporting the formation and use of memory representations within the specific task context.

Resolution of Visual Working Memory

The nature of visual working memory capacity limits has been a source of considerable debate within the adult literature (e.g., Bays & Husain, 2008; Wilken & Ma, 2004; Zhang & Luck, 2008; see Fukuda, Awh, & Vogel, 2010, for review). Part of this debate focuses on the resolution or precision of visual working memory representations. This question has more recently been addressed with developmental studies. In particular, Simmering and Patterson (2012) showed that strengthening connectivity within a related dynamic model led to increased resolution of visual working memory, as measured by color discrimination performance. In the model, this difference in resolution did not arise through the width of peaks in the working memory field, as might be suggested by the characterization of visual working memory "precision" in the literature (e.g., Burnett Heyes et al., 2012); rather, it was the strength of the inhibitory troughs projected to the perceptual field that determined how reliably colors could be identified as "different." Simmering and Patterson showed that children's ability to discriminate very similar colors separated by a short delay improved between 4 and 6 years, in parallel to the increases in capacity shown in the current sample, and as predicted by strengthening connectivity the dynamic model. Following this demonstration, Simmering and Miller (2016) tested whether these changes in capacity and resolution were related over development. Their study showed that 5- to 8-year-old children's capacity in change detection was predicted by their discrimination performance, but not by age. These empirical and computational results indicate an eighth characteristic of increasing real-time stability not address in Chapter 4: improved resolution of visual working memory over development.

A related question that has not yet been addressed within this framework, however, is whether the resolution per item changes as more items are held in memory. Behavioral evidence shows a trade-off between resolution and capacity, with the resolution per item decreasing as the number of items held in memory increases; such findings have been used to support a "flexible resource" perspective (e.g., Bays & Husain, 2008; Burnett Heyes et al., 2012). More recent evidence suggests that changes in resolution asymptote once a maximum number of items (typically three to four) has been reached; these results support a "discrete resource" account of capacity limits (see Fukuda et al., 2010, for review). From this perspective, each individual has a limited number of "slots" in which to store items, but differing amounts of a shared resource could be devoted to each item, allowing for differences in resolution among items with a fixed upper limit (Fukuda et al., 2010).

To evaluate how resolution might vary with the number of items held in the dynamic model, it is important to consider how precision or resolution is probed behaviorally (see below for discussion of electrophysiological measures of attention). First, Simmering and Patterson's (2012) color discrimination paradigm used participants' ability to detect small changes in colors as the metric of resolution (detecting smaller changes implies higher resolution). As noted in the description of their results above, their model simulations suggested that this effect did not arise through more precise representations (i.e., peak width), but through the associated inhibition that supported the comparison processes needed to detect a change. The simulations in Chapter 4 showed that, as the number of items in the working memory field increases, more inhibition projects to the perceptual field, which makes changes more difficult to detect overall. This leads to the prediction that color discrimination performance should be worse when more items are held in memory, not due to the width of peaks, but due to a reduced ability to detect small changes. Thus, the behavioral estimate of resolution would differ across set sizes without a corresponding change in the underlying representations.

The second type of task used to assess precision or resolution is a recall task, in which participants reproduce a continuous stimulus feature (i.e., color or orientation of a line) from memory, and precision is calculated from the variability in error magnitude across trials. This metric of precision is similar to a common measure in motor control and spatial recall, referred to as variable error in those domains (i.e., the standard deviation of errors across responses to the same target; e.g., Spencer & Hund, 2002). Because similar three-layer model architectures have been used to simulate spatial recall performance, it is possible to extrapolate from those simulation results to interpret precision in color recall. Variable error from behavioral data has been fit through quantitative simulations (Schutte & Spencer, 2009), but does not solely reflect the width of representations (i.e., peaks in the working memory field). Rather, some variation in responding arises through noise in the maintenance process over the memory delay. As such, the behavioral index of "precision" may reflect underlying variability in the real-time processes supporting maintenance, not just the nature of the representation.

Although these spatial recall simulations provide some insight into potential contributions to variable error other than representational precision, they have not addressed the implications for remembering

114

multiple items at once. Previous simulations of the change detection task, however, have shown that local excitatory and lateral inhibitory connections that underlie encoding and maintenance in the dynamic model allow for metric interactions among items held in working memory simultaneously. In particular, Johnson et al. (2014) showed more similarity of items within the memory array increased the likelihood of losing at item from memory (i.e., a peak "dying out" in the model) and more false alarm errors (in both the model and behavioral data); furthermore, more similarity between the new item on a change trial and other items from the memory array was related to higher miss rates.

How would these interactions among peaks within working memory affect variable error in a color recall task? Johnson (2008; see also Johnson, Ambrose, Dineva, & Spencer, 2016) showed that an uneven distribution of inhibition around a peak—which would arise from a second nearby item held in memory at the same time—caused bias in the peak away from the neighboring item (i.e., repulsion in memory; this effect is well documented between a single item held in memory and perceptual reference frames in spatial recall, both behaviorally and computationally, Spencer, Simmering, Schutte, & Schöner, 2007). Johnson demonstrated that systematically presenting two "near" colors and one "far" color together on each color recall trial led to predictable bias in the direction of recall error (i.e., showing repulsion from nearby colors), providing behavioral evidence for this mechanism of interactions among items in visual working memory. In most color recall tasks the selection of colors is random across trials, which would produce variability in whether another item was nearby or not, and the "direction" of the neighboring item in color-space when one was nearby. Thus, extrapolating from Johnson's findings, the different directions and magnitudes of the type of repulsion based on the (randomly-selected) distribution of target colors would lead to greater variable error, which in turn would produce a lower calculated precision score.

This section shows how theories that only address the nature of representations may not be sufficiently specific to evaluate against alternative explanations. Only through an analysis of how representations would produce the relevant behavior can we uncover other potential contributions to performance and errors. It remains to be tested whether the types of mechanisms described here—the role of inhibition in the ability to detect changes, or interactions among items in memory producing variability— could account for the full range of behavioral results, or if additional changes in the nature of the representations is also necessary. This highlights a central tenet of the cognitive dynamics theory: the way in which memory is used in service of behavior is *equally important* to understand as the nature of memory representations.

A second common question with regard to capacity limits is whether multiple features can be bound into so-called "integrated objects," which are then the units of capacity, or if different features of objects are represented additively, such that one object with two features would require the same capacity as two objects with one feature. Behavioral evidence suggests that neither of these extremes captures adults' performance in change detection tasks: in some conditions, multiple features can be remembered with no apparent cost (e.g., Luck & Vogel, 1997; Vogel et al., 2001), but in other conditions performance is moderately impaired for multi- versus single-feature items (e.g., Cowan, Blume, & Saults, 2013; Wheeler & Treisman, 2002). There is also some debate over whether binding requires additional processes, such as attention (Johnson, Hollingworth, & Luck, 2008). Furthermore, adults' performance on recall tasks shows some independence between features (i.e., one feature may be forgotten when the other feature is remembered; Bays, Wu, & Husain, 2011) but also some effect of remembering other features (i.e., resolution for each feature is lower when remembering two features compared to single-feature objects; Fougnie, Asplund, & Marois, 2010). The full pattern of results across tasks and conditions has not yet been explained by a single, comprehensive theory; rather, contradictory results are often presented to refute a theory, but without a thorough description of the source of discrepancies across conditions. This is a promising future avenue for computational work, which can provide the necessary specificity to test which types of representations and processes could capture the details of performance across variations in task parameters.

Two of the developmental theories described in Chapters 1 and 2 have implications for relating features within visual working memory. First, Oakes and colleagues (2006, 2009) proposed that infants' ability to retain multiple items within an array arises through the emerging ability to bind colors to locations. Second, the neural synchrony model from Raffone and Wolters (2001), cited by Riggs et al. (2011) as a potential mechanism for capacity increases, was originally proposed to account for the similarity in capacity limits between single- and multi-featured objects (e.g., Luck & Vogel, 1997). As the simulations in Chapter 4 demonstrated, such binding was not necessary to explain developmental increases in capacity in the change-preference and change detection tasks when only colors are tested. However, to account for performance when correspondence between color and location is required (e.g., Oakes et al., 2006), or with multiple features per object (e.g., Riggs et al., 2011), the processes involved in binding must be specified.

The processes necessary for binding features and space were not part of the dynamic model presented in Chapters 2 and 4, but initial steps toward this level of representation have been taken within the broader Dynamic Field

Theory framework by Schneegans, Spencer, and Schöner (2015). In their model, separate feature dimensions (e.g., color, shape, space) are represented in parallel four-layer architectures (similar to the three-layer architecture described here, but with the processes capture in the current perceptual field split across an attentional field and a contrast field; see also Schneegans, Lins, & Spencer, 2015). These features are then linked via two-dimensional feature-space fields that receive projections from the one-dimensional fields. For example, the two-dimensional color-space working memory field would receive projections from the color working memory field along one dimension and the space working memory field along the other dimension; where the activation from these fields intersects would specify which color was present at which location. In this model, multiple features of an object (e.g., color and shape) are not linked directly, but rather both features are linked to the shared spatial location. Mis-binding of features is possible when multiple objects are present, but this is limited through attentional processes (see Schneegans, Spencer, et al., 2015, for simulations of the circumstances under which mis-bindings are likely to occur).

The most stringent test of feature binding comes through change detection tasks that test binding changes (i.e., when two features swap between objects) versus changes to new features (i.e., a new color or shape on one object). Schneegens, Spencer, et al. (2015) demonstrated that the expanded Dynamic Field Theory architecture can detect binding changes—the swap in position of one feature between two objects—by virtue of the new feature-location binding. Rather than a new feature value driving a peak in the perceptual field, as shown in the simulations in Chapters 2 and 4, binding changes are detected in this model's feature-space fields. One challenge for this mechanism would be identifying such changes when an object is presented in a new location (e.g., Cowan et al., 2013); this type of probe could potentially be addressed with an updating mechanism such as that used in a dynamic neural field model of multi-object tracking (Spencer, Barich, Goldberg, & Perone, 2012). Thus far, this expanded model architecture has been used to demonstrate that binding changes can be detected through this manner of representation, but has not been tested quantitatively to see if it could produce the patterns of results shown in behavioral tasks. As such, it is not yet clear how this approach compares to existing explanations of feature binding in adults.

What are the implications of developmental increases in real-time stability for feature binding? Although the types of changes from Chapter 4 have not been implemented in this expanded Dynamic Field Theory architecture, a likely consequence of weaker connections within and between fields would be an increased likelihood of mis-binding features and/or forgetting features as peaks die out during the delay. Moreover, slower encoding would make it more difficult to stabilize peaks in the two-dimensional fields, as these fields require activation building first in the one-dimensional fields before projecting activation to the two-dimensional fields. Behavioral evidence shows that children as young as 3 years perform similarly on trials with single- versus multi-featured objects when testing only changes to new features; however, when performance was compared between trials requiring the detection of binding changes versus detection of new features, young children show binding impairments (Simmering, Johnson, Patterson, & Spencer, 2009; Simmering & Wood, 2016). Further behavioral and computational tests are needed to evaluate whether there are developmental changes in feature binding beyond the changes in visual working memory for single-feature objects.

Relating Attention and Visual Working Memory

A third area of interest is the role of attention in visual working memory capacity limits. Effects of attention are difficult to summarize due to notable differences in definitions and distinctions for multiple types of attention (see Anderson, 2011, for discussion). In this section, I consider three types of evidence that attention relates to visual working memory capacity: exogenous attentional cues can augment infants' looking performance; developmental and individual differences in infants' attention predict measures of working memory both concurrently and longitudinally; and individual differences in adults' control of attention correlates with capacity.

One study with infants has shown the effect of exogenous attention on infants' visual working memory performance. As reviewed in previous chapters, 6-month-old infants show no preference when tested on set size three trials in the change-preference task (Oakes et al., 2006, 2009; Ross-Sheehy et al., 2003). However, Ross-Sheehy, Oakes, and Luck (2010) showed that 5-month-old infants look longer to a set size three change display if attention is drawn to the item that is changing. This version of the paradigm compared looking time to changing streams (comparable to the change display in the current study) with attentional cues that indicated the changed color (valid) versus one of the unchanged colors (invalid) across trials. When the cue was rotation of the colored square, 5-month-old infants looked significantly longer to the valid versus invalid stream, suggesting that this cue supported memory for the items within the display (see Ross-Sheehy et al., 2010, for discussion of a different manipulation that did not augment infants' performance).

How could this type of manipulation be implemented in the dynamic model used here? Motion presumably serves as a spatial cue to direct the infant's gaze in the experiment, but the dynamic model does not include a representation of space within each display. Using the kind of architecture described in the previous section on feature binding, where space and color each provide inputs to a color-space field, a stronger spatial cue (through motion) would increase the overall input to the working memory field at the location of the cued item. This would, in turn, increase the likelihood of encoding the color of the item at that location in the working memory field, which would make the change easier to detect. Thus, exogenous attentional cues could be simulated as additional spatially specific input to the model.

A second notion of attention that is commonly discussed in the infant literature refers to the dynamics of looking behavior. Rose and colleagues quantify attention through switch rates in looking tasks and describe attention as an important component of looking behavior that predicts later cognitive functions (Rose, Feldman, & Jankowski, 2004; Rose et al., 2012). As shown in Chapter 4, the dynamic model architecture can produce different rates of switching through changes in the fixation system dynamics as well as in the underlying memory representations that contribute to looking behavior. The fixation dynamics in the model could be interpreted as attention, specifically, the parameter that influenced the fluctuation in the fixation nodes' resting levels based on their activation (i.e., h_{down} in Tables 4 and 5). In the simulations presented in Chapter 4, this parameter varied across age groups, but could also be set to vary between "individuals" (i.e., runs of the model) within an age group.

Simulations by Perone and Spencer (2014) suggests that this level of individual variation in processes may not be necessary, however. They simulated infants' performance in a visual paired comparison task that included objects that varied in both colors and shapes. Similar to infants' performance, analyses of their simulation results showed that the model's looking during familiarization—measured by switch rate, look duration, and peak look length—predicted whether the model would prefer the familiar or novel item at test. Importantly, Perone and Spencer used identical parameter values for each separate run of the model through the task, meaning that the "individual" differences arose through stochastic noise and the history-dependent nature of looking performance in the model (i.e., where the model looked determined the input to the model). These simulations, combined with the analyses of the dynamic model's performance in Chapter 4, suggest that the individual differences that Rose et al. (2004, 2012) have described as attention may depend on processes of encoding and comparing in visual working memory.

Lastly, studies with adults have shown that individual differences in attentional control correlate with capacity in the change detection task. For example, Vogel, McCollough, and Machizawa (2005) found that participants' capacity was predicted by their ability to filter out irrelevant stimuli from the memory array. To assess filtering, they used ERPs to measure contra-lateral delay activity, which had previously been shown to scale with the number of items held in memory (Vogel & Machizawa, 2004). Participants completed a change detection task in which memory arrays could contain two or four items; on some of the set size four trials, participants were instructed to ignore half of the items though a cue at the beginning of each trial. Filtering efficiency was calculated by comparing contra-lateral delay activity on the trials when two items were to be ignored to the other trial types: activity comparable to the set size two trials indicated good filtering, whereas activity comparable to the set size four trials indicated poor filtering. Results showed that filtering efficiency differed between high- and low-capacity individuals (defined by a median split), and that capacity estimates correlated with filtering efficiency. These results suggest that the ability to control what information gets into working memory contributes to individual differences in capacity limits.

Similarly, Fukuda and Vogel (2009) showed that individual differences in resistance to attentional capture (also measured through ERPs) correlated with capacity estimates from change detection. Their measure of attentional capture compared evoked responses to probes at target versus distractor locations in a cued target identification task. In particular, participants were instructed to attend to one of two cues (signaled by corresponding colors in different locations) to encode the identity of a shape presented later at the cued location. Across trials, either the valid or invalid location could be presented; the difference in amplitude of the ERP wave form between these two trial types was the attentional capture (i.e., more similarity corresponds to more capture). Thus, participants with strong evoked responses for the valid locations, and weak evoked responses for the invalid locations, showed the best resistance to attentional capture, which correlated with capacity.

Could this sense of attention be realized in a dynamic field model? In its current form, the model described in Chapters 2 and 4 had no mechanism explicitly serving as attention in the change detection task, and also no individual differences. It is possible that modulation of the existing parameters could simulate individual differences in capacity. For example, Buss and Spencer (2014) used a dynamic neural field architecture similar to the feature-binding model described above to capture children's perfor-mance in the dimensional change card sort task. In this task, children are told to sort cards by one feature (i.e., color or shape) in a first block of trials, then by the other feature in a second block of trials. Buss and Spencer simulated these instructions by boosting the resting level of the field associated with the correct feature (i.e., the color-space field on color trials and the shape-space field on shape trials); using this mechanism, they simulated results from 14 conditions of the card sort task. Exploratory simulations of the adult parameters reported in Chapter 4 showed that this type of boost to the resting levels in the three-layer architecture modulated capacity estimates, with higher estimates when the perceptual field or inhibitory layer had a higher resting level, but lower estimates when the working memory field had a higher level. It is possible that different combinations of resting levels across "individuals" could produce reliable differences in capacity.

Individual differences in capacity could also be simulated in the dynamic model by modifying the parameters that were strengthened over development in Chapter 4. Note that even without any sense of "individuals" in the model (i.e., each run of the model within a given "age group" included identical parameter values), the quantitative fits presented in Chapter 4 provided a satisfactory fit of variability as well as mean performance (see error bars in Figure 20; MAE for standard deviations ranged from 0.22 to 0.27 trials across age groups). Given the number of ways individual differences could be implemented in the dynamic model architecture, the question of whether the dynamic model could simulate individual differences is somewhat trivial. The more critical question is whether the neural indexes of attention described by Vogel et al. (2005) and Fukuda and Vogel (2009) could be measured analogously in the model. At present, there is no clear answer to this question. Although models within the Dynamic Field Theory framework build from neural population models (Amari, 1977), and other models within the framework have been used to predict ERP differences across conditions (e.g., McDowell, Jeka, Schöner, & Hatfield, 2002), the models used to simulate visual working memory performance are abstractions that do not map directly to neural areas (see Johnson, Spencer, & Schöner, 2009, for discussion). Furthermore, activation within a given field in the model may not be analogous neural activity; rather, activation projected from one field to another might be a more suitable comparison. More work needs to be done before this question can be addressed, and there are currently efforts to connect the Dynamic Field Theory framework more directly to neural measures (e.g., Spencer, Buss, & Magnotta, 2013; see also Buss, Magnotta, Schöner, & Spencer, 2016).

GENERALIZING THE COGNITIVE DYNAMICS THEORY AND REAL-TIME STABILITY HYPOTHESIS

Although the cognitive dynamics theory has led to novel insights into behavior and empirical predictions within research on visual working memory development, as described above, one of the primary motivations for this project was to build toward a general theoretical perspective that can be applied across a broad range of domains. This section considers two potential extensions, first to the types of working memory and development that were described in Chapter 1, then to cognitive development research more generally.

Chapter 1 reviewed behavioral phenomena and theoretical accounts from two domains of working memory research: visual working memory during infancy and children's performance on complex working memory tasks. One of the goals of the current empirical and computational work was to advance a process-based theory of working memory development that could be generalized to these two domains. To this end, the current section reviews the major findings from these domains and address how the cognitive dynamics theory and real-time stability hypothesis align with this part of the literature.

Recall from Chapter 1 that infant working memory has been assessed using tasks that require delayed reaching or looking to different stimuli over time. A number of the developmental changes in infants' performance in looking paradigms have already been modeled using dynamic neural fields, demonstrating that these effects could arise through increasing real-time stability: faster encoding (Perone & Spencer, 2013a,b, 2014; see also Chapter 4); stronger novelty preferences (including the early familiarity-to-novelty shift; Perone & Spencer, 2013a,b, 2014); more looks and switches between displays (Perone & Spencer, 2013a, 2014; see also Chapter 4). Both looking and reaching paradigms have also shown increases in the durability of memory, with older infants retaining information for longer delays. Some of these effects are driven by long-term memory (e.g., recognizing an object from a previous lab visit; Courage & Howe, 2001), whereas others depend more directly on working memory (e.g., reaching correctly after a longer delay; Diamond, 1985). Although neither of these effects has been modeled directly, the simulations from Chapter 4 can provide some insight. In particular, the developmental changes implemented in the dynamic model led to fewer "forgotten" items (i.e., peaks dropping out during maintenance; see Figures 22 and 23) over development, which would correspond to better durability if memory was probed after varying lengths of delay. The increased durability in long-term memory could arise through increases in strength and durability of working memory representations as well: in the dynamic model presented here, long-term memory is accumulated as a trace of the above-threshold activation from the working memory field. Thus, as items are represented more strongly and held longer in working memory (as shown in Chapter 4), the corresponding long-term memory representations would also be stronger. Together these simulations of various looking paradigms across infancy and early childhood suggest that the major developmental improvements noted during infancy—faster encoding, increased durability, stronger novelty preferences, and more switching—could all arise through a common underlying mechanism.

In addition to these developmental changes during infancy, Chapter 1 reviewed evidence from complex span tasks showing developmental improvements and correlations with higher cognitive skills. Recall that these tasks either require manipulation of information in memory (e.g., repeating a series of items backward) or switching between storage and processing tasks (e.g., counting sets of dots and storing the results from the series for later recall). Four potential sources of change have been proposed to account for developmental improvements in performance on complex tasks: faster processing speed, increased capacity, reduced decay, and more resistance to interference. Although the dynamic model used here cannot perform complex tasks in its current form due to the very different task structures and demands, simulations in Chapter 4 showed how three of these general characteristics of memory—capacity, decay, and interference—change developmentally. It is possible that the faster encoding speed noted in Chapter 4 could also provide the faster processing speed in complex tasks: due to the differences in task demands, however, this comparison is not straight-forward. More work is needed to adapt this type of modeling framework to encompass all of the processes required to perform complex span tasks.

The dynamic model presented here produced eight characteristics of developmental change in visual working memory—collectively described as increases in real-time stability—through a single underlying mechanism. Comparisons to other working memory tasks within infancy and later childhood suggest that these developmental processes could capture many of the improvements across those tasks and developmental periods as well. This synthesis across areas of research suggests *developmental continuity* in the processes underlying working memory performance from infancy through childhood. As noted in Chapter 1, separate studies have shown that cognitive skills are predicted by both infants' looking behavior and children's performance on complex span tasks, raising the question of whether the same working memory processes underlie performance between infancy and complex tasks. The empirical and computational work presented here suggests that they overlap at least partially, and perhaps completely. An important next step in this line of research is to understand how the processes in common between infant looking tasks and complex span tasks support higher cognitive functions.

Future Directions: Real-Time Stability as a General Construct

Beyond this proposed synthesis between infant looking paradigms and complex working memory tasks in childhood, a long-term goal of the cognitive dynamics theory is to extend the general concept of real-time stability across broader areas of research. Through dynamic systems approaches to motor development, related concepts of stability have been demonstrated in the development of reaching, locomotion, and spatial cognition. In the domain of reaching, Thelen and colleagues showed that successfully grasping an object requires bringing together multiple processes in the moment—holding the trunk stable, controlling both the direction and velocity of the arm's movement, opening and closing the hand at the right moment (Thelen et al., 1993; Thelen, Corbetta, & Spencer, 1996; Thelen & Spencer, 1998). These different components of reaching may develop at different rates, but are not independent and combine to produce mature reaching.

In the domain of locomotion, Adolph and colleagues have shown newly acquired behaviors, like crawling and walking during infancy, are relatively unstable and therefore more likely to fail when task conditions change. For example, a series of studies assessing how infants descend slopes showed that age was not an important predictor of whether infants would attempt to descend steep slopes; rather, infants with more experience with the form of locomotion (crawling vs. walking) were better at judging their ability to descend (Adolph, 1997; Adolph, Eppler, & Gibson, 1993; Adolph, Tamis-LeMonda, Ishak, Karasik, & Lobo, 2008). This difference was evident within individuals over time: infants with little walking experience would resist descending a too-steep slope when in a crawling posture (the more stable form of locomotion) but would attempt descent of the same angle of slope while walking. Thus, the relative stability of each form of locomotion predicted how well infants could adapt to different task demands.

Applications to spatial cognition provide the most direct analogy to the development of visual working memory (see Simmering & Schutte, 2015; Spencer et al., 2007, for reviews). Beginning with infancy, increasing real-time stability can account for developmental changes in the Piagetian A-not-B task. In this task context, unstable representations of the current hiding location leads to more frequent errors on A trials in 8- to 10-month-old infants (Schöner & Dineva, 2007), as well as perseverative responding on B trials in 10- to 12-month-old infants (see Simmering et al., 2008, for details). Later in development, more stable representations can be maintained more robustly over the short delay, supporting correct performance. This notion of stability led to the counter-intuitive prediction that even younger infants would *not* search perseveratively in the A-not-B task. This is because the accumulation of long-term memory on A trials (the source of such errors) requires sufficient stability in working memory. Clearfield, Diedrich, Smith, and Thelen (2006) showed that 5-month-old infants reach correctly on B trials, indicating that perseveration requires some underlying stability.

Beyond infancy, as connectivity continues to strengthen, peaks may sustain over longer delays and in the absence of continued visual input (i.e., without lids marking the hiding locations; Schutte, Spencer, & Schöner, 2003). Between the ages of 3 and 6 years, as children are able to perform more challenging recall tasks, four types of changes in spatial working memory tasks that arise through increasing real-time stability. First, the spatial range across which long-term memory influences working memory reduces: when recalling two nearby locations across trials, younger children's responses are biased toward previous locations at relatively large separations between locations, whereas older children's and adults only show such bias at small separations (Schutte et al., 2003). Second, children's memory for locations is biased by the perceived reference frames in the within the task space, with a complex pattern of change over development. This pattern has been quantitatively modeled within the Dynamic Field Theory framework using the spatial precision hypothesis (Schutte & Spencer, 2009). Third, these findings have been generalized to predict performance in a different task context, position discrimination, with children showing improved discrimination (similar to color discrimination results from Simmering & Patterson, 2012) as well as changing influences of perceptual reference frames over development (Simmering & Spencer, 2008). Fourth, Schutte and Spencer (2010) showed that children's spatial recall could be improved through increased perceptual structure in the task space, which augments real-time stability through stronger input.

Although the types of tasks and developmental effects that have been modeled in the Dynamic Field Theory framework differ between spatial cognition and visual working memory, they still represent a relatively narrow range of cognitive development research. The examples from motor development expand on this account further, but do not yet connect with areas traditionally considered "higher level" cognition. Some research has been used to expand this modeling framework in that direction, including accounts of rule use (as described above in the dimensional change card sort task; Buss & Spencer, 2014) and language development (Samuelson et al., 2009; Samuelson, Smith, Perry, & Spencer, 2011).

In the domain of word learning, Samuelson et al. (2009) showed that changes in the strength of input in a dynamic neural field model could simulate toddlers' attention to shape versus material in a novel noun generalization task. Furthermore, Samuelson et al. (2011) demonstrated how interactions between features and space provided a foundation for children to associate labels with objects that were separated in time, using a variant of the two-dimensional model architecture described briefly above. In these cases, model simulations provided an explanation for how children's behavior varied across task contexts—consistent with the cognitive dynamics perspective—but have not yet addressed questions of developmental change.

For the cognitive dynamics perspective and real-time stability to be expanded further, however, conceptual principles from this approach should be tested without depending on formal implementation in a model. This requires finding ways to assess and modify real-time stability empirically, to evaluate whether it is changing developmentally and how it contributes to task performance. The simulations in Chapter 4 provide a number of potential avenues for this type of exploration. First, a less-stable system builds representations more slowly and loses them more quickly; changing the length of stimulus presentations and delays can evaluate time-based changes in representations. Second, unstable memory representations may be used reliably for relatively simple behaviors, but not for more demanding behaviors. The cognitive development literature is filled with such examples of "decalage," in which children's performance differs across multiple tasks that purportedly rely on the same underlying processes. The example tasks from the current monograph showed mechanistically how such a difference can arise through the details of the task structures and behavioral responses; identifying such differences requires careful analysis of the processes necessary to perform each task. Third, manipulating task details to provide more support for memory representations could augment stability and allow younger children to perform more comparably across different tasks. This is exactly how Perone et al. (2015) improved children's performance in the dimensional change card sort task: providing children with additional color experience increased the stability of their color representations, which in turn supported their ability to sort cards along the color dimension. Increasing real-time stability suggests a developmental cascade of improvements: as working memory representations become more stable, more accurate long-term memory can be formed, and these representations can be used more reliably in service of other tasks.

CONCLUSIONS

The experiments and simulations presented here make two important contributions to the field of cognitive development. First, the cognitive dynamics theory and real-time stability hypothesis provide a specific, mechanistic account of visual working memory capacity over development and across behavioral tasks. This theory predicted that capacity estimates would differ across tasks despite the fact that both tasks rely on the same underlying memory system, and performance correlated across tasks. These results demonstrate the utility of computational models in formalizing theoretical constructs to test how tasks relate over development. Second, in the broader context of working memory research, this theory provides a potential explanation for why both infants' performance on looking tasks and children's performance on complex span tasks are related to later cognitive skills—the simulations in Chapter 4 suggest developmental continuity in the mechanisms supporting improvements in working memory. The critical next step for this application of the current theory is to investigate how the common processes across working memory tasks relate to performance on standardized tests of reasoning and general intelligence.

Future empirical and theoretical work is needed to connect these processes to the broader cognitive skills that are related to working memory functioning, but the theory presented here takes an important step toward providing the specificity needed to make meaningful connections across tasks. Theories must be expanded beyond a single task, domain, and developmental period in order to explain—and predict—how working memory changes within an individual over time (Simmering & Perone, 2013). If we do not understand how the tasks we use in the lab relate to one another, we cannot predict when training in lab tasks will produce lasting improvements in behaviors outside of the lab.

REFERENCES

This article is part of the issue "Working Memory Capacity in Context: Modeling Dynamic Processes of Behavior, Memory, and Development," Simmering, Vanessa (Issue Author). For a full listing of articles in this issue, see: http://onlinelibrary.wiley.com/doi/10.1111/mono.v81.3/issuetoc.

Aaronson, D., & Watts, B. (1987). Extensions of Grier's computational formulas for A' and B" to below-chance performance. *Psychological Bulletin,* **102**, 439–442.

Adolph, K. E. (1997). Learning in the development of infant locomotion. *Monographs of the Society for Research in Child Development,* **62**, 1–140.

Adolph, K. E., Eppler, M. A., & Gibson, E. J. (1993). Crawling versus walking infants' perception of affordances for locomotion over sloping surfaces. *Child Development,* **64**, 1158–1174.

Adolph, K. E., Tamis-LeMonda, C. S., Ishak, S., Karasik, L. B., & Lobo, S. A. (2008). Locomotor experience and use of social information are posture specific. *Developmental Psychology,* **44**, 1705–1714.

Alloway, T. P., Gathercole, S. E., & Pickering, S. J. (2006). Verbal and visuospatial short-term and working memory in children: Are they separable? *Child Development,* **77**(6), 1698–1716.

Alloway, T. P., Gathercole, S. E., Willis, C., & Adams, A.-M. (2004). A structural analysis of working memory and related cognitive skills in young children. *Journal of Experimental Child Psychology,* **87**, 85–106.

Amari, S. (1977). Dynamics of pattern formation in lateral-inhibition type neural fields. *Biological Cybernetics,* **27**, 77–87.

Anderson, B. (2011). There is no such thing as attention. *Frontiers in Psychology,* **2**, 246. http://doi.org/10.3389/fpsyg.2011.00246

Baddeley, A. D. (2000). The episodic buffer: A new component of working memory? *Trends in Cognitive Sciences* **4**, 417–423.

Baddeley, A. D. (2001). Is working memory still working? *American Psychologist,* **56**(11), 851–864.

Baddeley, A. D., & Hitch, G. J. (1974). Working memory. In G. Bower (Ed.), *Recent advances in learning and motivation* (Vol. 8). New York, NY: Academic Press.

DOI: 10.1111/mono.12254

128

Baillargeon, R. (1987). Object permanence in 3.5- and 4.5-month-old infants. *Developmental Psychology*, **23**, 655–664.

Baillargeon, R., & Graber, M. (1988). Evidence of location memory in 8-month-old infants in nonsearch AB task. *Development Psychology*, **24**, 502–511.

Barrouillet, P., Gavens, N., Vergauwe, E., Gaillard, V., & Camos, V. (2009). Working memory span development: A time-based resource-sharing model account. *Developmental Psychology*, **45**(2), 477–490.

Bays, P. M., & Husain, M. (2008). Dynamic shifts of limited working memory resources in human vision. *Science*, **321**, 851–854.

Bays, P. M., Wu, E. Y., & Husain, M. (2011). Storage and binding of object features in visual working memory. *Neuropsychologia*, **49**, 1622–1631. http://doi.org/10.1016/j.neuropsychologia.2010.12.023

Blaser, E., & Kaldy, Z. (2010). Infants get five stars on iconic memory tests: A partial report test of 6-month-old infants' iconic memory capacity. *Psychological Science*, **21**, 1643–1645.

Burnett Heyes, S., Zokaei, N., van der Staaij, I., Bays, P. M., & Husain, M. (2012). Development of visual working memory precision in childhood. *Developmental Science*, **15**(4), 528–539.

Buss, A. T., Magnotta, V., Schöner, G., & Spencer, J. P. (2016). Model-based fMRI reveals the structure-function mappings that underlie visual working memory. Manuscript Submitted for Publication.

Buss, A. T., & Spencer, J. P. (2014). The emergent executive: A dynamic field theory of the development of executive function. *Monographs of the Society for Research in Child Development*, **79**(2), 1–103.

Case, R. (1995). Capacity based explanations of working memory growth: A brief history and a reevaluation. In F. M. Weinert & W. Schneider (Eds.), *Memory performance and competencies: Issues in growth and development* (pp. 23–44). Mahwah, NJ: Erlbaum.

Clearfield, M. W., Smith, L. B., Diedrich, F. J., & Thelen, E. (2006). Young infants reach correctly on the A-not-B task: On the development of stability and perseveration. *Infant Behavior & Development*, **29**(3), 435–444.

Cohen, L. B., Atkinson, D. J., & Chaput, H. H. (2000). *Habit 2000: A new program for testing infant perception and cognition.* Austin: University of Texas.

Colombo, J., & Mitchell, D. W. (2009). Infant visual habituation. *Neurobiology of Learning and Memory*, **92**(2), 225–234.

Conway, A. R. A., Kane, M. J., & Engle, R. W. (2003). Working memory capacity and its relation to general intelligence. *TRENDS in Cognitive Sciences*, **7**(12), 547–552.

Courage, M. L., & Howe, M. L. (2001). Long-term retention in 3.5-month-olds: Familiarization time and individual differences in attentional style. *Journal of Experimental Child Psychology*, **79**(3), 271–293. http://doi.org/10.1006/jecp.2000.2606

Cowan, N. (2001). The magical number 4 in short-term memory: A reconsideration of mental storage capacity. *Behavioral and Brain Sciences*, **24**, 87–185.

Cowan, N. (2005). *Working memory capacity.* Hove, East Sussex, UK: Psychology Press.

Cowan, N. (2007). What infants can tell us about working memory development. In L. M. Oakes & P. J. Bauer (Eds.), *Short- and long-term memory in infancy and early childhood: Taking the first steps toward remembering* (pp. 126–152). New York, NY: Oxford University Press.

Cowan, N. (2010). The magical mystery four: How is working memory capacity limited, and why? *Current Directions in Psychological Science*, **19**, 51–57.

Cowan, N. (2013). Short-term and working memory in childhood. In *The Wiley Handbook on the Development of Children's Memory* (pp. 202–229). West Sussex, UK: Wiley-Blackwell.

Cowan, N., AuBuchon, A. M., Gilchrist, A. L., Ricker, T. J., & Saults, J. S. (2011). Age differences in visual working memory capacity: Not based on encoding limitations. *Developmental Science, 14*, 1066–1074. http://doi.org/10.1111/j.1467-7687.2011.01060.x

Cowan, N., Blume, C. L., & Saults, J. S. (2013). Attention to attributes and objects in working memory. *Journal of Experimental Psychology: Learning, Memory, and Cognition, 39*(3), 731–747. http://doi.org/10.1037/a0029687

Cowan, N., Elliott, E. M., Saults, J. S., Morey, C. C., Mattox, S., Hismjatullina, A., et al. (2005). On the capacity of attention: Its estimation and its role in working memory and cognitive aptitudes. *Cognitive Psychology, 51*, 42–100. http://doi.org/10.1016/j.cogpsych.2004.12.001

Cowan, N., Elliott, E. M., Saults, J. S., Nugent, L. D., Bomb, P., & Hismatullina, A. (2006). Rethinking speed theories of cognitive development: Increasing the rate of recall without affecting accuracy. *Psychological Science, 17*(1), 67–73.

Cowan, N., Fristoe, N. M., Elliott, E. M., Brunner, R. P., & Saults, J. S. (2006). Scope of attention, control of attention, and intelligence in children and adults. *Memory & Cognition, 34*(8), 1754–1768. http://doi.org/10.3758/BF03195936

Cowan, N., Hismjatullina, A., AuBuchon, A. M., Saults, J. S., Horton, N., Leadbitter, K., & Towse, J. N. (2010). With development, list recall includes more chunks, not just larger ones. *Developmental Psychology, 46*(5), 1119–1131.

Cowan, N., Morey, C. C., AuBuchon, A. M., Zwilling, C. E., & Gilchrist, A. L. (2010). Seven-year-olds allcoate attention like adults unless working memory is overloaded. *Developmental Science, 13*(1), 120–133.

Cowan, N., Morey, C. C., Chen, Z., Gilchrist, A. L., & Saults, J. S. (2008). Theory and measurement of working memory capacity limits. *The Psychology of Learning and Motivation, 49*, 49–104. http://doi.org/10.1016/S0079-7421(08)00002-9

Cowan, N., Ricker, T. J., Clark, K. M., Hinrichs, G. A., & Glass, B. A. (2015). Knowledge cannot explain the developmental growth of working memory capacity. *Developmental Science, 18*(1), 132–145. http://doi.org/10.1111/desc.12197

Crone, E. A., Wendelken, C., Donohue, S., van Leijenhorst, L., & Bunge, S. A. (2006). Neurocognitive development of the ability to manipulate information in working memory. *Proceedings of the National Academy of Sciences of the United States of America, 103*(24), 9315–9320. http://doi.org/10.1073/pnas.0510088103

Deco, G., & Rolls, E. T. (2005). Sequential memory: A putative neural and synaptic dynamical mechanism. *Journal of Cognitive Neuroscience, 17*(2), 294–307.

Dempster, F. (1981). Memory span: Sources of individual and developmental differences. *Psychological Bulletin, 89*(1), 63–100.

Diamond, A. (1985). Development of the ability to use recall to guide action, as indicated by infants' performance on AB. *Child Development, 56*, 868–883.

Diamond, A., & Goldman-Rakic, P. S. (1989). Comparison of human infants and rhesus monkeys on Piaget's AB task: Evidence for dependence on dorsolateral prefrontal cortex. *Experimental Brain Research, 74*, 24–40.

Edin, F., Klingberg, T., Johansson, P., McNab, F., Tegnér, J., & Compte, A. (2009). Mechanism for top-down control of working memory capacity. *Proceedings of the National Academy of Sciences, 106*(16), 6802–6807.

Erlhagen, W., & Schöner, G. (2002). Dynamic field theory of movement preparation. *Psychological Review*, **109**(3), 545–572. DOI: 10.1037//0033-295X.109.3.545

Fagan, J. F. (1970). Memory in the infant. *Journal of Experimental Child Psychology*, **9**(2), 217–226.

Feigenson, L. (2007). Continuity of format and representation in short term memory development. In L. M. Oakes & P. J. Bauer (Eds.), *Short- and long-term memory in infancy and early childhood: Taking the first steps toward remembering* (pp. 51–74). New York, NY: Oxford University Press.

Feigenson, L., & Carey, S. (2003). Tracking individuals via object-files: Evidence from infants' manual search. *Developmental Science*, **6**, 568–584.

Feigenson, L., & Carey, S. (2005). On the limits of infants' quantification of small object arrays. *Cognition*, **97**, 295–313.

Feigenson, L., & Halberda, J. (2008). Conceptual knowledge increases infants' memory capacity. *Proceedings of the National Academy of Sciences*, **105**(29), 9926–9930.

Fougnie, D., Asplund, C. L., & Marois, R. (2010). What are the units of storage in visual working memory? *Journal of Vision*, **10**(12), 27. http://doi.org/10.1167/10.12.27

Fukuda, K., Awh, E., & Vogel, E. K. (2010). Discrete capacity limits in visual working memory. *Current Opinion in Neurobiology*, **20**, 177–182.

Fukuda, K., & Vogel, E. K. (2009). Human variation in overriding attentional capture. *Journal of Neuroscience*, **29**(27), 8726–8733.

Gathercole, S. E., Pickering, S. J., Ambridge, B., & Wearing, H. (2004). The structure of working memory from 4 to 15 years of age. *Development Psychology*, **40**(2), 177–190.

Gibson, B. S., Gondoli, D. M., Johnson, A. C., Steeger, C. M., & Morrissey, R. A. (2012). The future promise of Cogmed working memory training. *Journal of Applied Research in Memory and Cognition*, **1**(3), 214–216. http://doi.org/0.1016/j.jarmac.2012.07.003

Gogtay, N., Giedd, J. N., Lusk, L., Hayashi, K. M., Greenstein, D., Vaituzis, A. C., … Thompson, P. M. (2004). Dynamic mapping of human cortical development during childhood through early adulthood. *Proceedings of the National Academy of Sciences*, **101**, 8174–8179.

Grahn, C., Cooper, T. L., Miller, H. E., & Simmering, V. R. (2015). *Developmental changes in the effects of similarity on visual working memory*. Poster presented at the 71st Biennial Meeting of the Society for Research in Child Development, Philadelphia, PA.

Grier, J. B. (1971). Nonparametric indexes for sensitivity and bias: Computing formulas. *Psychological Bulletin*, **75**, 410–429.

Hitch, G. J., Woodin, M. E., & Baker, S. (1989). Visual and phonological components of working memory in children. *Memory & Cognition*, **17**(2), 175–185.

Hulme, C., & Melby-Lervåg, M. (2012). Current evdence does not support the claims made for CogMed working memory training. *Journal of Applied Research in Memory and Cognition*, **1**(3), 197–200. http://doi.org/10.1016/j.jarmac.2012.06.006

Hulme, C., & Tordoff, V. (1989). Working memory development: The effects of speech rate, word length, and acoustic similarity on serial recall. *Journal of Experimental Child Psychology*, **47**(1), 72–87. http://doi.org/10.1016/0022-0965(89)90063-5

Huttenlocher, P. R. (1979). Synaptic density in human frontal cortex-developmental changes and effects of aging. *Brain Research*, **163**, 195–205.

Huttenlocher, P. R. (1990). Morphometric study of human cerebral cortex development. *Neuropsychologia*, **28**, 517–527.

Huttenlocher, P. R. (1994). Synaptogenesis, synaptic elimination, and neural plasticity in human cerebral cortex. In C. A. Nelson (Ed.), *Threats to optimal development: Integrating biological, psychological, and social risk factors* (Vol. 27, pp. 35–54). Hillsdale, NJ: Erlbaum.

Jernigan, T. L., Trauner, D. A., Hesselink, J. R., & Tallal, P. A. (1991). Maturation of human cerebrum observed in vivo during adolescence. *Brain, 114,* 2037–2049.

Johnson, J. S. (2008). *A dynamic neural field model of visual working memory and change detection* (Unpublished doctoral dissertation). Iowa City, IA: University of Iowa.

Johnson, J. S., Ambrose, J. P., Dineva, E., & Spencer, J. P. (2016). *Neural interactions in working memory cause variable precision and similarity-based feature repulsion.* Manuscript in Preparation.

Johnson, J. S., Hollingworth, A., & Luck, S. J. (2008). The role of attention in the maintenance of feature bindings in visual short-term memory. *Journal of Experimental Psychology: Human Perception and Performance, 34,* 41–55.

Johnson, J. S., & Simmering, V. R. (2015). Integrating perception and working memory in a three-layer dynamic field architecture. In G. Schöner, J. P. Spencer, & the DFT Research Group (Eds.), *Dynamic thinking: A primer on dynamic field theory* (pp. 151–168). New York, NY: Oxford University Press.

Johnson, J. S., Simmering, V. R., & Buss, A. T. (2014). Beyond slots and resources: Grounding cognitive concepts in neural dynamics. *Attention, Perception, & Psychophysics, 76*(6), 1630–1654. http://doi.org/10.3758/s13414-013-0596-9

Johnson, J. S., Spencer, J. P., Luck, S. J., & Schöner, G. (2009). A dynamic neural field model of visual working memory and change detection. *Psychological Science, 20,* 568–577.

Johnson, J. S., Spencer, J. P., & Schöner, G. (2009). A layered neural architecture for the consolidation, maintenance, and updating of representations in visual working memory. *Brain Research, 1299,* 17–32.

Kane, M. J., Hambrick, D. Z., Tuholski, S. W., Wilhelm, O., Payne, T. W., & Engle, R. W. (2004). The generality of working memory capacity: A latent-variable approach to verbal and visuospatial memory span and reasoning. *Journal of Experimental Psychology: General, 113*(2), 189–217.

Kavšek, M. (2004). Predicting later IQ from infant visual habituation and dishabituation: A meta-analysis. *Journal of Applied Developmental Psychology, 25*(3), 369–393.

Klingberg, T., Forssberg, H., & Westerberg, H. (2002). Training of working memory in children with ADHD. *Journal of Clinical and Experimental Neuropsychology, 24*(6), 781–791.

Lin, P.-H., & Luck, S. J. (2009). The influence of similarity on visual working memory representations. *Visual Cognition, 17*(3), 356–372.

Lipinski, J., Simmering, V. R., Johnson, J. S., & Spencer, J. P. (2010). The role of experience in location estimation: Target distributions shift location memory biases. *Cognition, 115,* 147–153.

Logie, R. H. (2012). Cognitive training: Strategies and the multicomponent cognitive system. *Journal of Applied Research in Memory and Cognition, 1*(3), 206–207. http://doi.org/10.1016/j.jarmac.2012.07.006

Luciana, M., Lindeke, L., Georgieff, M., Mills, M., & Nelson, C. A. (1999). Neurobehavioral evidence for working-memory deficits in school-aged children with histories of prematurity. *Developmental Medicine & Child Neurology, 41*(8), 521–533.

Luck, S. J., & Vogel, E. K. (1997). The capacity of visual working memory for features and conjunctions. *Nature, 390,* 279–281. http://doi.org/10.1038/36846

Makovski, T., Watson, L. M., Koutstaal, W., & Jiang, Y. V. (2010). Method matters: Systematic effects of testing procedure on visual working memory sensitivity. *Journal of Experimental Psychology: Learning, Memory, and Cognition, 36*(6), 1466–1479.

Marchman, V. A., & Fernald, A. (2008). Speed of word recognition and vocabulary knowledge in infancy predict cognitive and language outcomes in later childhood. *Developmental Science, 11*(3) F9–F16. http://doi.org/10.1111/j.1467-7687.2008.00671.x

Marcovitch, S., & Zelazo, P. D. (1999). The A-not-B error: Results from a logistic meta-analysis. *Child Development, 70,* 1297–1313.

McCall, R. B. (1994). What process mediates predictions of childhood IQ from infant habituation and recognition memory? Speculations on the roles of inhibition and rate of information processing. *Intelligence, 18*(2), 107–125. http://doi.org/10.1016/0160-2896 (94)90022-1

McCall, R. B., & Carriger, M. S. (1993). A meta-analysis of infant habituation and recognition memory performance as predictors of later IQ. *Child Development, 64*(1), 57–79.

McDowell, K., Jeka, J. J., Schöner, G., & Hatfield, B. D. (2002). Behavioral and electrocortical evidence of an interaction between probability and task metrics in movement preparation. *Experimental Brain Research, 144,* 303–313.

McMurray, B., Horst, J. S., & Samuelson, L. K. (2012). Word learning emerges from the interaction of online referent selection and slow associative learning. *Psychological Review, 119*(4), 831–877. http://doi.org/10.1037/a0029872

Melby-Lervåg, M., & Hulme, C. (2013). Is working memory training effective? A meta-analytic review. *Developmental Psychology 49*(2), 270–291. http://doi.org/10.1037/a0028228

Miles, C., Morgan, M. J., Milne, A. B., & Morris, E. D. M. (1996). Developmental and individual differences in visual memory span. *Current Psychology, 15*(1), 53–67.

Miyake, A., Friedman, N. P., Rettinger, D. A., Shah, P., & Hegarty, M. (2001). How are visuospatial working memory, executive functioning, and spatial abilities related? A latent-variable analysis. *Journal of Experimental Psychology: General, 130*(4), 621–640.

Morton, J. B., & Munakata, Y. (2002a). Active versus latent representations: A neural network model of perseveration, dissociation, and decalage. *Developmental Psychobiology, 40,* 255–265.

Morton, J. B., & Munakata, Y. (2002b). Are you listening? Exploring a developmental knowledge-action dissociation in a speech interpretation task. *Developmental Science, 5*(4), 435–440.

Munakata, Y. (1998). Infant perseveration and implications for object permanence theories: A PDP model of the AB task. *Developmental Science, 1*(2), 161–184.

Munakata, Y., McClelland, J. L., Johnson, M. H., & Siegler, R. S. (1997). Rethinking infant knowledge: Toward an adaptive process account of successes and failures in object permanence tasks. *Psychological Review, 104,* 686–713.

Oakes, L. M., Baumgartner, H. A., Barrett, F. S., Messenger, I. M., & Luck, S. J. (2013). Developmental changes in visual short-term memory in infancy: evidence from eye-tracking. *Frontiers in Developmental Psychology, 4,* 697. http://doi.org/10.3389/fpsyg.2013.00697

Oakes, L. M., Messenger, I. M., Ross-Sheehy, S., & Luck, S. J. (2009). New evidence for rapid development of color-location binding in infants' visual short-term memory. *Visual Cognition, 17,* 67–82.

Oakes, L. M., Ross-Sheehy, S., & Luck, S. J. (2006). Rapid development of feature binding in visual short-term memory. *Psychological Science, 17*(9), 781–787.

Oberauer, K., & Lewandowsky, S. (2011). Modeling working memory: A computational implementation of the Time-Based Resource-Sharing theory. *Psychonomic Bulletin and Review*, **18**, 10–45.

Olsson, H., & Poom, L. (2005). Visual memory needs categories. *Proceedings of the National Academy of Science USA*, **102**(24), 8776–8780. http://doi.org/10.1073/pnas.0500810102

Overman, W. H., Bachevalier, J., Sewell, F., & Drew, J. (1993). A comparison of children's performance on two recognition memory tasks: Delayed nonmatch-to-sample versus visual paired-comparison. *Developmental Psychobiology*, **26**(6), 345–357.

Pashler, H. (1988). Familiarity and visual change detection. *Perception and Psychophysics*, **44**, 369–378. http://doi.org/10.3758/BF03210419

Pelphrey, K. A., & Reznick, J. S. (2003). Working memory in infancy. In R. V. Kail (Ed.), *Advances in child development and behavior* (Vol. 31, pp. 173–231). New York, NY: Academic Press.

Perone, S., Molitar, S., Buss, A. T., Spencer, J. P., & Samuelson, L. K. (2015). Enhancing the executive functions of 3-year-old children performing the dimensional change card sort task. *Child Development*, **86**(3), 812–827. http://doi.org/10.1111/cdev.12330

Perone, S., Simmering, V. R., & Spencer, J. P. (2011). Stronger neural dynamics capture changes in infants' visual working memory capacity over development. *Developmental Science*, **14**, 1379–1392. http://doi.org/10.1111/j. 1467-7687. 2011.01083.x

Perone, S., & Spencer, J. P. (2013a). Autonomous visual exploration creates developmental change in familiarity and novelty seeking behaviors. *Frontiers in Cognitive Science*, **4**, 648. http://doi.org/10.3389/fpsyg.2013.00648

Perone, S., & Spencer, J. P. (2013b). Autonomy in action: Linking the act of looking to memory formation in infancy via dynamic neural fields. *Cognitive Science*, **37**, 1–60. http://doi.org/10.1111/cogs.12010

Perone, S., & Spencer, J. P. (2014). The co-development of looking dynamics and discrimination performance. *Developmental Psychology*, **50**(3), 837–852. http://doi.org/10.1037/a0034137

Pickering, S. J. (2001). The development of visuo-spatial working memory. *Memory*, **9**, 423–432.

Raffone, A., & Wolters, G. (2001). A cortical mechanism for binding in visual working memory. *Journal of Cognitive Neuroscience*, **13**, 766–785.

Raghubar, K. P., Barnes, M. A., & Hecht, S. A. (2010). Working memory and mathematics: A review of developmental, individual difference, and cognitive approaches. *Learning and Individual Differences*, **20**, 110–122. http://doi.org/10.1016/j.lindif.2009.10.005

Reznick, J. S. (2007). Working memory in infants and toddlers. In L. M. Oakes & P. J. Bauer (Eds.), *Short- and long-term memory in infancy and early childhood: Taking the first steps toward remembering* (pp. 3–26). New York, NY: Oxford University Press.

Reznick, J. S. (2009). Working memory in infants and toddlers. In M. L. Courage & N. Cowan (Eds.), *The development of memory in infancy and childhood*. Hove, East Sussex, UK: Psychology Press.

Riggs, K. J., McTaggart, J., Simpson, A., & Freeman, R. P. J. (2006). Changes in the capacity of visual working memory in 5- to 10-year-olds. *Journal of Experimental Child Psychology*, **95**, 18–26. http://doi.org/10.1016/j.jecp.2010.11.006

Riggs, K. J., Simpson, A., & Potts, T. (2011). The development of visual short-term memory for multifeature items during middle childhood. *Journal of Experimental Child Psychology*, **108**, 802–809. http://doi.org/10.1016/j.jecp.2010.11.006

Rose, S. A., & Feldman, J. F. (1997). Memory and speed: Their role in the relation of infant information processing to later IQ. *Child Development, 68*, 630–641.

Rose, S. A., Feldman, J. F., & Jankowski, J. J. (2004). Infant visual recognition memory. *Developmental Review, 24*, 74–100.

Rose, S. A., Feldman, J. F., & Jankowski, J. J. (2002). Processing speed in the 1st year of life: A longitudinal study of preterm and full-term infants. *Developmental Psychology, 38*, 895–902. http://doi.org/10.1037/0012-1649.38.6.895

Rose, S. A., Feldman, J. F., & Jankowski, J. J. (2007). Developmental aspects of visual recognition memory in infancy. In L. M. Oakes & P. J. Bauer (Eds.), *Short- and long- term memory in infancy and early childhood: Taking the first steps toward remembering* (pp. 153–178). New York, NY: Oxford University Press.

Rose, S. A., Feldman, J. F., & Jankowski, J. J. (2012). Implications of infant cognition for executive functions at age 11. *Psychological Science, 23*(11), 1345–1355. http://doi.org/10.1177/0956797612444902

Rose, S. A., Feldman, J. F., Jankowski, J. J., & Van Rossem, R. (2005). Pathways from prematurity and infant abilities to later cognition. *Child Development, 76*(6), 1172–1184.

Ross-Sheehy, S., Oakes, L. M., & Luck, S. J. (2003). The development of visual short-term memory capacity in infants. *Child Development, 74*, 1807–1822.

Ross-Sheehy, S., Oakes, L. M., & Luck, S. J. (2010). Exogenous attention influences visual short-term memory in infants. *Developmental Science, 14*(3), 490–501.

Rouder, J. N., Morey, R. D., Morey, C. C., & Cowan, N. (2011). How to measure working memory capacity in the change detection paradigm. *Psychonomic Bulletin and Review, 18*, 324–330.

Samuelson, L. K., Schutte, A. R., & Horst, J. S. (2009). The dynamic nature of knowledge: Insights from a dynamic field model of children's novel noun generalization. *Cognition, 110*, 322–345. http://doi.org/10.1016/j.cognition.2008.10.017

Samuelson, L. K., Smith, L. B., Perry, L. K., & Spencer, J. P. (2011). Grounding word learning in space. *PLoS One, 6*(12), e28095.

Schlesinger, M., & McMurray, B. (2012). The past, present, and future of computational models of cognitive development. *Cognitive Development, 27*(4), 326–348.

Schneegans, S., Lins, J., & Spencer, J. P. (2015). Integration and selection in multidimensional dynamic fields. In G. Schöner, J. P. Spencer, & the DFT Research Group (Eds.), *Dynamic thinking: A primer on dynamic field theory* (pp. 121–150). New York, NY: Oxford University Press.

Schneegans, S., Lins, O. G., & Schöner, G. (2015). Embedding dynamic field theory in neurophysiology. In G. Schöner, J. P. Spencer, & the DFT Research Group (Eds.), *Dynamic thinking: A primer on dynamic field theory* (pp. 61–94). New York, NY: Oxford University Press.

Schneegans, S., Spencer, J. P., & Schöner, G. (2015). Integrating "what" and "where": Visual working memory for objects in a scene. In G. Schöner, J. P. Spencer, & the DFT Research Group (Eds.), *Dynamic thinking: A primer on dynamic field theory* (pp. 197–226). New York, NY: Oxford University Press.

Schöner, G., & Dineva, E. (2007). Dynamic instabilities as mechanisms for emergence. *Developmental Science, 10*, 69–74.

Schoner, G., Reimann, H., & Lins, J. (2015). Neural dynamics. In G. Schöner, J. P. Spencer, & the DFT Research Group (Eds.), *Dynamic thinking: A primer on dynamic field theory* (pp. 5–34). New York, NY: Oxford University Press.

Schöner, G., Spencer, J. P., & the DFT Research Group (Eds.). (2015). *Dynamic thinking: A primer on dynamic field theory*. New York, NY: Oxford University Press.

Schöner, G., & Thelen, E. (2006). Using dynamic field theory to rethink infant habituation. *Psychological Review*, **113**(2), 273–299.

Schutte, A. R., Simmering, V. R., & Ortmann, M. R. (2011). Keeping behavior in context: A dynamic systems account of a transition in spatial recall biases. *Spatial Cognition and Computation*, **11**(4), 313–342.

Schutte, A. R., & Spencer, J. P. (2002). Generalizing the dynamic field theory of the A-not-B error beyond infancy: Three-year-olds' delay- and experience-dependent location memory biases. *Child Development*, **73**, 377–404.

Schutte, A. R., & Spencer, J. P. (2009). Tests of the dynamic field theory and the spatial precision hypothesis: Capturing a qualitative developmental transition in spatial working memory. *Journal of Experimental Psychology: Human Perception and Performance*, **35**, 1698–1725.

Schutte, A. R., & Spencer, J. P. (2010). Filling the gap on developmental change: Tests of a dynamic field theory of spatial cognition. *Journal of Cognition and Development*, **11**, 328–355. http://doi.org/10.1080/15248371003700007

Schutte, A. R., Spencer, J. P., & Schöner, G. (2003). Testing the dynamic field theory: Working memory for locations becomes more spatially precise over development. *Child Development*, **74**(5), 1393–1417.

Shipstead, Z., Hicks, K. L., & Engle, R. W. (2012). Cogmed working memory training: Does the evidence support the claims? *Journal of Applied Research in Memory and Cognition*, **1**(3), 185–193. http://doi.org/10.1016/j.jarmac.2012.06.003

Shipstead, Z., Redick, T. S., & Engle, R. W. (2010). Does working memory training generalize? *Psychologica Belgica*, **50**(3–4), 245–276.

Shipstead, Z., Redick, T. S., & Engle, R. W. (2012). Is working memory training effective? *Psychological Bulletin*, **138**(4), 628–654. http://doi.org/10.1037/a0027473

Simmering, V. R. (2012). The development of visual working memory capacity in early childhood. *Journal of Experimental Child Psychology*, **111**, 695–707. http://doi.org/10.1016/j.jecp.2011.10.007

Simmering, V. R., Andrews, C. M., & Cooper, T. L. (2016). *Developmental increases in real-time stability predict changes in the effect of similarity in visual working memory*. Manuscript Submitted for Publication.

Simmering, V. R., Johnson, J. S., Patterson, C. M., & Spencer, J. P. (2009). When objects disintegrate: Young children do not bind features in visual working memory. In N. Taatgen, H. van Rijn, L. Schomaker, & J. Nerbonne (Eds.), *Proceedings of the Thirty-First Annual Cognitive Science Society*. Amsterdam, Netherlands: Cognitive Science Society.

Simmering, V. R., & Miller, H. E. (2016). Developmental improvements in visual working memory resolution and capacity share from a common source. *Attention, Perception, & Psychophysics*, http://doi.org/10.3758/s13414-016-1163-y

Simmering, V. R., Miller, H. E., & Bohache, K. (2015). Different developmental trajectories across feature types support a dynamic field model of visual working memory development. *Attention, Perception, & Psychophysics*, **77**(4), 1170–1188. http://doi.org/10.3758/s13414-015-0832-6

Simmering, V. R., & Patterson, R. (2012). Models provide specificity: Testing a proposed mechanism of visual working memory capacity development. *Cognitive Development*, **27**(4), 419–439. http://doi.org/10.1016/j.cogdev.2012.08.001

Simmering, V. R., & Perone, S. (2013). Working memory capacity as a dynamic process. *Frontiers in Developmental Psychology, 3*, 567. http://doi.org/10.3389/fpsyg.2012.00567

Simmering, V. R., & Schutte, A. R. (2015). Developmental dynamics: The spatial precision hypothesis. In G. Schöner, J. P. Spencer, & the DFT Research Group (Eds.), *Dynamic thinking: A primer on dynamic field theory* (pp. 251–270). New York, NY: Oxford University Press.

Simmering, V. R., Schutte, A. R., & Spencer, J. P. (2008). Generalizing the dynamic field theory of spatial cognition across real and developmental time scales. *Brain Research, **1202***, 68–86. http://doi.org/10.1016/j.brainres.2007.06.081

Simmering, V. R., & Spencer, J. P. (2008). Generality with specificity: The dynamic field theory generalizes across tasks and time scales. *Developmental Science, **11***(4), 541–555. http://doi.org/10.1111/j.1467-7687.2008.00700.x

Simmering, V. R., & Wood, C. M. (2016). *The importance of real-time stability for visual working memory performance: Young children's feature binding can be improved through perceptual structure.* Manuscript Submitted for Publication.

Smith, L. B., Colunga, E., & Yoshida, H. (2010). Knowledge as process: Contextually cued attention and early word learning. *Cognitive Science, **34***(7), 1287–1314. http://doi.org/10.1111/j.1551-6709.2010.01130.x

Smith, L. B., Thelen, E., Titzer, R., & McLin, D. (1999). Knowing in the context of acting: The task dynamics of the A-not-B error. *Psychological Review, **106***, 235–260.

Sokolov, E. N. (1963). *Perception and the conditioned reflex.* New York, NY: Pergamon Press.

Spencer, J. P., Barich, K., Goldberg, J., & Perone, S. (2012). Behavioral dynamics and neural grounding of a dynamic field theory of multi-object tracking. *Journal of Integrative Neuroscience, **11***, 339–362.

Spencer, J. P., Buss, A. T., & Magnotta, V. (2013). *Testing hemodynamic predictions of a dynamic neural field model of visual working memory.* Presented at the Vision Sciences Society, Naples, FL.

Spencer, J. P., Clearfield, M., Corbetta, D., Ulrich, B., Buchanan, P., & Schöner, G. (2006). Moving toward a grand theory of development: In memory of Esther Thelen. *Child Development, **77***, 1521–1538.

Spencer, J. P., & Hund, A. M. (2002). Prototypes and particulars: Geometric and experience-dependent spatial categories. *Journal of Experimental Psychology: General, **131***, 16–37.

Spencer, J. P., & Hund, A. M. (2003). Developmental continuity in the processes that underlie spatial recall. *Cognitive Psychology, **47***(4), 432–480.

Spencer, J. P., & Schutte, A. R. (2004). Unifying representations and responses: Perseverative biases arise from a single behavioral system. *Psychological Science, **15***(3), 187–193.

Spencer, J. P., Simmering, V. R., & Schutte, A. R. (2006). Toward a formal theory of flexible spatial behavior: Geometric category biases generalize across pointing and verbal response types. *Journal of Experimental Psychology: Human Perception & Performance, **32***, 473–490.

Spencer, J. P., Simmering, V. R., Schutte, A. R., & Schöner, G. (2007). What does theoretical neuroscience have to offer the study of behavioral development? Insights from a dynamic field theory of spatial cognition. In J. M. Plumert & J. P. Spencer (Eds.), *The emerging spatial mind* (pp. 320–361). New York, NY: Oxford University Press.

Thelen, E., Corbetta, D., Kamm, K., Spencer, J. P., Schneider, K., & Zernicke, R. F. (1993). The transition to reaching: Mapping intention and intrinsic dynamics. *Child Development, **64***, 1058–1098.

Thelen, E., Corbetta, D., & Spencer, J. P. (1996). Development of reaching during the first year: Role of movement speed. *Journal of Experimental Psychology: Human Perception and Performance*, **22**(5), 1059–1076.

Thelen, E., & Smith, L. B. (1994). *A dynamic systems approach to the development of cognition and action*. Cambridge: MIT Press.

Thelen, E., & Spencer, J. P. (1998). Postural control during reaching in young infants: A dynamic systems approach. *Neuroscience and Biobehavioral Reviews*, **22**(4), 507–514.

Todd, J. J., & Marois, R. (2005). Posterior paricortex activity predicts individual differences in visual short-term memory capacity. *Cognitive, Affective, & Behavioral Neuroscience*, **5**(2), 144–155. http://doi.org/10.3758/CABN.5.2.144

Towse, J. N., & Hitch, G. J. (2007). Variation in working memory due to normal development. In C. Jarrold, A. Miyake, & J. N. Towse (Eds.), *Variations on working memory* (pp. 109–133). New York, NY: Oxford University Press.

Unsworth, N., & Engle, R. W. (2007). On the division of short-term and working memory: An examination of simple and complex span and their relation to higher order abilities. *Psychological Bulletin*, **133**(6), 1038–1066.

Vogel, E. K., & Machizawa, M. G. (2004). Neural activity predicts individual differences in visual working memory capacity. *Nature*, **428**, 748–751.

Vogel, E. K., McCollough, A. W., & Machizawa, M. G. (2005). Neural measures reveal individual differences in controlling access to working memory. *Nature*, **438**, 500–503.

Vogel, E. K., Woodman, G. F., & Luck, S. J. (2001). Storage of features, conjunctions, and objects in visual working memory. *Journal of Experimental Psychology: Human Perception and Performance*, **27**, 92–114.

Wass, S. V., Scerif, G., & Johnson, M. J. (2012). Training attentional control and working memory – Is younger, better? *Developmental Review*, **32**(4), 360–387.

Wei, Z., Wang, X.-J., & Wang, D.-H. (2012). From distributed resources to limited slots in multiple-item working memory: A spiking network model with normalization. *Journal of Neuroscience*, **32**, 11228–11240. http://doi.org/10.1523/JNEUROSCI. 0735-12.2012

Westermann, G., & Mareschal, D. (2004). From parts to wholes: Mechanisms of development in infant visual object processing. *Infancy*, **5**(2), 131–151.

Westermann, G., & Mareschal, D. (2012). Mechanisms of developmental change in infant categorization. *Cognitive Development*, **27**(4), 367–382. http://doi.org/10.1016/j.cogdev. 2012.08.004

Wheeler, M., & Treisman, A. M. (2002). Binding in short-term visual memory. *Journal of Experimental Psychology: General*, **131**, 48–64. http://doi.org/10.1037/0096-3445.131.1.48

Wilken, P., & Ma, W. J. (2004). A detection theory account of change detection. *Journal of Vision*, **4**(12), 1120–1135.

Zelazo, P. D. (2006). The dimensional change card sort (DCCS): A method of assessing executive function in children. *Nature Protocols*, **1**, 297–301.

Zhang, W., & Luck, S. J. (2008). Discrete fixed-resolution representations in visual working memory. *Nature*, **453**, 233–235.

Zhang, W., & Luck, S. J. (2009). Sudden death and gradual decay in visual working memory. *Psychological Science*, **20**(4), 423–428.

Zosh, J. M., & Feigenson, L. (2012). Memory load affects object individuation in 18-month old infants. *Journal of Experimental Child Psychology*, **113**, 322–336.

APPENDIX

This article is part of the issue "Working Memory Capacity in Context: Modeling Dynamic Processes of Behavior, Memory, and Development," Simmering, Vanessa (Issue Author). For a full listing of articles in this issue, see: http://onlinelibrary.wiley.com/doi/10.1111/mono.v81.3/issuetoc.

This section describes the equations that govern activation in the five fields of the unified model used in the present monograph. The three-layer model described by Johnson et al. (2014) consists of an excitatory field, $u(x, t)$, which receives afferent sensory input, $S(x, t)$; a shared inhibitory field, $v(x, t)$; and second excitatory field, $w(x, t)$ that receives excitatory input, primarily from the first excitatory field but also a weak copy of the sensory input. These excitatory fields were connected to response nodes d and s, indicating "different" and "same" responses in the change detection task; activation to these nodes was controlled by a gate node, g. To simulate the change-preference task, I added the two Hebbian fields from Perone et al. (2011), which held excitatory traces left by above-threshold activation in u and w, and fixation nodes l, r, c, and a. Although these equations share many components, I describe each separately to highlight the unique contributions to the dynamics of each field.

PERCEPTUAL FIELD

Activation in the first field, $PF(u)$, is captured by:

DOI: 10.1111/mono.12255
© 2016 The Society for Research in Child Development, Inc.

$$\tau_u \dot{u}(x, t) = -u(x, t) + h_u + uStim(x, t)$$

$$+ \int c_{uu}(x - x')\Lambda_{uu}(u(x', t))\,dx'$$

$$- \int c_{uv}(x - x')\Lambda_{uv}(v(x', t))\,dx'$$

$$+ \int c_{uH}(x, x')H_u(x, t)\,dx'$$

$$+ [a_{ud}\Lambda_{ud}(r_d(t)) + (c_{ud}*r_d)]$$

$$+ [c_{uf}\Lambda_{uf}(f_l(t)) + c_{uf}\Lambda_{uf}(f_r(t))]$$

$$+ noise.$$

where $\dot{u}(x, t)$ is the rate of change of the activation level for each node across the spatial dimension, x, as a function of time, t. The constant τ_u determines the time scale of the dynamics (Erlhagen & Schöner, 2002). The first factor that contributes to the rate of change of activation in PF(u) is the current activation in the field, $-u(x, t)$, at each site x. This component is negative so that activation changes in the direction of the resting level h_u. The resting level included colored noise, which was determined by the equation $\tau_h \dot{h}(t) = -h(t) + q_h * noise$, in which the current resting state is increased or decreased by a random amount ($q_h * noise$) at each time step. This is termed colored noise because the value at each time step is partially determined by the value at the previous time step; this contrasts with white noise, which is independent across time steps.

Inputs to the model take the form of a Gaussian distribution, $uStim(x, t) = c\,\exp\left[-\frac{(x - x_{center})^2}{2\sigma^2}\right]\chi^{(t)}$, with the positions of colors centered at x_{center}, input widths of σ, and strengths c. These inputs are turned on and off through time as items appear and then disappear in the display. This time interval is specified by the pulse function $\chi^{(t)}$. Note that input in the change-preference task corresponds to only one of the two displays, depending on which fixation node is active; this is achieved mathematically by multiplying the thresholded activation of the left and right nodes by the respective stimulus input. Thus, $uStim(x, t) = S_l(x, t)\Lambda(f_l) + S_r(x, t)\Lambda(f_r)$, with f_l and f_r equaling 0 when activation of that node is below 0 or 1 when it is above 0; note that competition between nodes is such that both cannot simultaneously have above-threshold activation.

Activation in PF(u) is also influenced by the local excitation-lateral inhibition interaction profile, defined by self-excitatory projections,

140

$\int c_{uu}(x - x')\Lambda_{uu}(u(x', t))dx'$, and inhibitory projections from $\mathrm{Inhib}(v)$, $\int c_{uv}(x - x')\Lambda_{uv}(v(x', t))dx'$. These interactions are specified by the convolution of a Gaussian kernel with a sigmoidal threshold function. In particular, the Gaussian kernel was defined as $c(x - x') = c \exp\left[-\frac{(x-x')^2}{2\sigma^2}\right] - k$, where the σ determines the neighboring nodes across which interactions propagate, c determines the strength, and k sets the resting level. Note that k was set to 0 for all excitatory convolutions. Only nodes with above-thoreshold activaiton (i.e., above 0) participate in interactions, as determined by a sigmoidal function, $\Lambda(u) = \frac{1}{1+\exp[-\beta u]}$, where β is the slope of the sigmoid, that is, the degree to which nodes close to threshold (i.e., 0) contribute to the activation dynamics. Lower slope values permit graded activation near threshold to influence performance, while higher slope values ensure that only above-threshold activation contributes to the activation dynamics. At extreme slope values, the sigmoid function approaches a step function. For all simulations presented here, $\beta = 0.5$.

Activation in $\mathrm{PF}(u)$ is influenced by input from the corresponding Hebbian field $H_{\mathrm{PF}}(u_H)$, as defined by $\int c_{uH}(x, x')H_u(x, t)dx'$ (see below for u_H equation). This input is determined by the convolution of a Gaussian projection, $c_{uH}(x, x')$, which determines the neighborhood of nodes across which Hebbian traces have an influence, and the strength of the trace within the Hebbian field, $H_u(x, t)$.

Next, a global input to $\mathrm{PF}(u)$ is projected from the "different" response node (r_d) in the change detection task, or from the *left* or *right* fixation nodes (f_l and f_r) in the change-preference task, when the activation of one of these nodes is above zero. Note that the response nodes were never active during the change-preference task, and the fixation nodes were never active during the change detection task, reflecting the overall differences between these tasks (i.e., stimuli on one versus two displays, whether an explicit response was required).

Lastly, activation within the field is influenced by the addition of a stochastic component consisting of spatially correlated noise, $noise = q \int dx' g_{noise}(x, x')\xi(x', t)$. Noise was added to the simulations by convolving a noise field composed of independent noise sources with a Gaussian kernel specified by: $g_{noise}(x, x') = \frac{1}{\sqrt{2\sigma_{noise}}}\exp\left[-\frac{(x-x')^2}{2\sigma_{noise}^2}\right]$, where σ_{noise} is the spatial spread of the noise kernel. For discussion of the differences between spatially correlated noise and Gaussian white noise, see Schutte et al. (2003).

INHIBITORY FIELD

The second field of the model, $\mathrm{Inhib}(v)$, is specified by the following equation:

$$\tau_v \dot{v}(x, t) = -v(x, t) + h_v$$

$$+ \int c_{vu}(x - x')\Lambda_{vu}(u(x', t))dx'$$

$$+ \int c_{vw}(x - x')\Lambda_{vw}(w(x', t))dx'$$

$$+ noise.$$

As before, $\dot{v}(x, t)$ specifies the rate of change of activation across the population of feature-selective nodes, x, as a function of time, t; the constant τ sets the time scale (note that the time scale for inhibition is faster than for the excitatory fields, i.e., $\tau_v < \tau_u$); $v(x, t)$ captures the current activation of the field; and h_v sets the resting level of nodes in the field. As with PF(u), colored noise was added to the resting level. Inhib(v) receives activation from two projections: one from PF(u), $\int c_{vu}(x - x')\Lambda_{vu}(u(x', t))dx'$; and one from WM($w$), $\int c_{vw}(x - x')\Lambda_{vw}(w(x', t))dx'$.

As described above, these projections are defined by the convolution of a Gaussian kernel with a sigmoidal threshold function (equations listed above). Finally, this field also receives spatially correlated noise, as described above. This noise is independent from the noise sources in the other fields of the model.

WORKING MEMORY FIELD

The third field of the model, WM(w), is governed by the following equation:

$$\tau \dot{w}(x, t) = -w(x, t) + h_w + wStim(x, t)$$

$$+ \int c_{ww}(x - x')\Lambda_{ww}(w(x', t))dx'$$

$$- \int c_{wv}(x - x')\Lambda_{wv}(v(x', t))dx'$$

$$+ \int c_{wu}(x - x')\Lambda_{wu}(u(x', t))dx'$$

$$+ \int c_{wH}(x, x')H_w(x, t)dx'$$

$$+[a_{ws}\Lambda_{ws}(r_s(t)) + (c_{ws}*r_s)]$$

$$+noise.$$

As in the previous equations, $\dot{w}(x, t)$ is the rate of change of activation across the population of spatially-tune nodes, x, as a function of time, t; the constant τ sets the time scale; $w(x, t)$ captures the current activation of the field; and h_w sets the resting level. As with $PF(u)$, colored noise was added to the resting level. This field also receives direct target inputs, $wStim(x, t)$, although the strength of this input is weaker than the direct input to $PF(u)$, as noted in Tables 4 and 5. As with $PF(u)$, this input turns on and off over time to correspond to the task structure, and input in the change-preference task corresponds to only one of the two displays, depending on which fixation node is active (i.e., $wStim(x, t) = .S_l(x, t)\Lambda(f_l) + S_r(x, t)\Lambda(f_r)$).

$WM(w)$ also receives self-excitation, $\int c_{ww}(\mathrm{x} - x')\Lambda_{ww}(w(x', t))dx'$, lateral inhibition from $Inhib(v)$, $\int c_{wv}(x - x')\Lambda_{wv}(v(x', t))dx'$, excitatory input from $PF(u)$, $\int c_{wu}(x - x')\Lambda_{wu}u(x', t)dx'$, and excitatory input from the corresponding Hebbian field $H_{WM}(w_H)$. Next, a global input to $WM(w)$ is projected from the "same" response node (r_s) in the change detection task when the activation of this node is above zero. Note that the response nodes were never active during the change-preference task, as described above. Finally, this field also receives spatially correlated noise, as described above. Again, this noise is independent from the noise sources in the other fields of the model.

HEBBIAN FIELDS

The Hebbian fields, $H_{PF}(u_H)$ and $H_{WM}(w_H)$, are governed by the active states of the associated excitatory field (for simplicity, only the $H_{PF}(u_H)$ equation is shown, as the $H_{WM}(w_H)$ equation is analogous):

$$\tau_{ltm}\dot{u}_{ltm}(x, t) = \dot{u}_{ltmbuild}(x, t) + \dot{u}_{ltmdecay}(x, t)$$

The rate of change of activation, $\dot{u}_{ltm}(x, t)$, for each node in the long-term memory field across the spatial dimension, x, as a function of time, t, is specified by two components: the build-up of activation, $\dot{u}_{ltmbuild}$, and the decay of activation, $\dot{u}_{ltmdecay}$. These components were specified as follows:

$$\tau_{ltmbuild}\dot{u}_{ltmbuild}(x, t) = [u_{ltm}(x, t) + \Lambda(u(x, t)] \cdot \theta(u(x, t));$$

$$\tau_{ltmdecay}\dot{u}_{ltmdecay}(x, t) = u_{ltm}(x, t) \cdot [1 - \theta(u(x, t))].$$

The shunting function θ ($\theta = 1$ if $u(x, t) > 0$ and $\theta = 0$ otherwise) determines where the activation is built up and maintained in u_H. The build-up rate is relatively fast while the decay rate is much slower; this allows previous memory to be maintained over longer periods. Separating the build-up and decay mechanisms approximates accumulation and depression of synaptic change (Deco & Rolls, 2005).

RESPONSE NODES

The nodes in the response field are governed by the following equations:

$$\tau \dot{r}_d(t) = -r_d + h_d + c_{dd}\Lambda_d(r_d) - c_{sd}\Lambda_s(r_s) + a_{dg}\Lambda_{dg}(g(t))$$
$$+ \Lambda_{dg}(g(t)) \int c_{du}\Lambda_u(u(x', t))dx' + noise$$

$$\tau \dot{r}_s(t) = -r_s + h_s + c_{ss}\Lambda_s(r_s) - c_{sd}\Lambda_d(r_d) + a_{sg}\Lambda_{sg}(g(t))$$
$$+ \Lambda_{sg}(g(t)) \int c_{sw}\Lambda_w(w(x', t))dx' + noise.$$

The rate of change of each node's activation, $\dot{r}$ (where the constant τ determines the timescale and the subscripts d and s denote the "different" and "same" nodes, respectively), is determined by the current activation level, $-r$, and the resting level of the node activation, h_d or h_s. Each node has a self-excitatory connection, $c_{dd}\Lambda_d(r_d)$ or $c_{ss}\Lambda_s(r_s)$, and receives inhibition from the other node, $c_{ds}\Lambda_{ds}(r_s)$ or $c_{sd}\Lambda_{sd}(r_d)$. Additionally, the change node receives summed excitatory input from PF(u), $\int c_{du}\Lambda_u(u(x', t))dx'$, and the no change node receives summed excitatory input from WM(w), $\int c_{sw}\Lambda_w(w(x', t))dx'$. These inputs are only on when the activation of the gate node is above zero, achieved by multiplying by $\Lambda_{dg}(g(t))$ or $\Lambda_{sg}(g(t))$.

The gating system, given by the following equation, served as an indication of when a response was required in the task.

$$\tau \dot{r}_g(t) = -r_g + h_g + c_{gg}\Lambda_g(r_g) + \int c_{gw}\Lambda_w(w(x', t))dx' + c_{tar} + c_{trans}$$
$$+ noise.$$

This system consisted of a single node that received input from the stimulus presentation and WM(w); as such, activation of this node only passed threshold when one or more items (peaks) was held in WM(w) and the stimulus was present. These inputs, combined with input from WM(w) drove activation of the gate node above threshold; throughout each trial, this node's activation was sigmoided and multiplied by the activation from PF(u) and WM(w) to the decision nodes. In this case, activation from the fields to the decision nodes was only robust when the gate node was activated above threshold.

144

Lastly, noise in these three equations represents white noise added to the activation of the node at each time step. The noise sources are independent for each node.

As noted briefly in Chapter 4, these response nodes did not always generate a single response on every trial. Specifically, with the weaker connection strengths to fit children's data (as described below), the response system was less stable and produced two types of response instabilities. First, the model occasionally failed to generate any response (i.e., neither neuron surpassed 0 activation on two trials with 3-year-old parameters and one trial with the 4-year-old parameters). Second, both the "same" and "different" neurons rose above threshold at different points during the test array presentation on some trials (i.e., different followed by same on four trials with the 4-year-old parameters and three trials with the 5-year-old parameters; same followed by different on one trial each with the 4- and 5-year-old parameters). Note that each parameter set was tested for 1,200 trials, indicating that these responses system errors were very rare ($<.005\%$). Trials with no response were treated as "guesses" and the model's response was randomly generated. For trials when both neurons passed threshold sequentially, the first responses was recorded. This could be interpreted as the model "changing its mind", which was a behavior some young children exhibited in Experiments 2 and 3, in which cases the first response was entered.

FIXATION NODES

Nodes in the fixation system are specified by the following equations:

$$\tau_f \dot{f}_l(t) = -f_l + h_f + c_{ll}\Lambda_l(f_l) - c_{lr}\Lambda_r(f_r) - c_{lc}\Lambda_c(f_c) - c_{la}\Lambda_a(f_a) + c_T$$
$$+ c_B + c_C + \Lambda_{fl}(f_l)\int c_{lu}\Lambda_u(u(x',t))dx'$$

$$\tau_f \dot{f}_r(t) = -f_r + h_f + c_{rr}\Lambda_r(f_r) - c_{rl}\Lambda_l(f_l) - c_{lr}\Lambda_r(f_r) - c_{ra}\Lambda_a(f_a) + c_T$$
$$+ c_B + c_C + \Lambda_{fr}(f_r)\int c_{ru}\Lambda_u(u(x',t))dx'$$

$$\tau_f \dot{f}_a(t) = -f_a + h_f + c_{aa}\Lambda_a(f_a) - c_{al}\Lambda_l(f_l) - c_{ar}\Lambda_r(f_r) - c_{ac}\Lambda_c(f_c) + c_T + c_B$$

$$\tau_f \dot{f}_c(t) = -f_c + h_f + c_{cc}\Lambda_c(f_c) - c_{cl}\Lambda_l(f_l) - c_{cr}\Lambda_r(f_r) - c_{ca}\Lambda_a(f_a) + c_{AG}.$$

The rate of change of each node's activation, $\dot{f}$ (where the constant τ_f denotes the time scale, and subscripts l, r, a, and c indicate the *left, right, away,* and *center* nodes, respectively) is determined by the current level of activation, f, and resting level of the node, h. The resting level of each node is dynamic and is specified by:

$$\tau_h \dot{h}_f(t) = -ah_f + h_{rest} + \Lambda_f(h_f) \cdot h_{down},$$

with a slope (a). Note that the dynamic resting level of the node decreases toward the attractor specified by h_{down} when activation of the node (f) surpasses threshold (i.e., 0). When activation of the node drops below threshold, the resting level dynamically returns to the attractor specified by h_{rest}. This allows the fixation system to be exploratory, and prevents fixation from getting "stuck" with one node continuing to remain above threshold. These dynamics, combined with the task-relevant input and activation from the perceptual field (described below), lead to a fixation system that autonomously explores its environment and responds to familiarity and novelty (see also Perone & Spencer, 2013a,b, 2014).

The fixation nodes also receive nonspecific input to draw fixation to a stimulus. In particular, to indicate the onset of a stimulus, a transient attentional capture (c_T) is sent to the *fixation* nodes. Moreover, all nodes received constant input, c_{lC}/c_{rC}, corresponding to the salience of the stimulus being presented. For the *left* and *right* nodes, this reflected that something has been presented on one of the displays; for the center and away node, the input was much weaker to reflect the possibility that visual features other than the displays might capture attention and draw fixation away from the experimental apparatus. At each time step, independent white noise was applied to the inputs c_{lC} and c_{rC}. Additionally, the *left* and *right* fixation nodes received a small transient boost (c_B) associated with the onset of the arrays following each "blank" delay.

Lastly, the left and right fixation nodes receive excitatory input from PF(u), $\Lambda_{fl}(f_l) \int c_{lu}\Lambda_u(u(x', t))dx'$ or $\Lambda_{fr}(f_r) \int c_{ru}\Lambda_u(u(x', t))dx'$, which is the sum of above-threshold activation in PF(u) across all sites, x, at time, t, and is gated by the thresholded activation in the respective fixation node, $\Lambda_{fl}(f_l)$ or $\Lambda_{fr}(f_r)$. Thus, activation in PF(u) only contributes to the activation of left and right fixation nodes when the node is in the "on" state. Note that because there are no task-relevant features associated with the attention getter or the rest of the testing room, activation in PF(u) does not contribute to the activation of the center and away nodes.

PARAMETERS FROM SIMULATIONS IN CHAPTER 2

The simulations in Chapter 2 provided qualitative predictions relating performance across the change detection and change-preference tasks. Unless otherwise noted, all simulations used the parameters tuned by Johnson et al. (2014) to fit adults' change detection performance. However, their architecture did not include Hebbian fields; for the current simulations, parameters for these fields were set to values tuned to fit adults' spatial recall performance (Lipinski et al., 2010). The change detection parameters used to generate Figures 7–9 were identical to those presented in Table 4 with one exception: $h_s = -4.35$. For Figure 10, the infant fixation parameters from Perone et al. (2011) were used. These were identical to the parameters presented in Table 5 with the following five exceptions: $c_{FF} = 2$, $c_{F-} = 2.5$, $c_{lC} = c_{rC} = 6.16$, $c_{lu} = c_{ru} = 0.295$, $h_{down} = 3.1$. To approximate early childhood for the simulations in Figures 11 and 12, I scaled a subset of the parameters by 0.5, resulting in the following values (all others were identical to the parameters in Table 4): $c_{uu} = 1$, $c_{uv} = 0.925$, $c_{wv} = 0.1625$, $c_{ww} = 1.575$, $c_{ustim} = 15$, $c_{wstim} = 3$, $\sigma_{ustim} = \sigma_{wstim} = 4.5$. For all simulations in Chapter 2, the task structures were as described in Chapter 4.

ACKNOWLEDGMENTS

This article is part of the issue "Working Memory Capacity in Context: Modeling Dynamic Processes of Behavior, Memory, and Development," Simmering, Vanessa (Issue Author). For a full listing of articles in this issue, see: http://onlinelibrary.wiley.com/doi/10.1111/mono.v81.3/issuetoc.

Thanks to the families and students who participated in this research. The behavioral data presented here were part of the author's dissertation, which was funded by a fellowship from the University of Iowa Graduate College. Portions of the data were presented at the 16th International Conference on Infant Studies in Vancouver, BC, the 30th Annual Meeting of the Cognitive Science Society in Washington, DC, and the 68th Biennial Meeting of the Society for Research in Child Development in Denver, CO. Special thanks go to: John P. Spencer for input and guidance during the conceptualization of the project; Shannon Ross-Sheehy for providing materials and analysis details for the looking paradigm; Jeffrey S. Johnson for programming the change detection tasks; Valerie Vorderstrasse and Chelsey M. (Patterson) Wood for assistance with data collection; Nicholas J. Fox and Sammy Perone for help coding and analyzing looking data; Martha W. Alibali, Karl Rosengren, and John P. Spencer for input on previous versions of this manuscript; and Jessica Horst, Heather Kirkorian, Audra Sterling, and Haley Vlach for support and encouragement during the writing and revision process.

DOI: 10.1111/mono.12256

COMMENTARY

EXPLORING THE POSSIBLE AND NECESSARY IN WORKING MEMORY
DEVELOPMENT

Nelson Cowan

This article is part of the issue "Working Memory Capacity in Context: Modeling Dynamic Processes of Behavior, Memory, and Development," Simmering, Vanessa (Issue Author). For a full listing of articles in this issue, see: http://onlinelibrary.wiley.com/doi/10.1111/mono.v81.3/issuetoc.

This commentary considers Vanessa Simmering's monograph on a dynamic-systems theoretical approach to understanding working memory development, with reference to the past, present, and future. In the section on the past, I attempt to provide a further historical context for the work, discussing from where it stemmed and how it is unique. In a second section, I contemplate the purpose of the present modeling. The aim of the monograph may be primarily to establish a simple possible account of development based on neural connection strength and dynamic principles; it should not be judged as a proposal of what is necessarily true. Finally, in the section on the future, I suggest some phenomena that dissociate performance levels from stability over time and, therefore, appear to require modifications of the theory. Several suggestions are made as to where further refinement of the modeling effort could lead.

Upon my arrival at the University of Missouri, where I have worked for most of my career, I was assigned to a laboratory recently vacated by Esther

---

Corresponding author: Nelson Cowan, Department of Psychological Sciences, University of Missouri, McAlester Hall, Columbia, MO 65211; email: cowann@missouri.edu
DOI: 10.1111/mono.12257

Thelen, a foremother of the present-day interest in dynamic systems theory as applied to child development. When Esther moved out of her infant-stepping lab, she left attached to the door one of my favorite cartoons, which I have since misplaced but have thought of often. It featured a beaver talking to another animal, with an enormous hydroelectric dam in the background. Of this structure the beaver remarked, "Well, I didn't actually build it, but it was based on my ideas." The dynamic systems modeling of processes underlying working memory from infancy through childhood in the present monograph by Vanessa Simmering might be viewed as a hydroelectric version of earlier beaver dams. My contribution is to comment on how the dam is related to past work (the history), how well it is operating (the modeling), and where we might go from here (the persistent questions).

THE PAST: A LITTLE HISTORY

As series of important beaver dams, first there are the empirical phenomena. Working memory is a critical process in human cognition, representing the small amount of information that can be held in mind and used in the service of many processes: remembering the early part of a sentence long enough to integrate it with what comes later, carrying a digit when doing mental addition, using mental imagery to rotate puzzle pieces to see which ones might fit together, or in an infant, perhaps comparing a babbled utterance to an adult model or retaining memory of Mom as she disappears behind a door. The study of working memory may be as old as the study of memory generally. Ebbinghaus (1885/1913) is typically credited with initiating the scientific study of memory, in his groundbreaking research in which he repeatedly tested himself until he learned series of nonsense syllables. What is germane here is his finding that, although a list of 12 syllables could be learned only after 16 repetitions, a shorter list of 7 syllables could be learned in a single presentation or, as he put it (p. 33), a "first fleeting grasp" of the items. Studies of the childhood development of immediate memory soon followed in the form of memory span experiments (Bolton, 1892; Jacobs, 1887).

Miller, Galanter, and Pribram (1960) introduced the term "working memory" to describe memory for one's near and distant future plans, and Sperling (1960) greatly expanded our understanding of temporary memory in general, and specifically in the case of visual stimuli. Baddeley and Hitch (1974) popularized the term working memory and applied it to a multicomponent system with devoted automatic buffers (verbal and by implication nonverbal visual) as well as an attention-demanding central resource comprising executive processes. Tests of limited resources were later extended to infant and child development by numerous investigators, for

150

example, in tests of a relation between memory and processing speed in children (Case, Kurland, & Goldberg, 1982; Hulme, Thomson, Muir, & Lawrence, 1984). More recent and closely germane strands of the developmental research history are well-covered in the monograph.

A complementary set of key beaver dams are the theoretical explanations of the development of working memory and cognition. As noted in the monograph, many investigators have offered verbal and pictorial explanations for how working memory operates, or how it develops. That is still a far cry from a principled, mathematical model of how working memory develops. One can imagine that certain verbal or pictorial models lead to particular predictions, but sometimes this kind of speculation depends on assumptions that have not been made clear, and sometimes are not fully appreciated even by the investigator doing the speculating. Mathematical modeling leaves less room for unappreciated assumptions because one needs to fill in the assumptions to yield the desired mathematical result.

Work using equations to specify psychological processes seems to have begun with Ernst Weber and Gustav Fechner in the late 1800s. Estes (1950) was perhaps the first to show that mathematical precision could be brought to the task of stating models of learning and memory in a more rigorous fashion, and many related approaches have followed. Investigators sometimes called neo-Piagetian (McLaughlin, 1963; Pascual-Leone & Smith, 1969) used concepts of temporary memory and information processing to explain conceptual development in childhood, including some mathematical specification. Others have pioneered various principles that were incorporated into the present modeling, such as the principle of lateral inhibition applied to cognitive concepts in memory by Walley and Weiden (1973).

THE PRESENT USE OF MATHEMATICAL MODELING

Before discussing the topic of mathematical modeling further, I would note that my qualifications to this topic include being all over the map in terms of my attitude. I have a love–hate relationship with modeling. I can see important pitfalls of mathematical modeling, and I can see enormous benefits. I have ignored some mathematical models that I am expected to know, and I have done mathematical modeling myself (generally with technical help). However one feels when reading or trying to read a mathematically involved work like the present monograph, I am probably sympathetic.

To become a connoisseur of mathematical modeling, one must first appreciate that there are multiple aims of the modeling, and the correct aim must be attributed for a model to be appreciated. The present modeling shows how certain theoretical accounts of working memory development are *possible*, not necessarily how they are necessary. Is it possible to explain why

151

children do steadily better in working memory tasks as they get older? Why some materials are remembered better than others? Why what develops may include both the number of items in working memory (e.g., how many colors) and the precision by which those items are represented (the fidelity of the remembered shades)? Can we understand why performance depends to some extent on the individual and to some extent on the task he or she is to carry out? How about dependence on the similarity of items to be remembered and the interference between them (cf., Oberauer, Lewandowsky, Farrell, Jarrold, & Greaves, 2012)? Can all of these factors be understood with the same simple principles, tying together development from infancy through childhood? In the present work, these questions are all answered in the affirmative. A working assumption is made that, as infants and children develop, the connectivity in the neural architecture is strengthened. At least with one reasonable architecture, the simple principle of connectivity is said to account for all of these phenomena.

For the modeling results to be useful, their limits must be understood. There need be no claim that the details of the architecture are in fact correct. Perhaps a completely different model would also explain the facts equally well. What can be established, though, is that the model, though itself complex in its mathematical details, is essentially an argument for simplicity. Before, there may have been a perceived need for different principles to explain the infant and child data. Several complex mechanisms might have been thrown in to explain separately the development of capacity in terms of the number of items represented in working memory and the precision of the representations. Instead, these details can be seen as falling out of the same architecture with the principle of increasing connectivity, leading to increasing stability of the representations.

One naturally hopes that what has been proven possible in one's model eventually proves to be the actual case, or even proves to be necessary to account for the results. Then one could be considered "right." Even without being right, modeling work is useful as it sharpens up the concepts being discussed, which aids in evaluating them.

What the model does best is to strengthen the plausibility of a dynamic systems approach. As stated in the monograph, "Within dynamic systems theory, the focus is on how behavior emerges from multiple underlying causes, encouraging researchers to explore the various contributions to behavior, and to evaluate the robustness of behavior relative to the circumstances required to support them." This mundane-sounding theoretical statement actually runs counter to the thinking of Jean Piaget, who tended to believe that once a mental structure was fully acquired, it was robustly demonstrated across task demands. The neo-Piagetians would have disagreed. Once, as a teaching assistant during graduate school in the later 1970s, I confirmed to my own satisfaction the neo-Piagetian stance. By mid-childhood, children are supposed to understand that water poured from a squat beaker to a thin one does not change in volume, and that clay rolled from a ball into a sausage shape does not change in volume either. With undergraduate students, I upped the level of complexity by asking what would happen if heavy clay in a ball shape versus a sausage shape were totally submerged into identical beakers of water. Many college students incorrectly predicted that the sausage-shaped clay would raise the water level more, a failure of the conservation-of-matter principle in a complex context.

The model also shows that there is room for error in the encoding, maintenance, processing, decision, and response phases of a task. We may choose only one of these as the source of error in a particular simplified model, but no model of behavior across contexts can survive without coming to grips with processing during all of the phases of the task.

FOR THE FUTURE: SOME UNANSWERED QUESTIONS

The first and perhaps foremost unanswered question I have is how long the model can persist before the need to modify it sets in. When the model does have to be modified, how extreme will the modification have to be? How many detailed facts can the model account for and still elegantly show that the increasing-connectivity principle accounts for the development of working memory across tasks?

There is some mystery left for me with regards to the effect of the similarity of the items to be remembered. It was stated that "When multiple peaks form near one another, their related inhibition combines, making it more difficult to form new peaks." Some of the sources cited, however, indicate that sets of more similar items, such as several shades of green, can be remembered better than sets of less similar items, such as different colors together (e.g., Lin & Luck, 2009). I cannot figure out how to reconcile the principle with the findings.

Although the developmental results that were accounted for are rich and varied, they do generally seem to involve just about every aspect of working memory performance getting better with age. That pattern of development in itself has been referred to as "the dull hypothesis" (Perfect & Maylor, 2000); the dull hypothesis can be rejected when one finds an interaction between tasks and age groups. To some extent, in the present approach, the dull hypothesis is rejected in the fitting of the model to young children in two tasks, the typical infant task and the typical child task.

In the future, however, it may be necessary to reject the dull hypothesis more severely. Among the predictions of the model is that with development, memory representations gain more stability and, therefore, are preserved better across a retention interval; that is, in more mature participants, the representations decay less than they do in younger ones. In general, though, we have not found that decay difference across age groups. In one procedure (Cowan, Nugent, Elliott, & Saults, 2000), children were tested on memory for lists of digits that were ignored at the time of their presentation and then occasionally were cued for recall 1, 5, or 10 sec after the last digit in the list. With the list length adjusted to each individual's span, the rates of decay of the list across 10 sec did not change significantly between 7 and 20 years. There was, however, a large age effect restricted to the final serial position, which could be accounted for by age differences in either sensory memory persistence or covert attention-shifting to the end of the list. There is a similar finding of an age difference in the decay of isolated tone information (Keller & Cowan, 1994). Using spatial arrays of unfamiliar characters, followed by a mask to reduce the use of sensory memory, Cowan, Ricker, Clark, Hinrichs, and Glass (2015) found no difference between 7-year-olds and college students in the rate of decay of memory for array characters across 10 sec. Taken together, these results suggest that a key principle of the model may not apply in the same way to sensory and conceptual information.

To understand age differences in the decay of information, perhaps one needs to specify the mechanism that produces stabilization. Camos and Barrouillet (2011) have studied the ability to use spare time to refresh working memory representations. They presented series of animal pictures to be remembered and, between each pair of animals, either one or two colored spots to be named. An important change occurred between 6 and 7 years of age. In 6-year-olds (kindergarteners), performance was better when the total time between animals was shorter. In 7-year-olds (first-graders), performance was better when the proportion of time between animals that was free for refreshing was high, no matter whether the total time was short or long. The results suggested that 6-year-olds do not use the refreshing process and, therefore, are subject to steady decay, whereas decay is counteracted by refreshing in 7-year-olds. This study differs from the ones by Cowan et al. (2000, 2015) in that those studies presented conditions for which refreshing would be difficult or impossible (because the items were unattended digits or attended arrays of unfamiliar characters). In all, the results suggest that age differences in instability of representations might often be attributed to the growing effectiveness of attention-demanding refreshing processes. The idea is that only in tasks in which older participants can refresh items can they stabilize their working memory representations during the maintenance period better than younger, less mature participants.

The notion that attention-based processes are used for refreshing does not contradict the model presented in the present monograph, but it does appear to restrict the scope of the model. The scope may have to be restricted to situations in which there are age differences in a process that can be mapped onto better stability of the traces. For some stimuli, in some age groups, such as letters in children 5–7 years old, there will be age differences in knowledge that can result in differences in stability of the representations that are already manifest at the time of encoding. For other stimuli, age differences occur at the time of maintenance through refreshing. These sorts of differences would be expected to produce age differences in decay. For stimuli that are neither encoded nor refreshed advantageously by older age groups, there may be no difference in decay.

The finding of no age difference in decay is interesting when it is obtained with the list length adjusted to the participant's ability (e.g., Cowan et al., 2000) or with age groups at different levels of performance despite no decay differences (e.g., Cowan et al., 2015). The intriguing thing here is that age group effects in performance level and decay are dissociated. It is unclear to me how to modify the present dynamic systems model to produce this dissociation. It seems as if the "self-sustaining" state of working memory may be self-sustaining in some ways based on automatic processes (such as encoding clarity that may often favor more mature participants who have more knowledge) and self-sustaining in other ways only when voluntary strategies can be implemented (such as memory persistence over time, which may favor more mature participants only for stimuli that lend themselves to refreshing or rehearsal processes).

Beyond empirical issues such as this, it is possible to use modeling in a more specific manner than was done in the present monograph. Many researchers attempt to produce models that match the data so closely that they can present a pattern of predicted results in one panel of a figure and a panel of obtained results next to it. In this kind of approach, to get the data and model to resemble one another so closely, there are usually a host of auxiliary assumptions resulting in parameters in the equations with arbitrary values. The strength of the approach is that there can be no doubt that one can get the actual pattern of results from the model; the down side is that one still has to figure out how much of the success comes from parameters that reflect basic principles of the model (e.g., connection strength) and how much of the success depends instead on parameters that were supposed to be incidental or unimportant but actually are doing the heavy lifting, forcing the model to match the data in a manner that has little to do with its stated principles. A related problem is that it is difficult to get these more specific models to account for a variety of circumstances as the present modeling does; for example, I have seen serial recall models that could not be modified in a foreseeable way to account for free recall.

In the more specific modeling approaches, one often compares multiple models that differ in important ways and finds out which model fits the data better according to standard fit statistics. In the present dynamic systems approach, it would be possible to present models with connectivity that develops at different rates for different layers in the model, which may make the model more complex but may be consistent with evidence that different parts of the brain develop at different rates (Sowell et al., 2003; Thomason et al., 2008). Some fit statistics (such as AIC and BIC) are designed to penalize models for extra complexity and see if the more complex models are worth it.

Finally, modeling is a tricky exercise when one takes the popular approach of comparing two or more possible models to determine which model is more apt. In a recent effort (Cowan et al., 2016), we tried out models of how adults perform in a new task in which they were presented with two arrays of colored spots in succession, and asked to judge how many of the array items changed color between a studied display and a test display. In our first modeling approach, a separate decision was assumed to be made by the participant for each array item. The model fit the pattern of means beautifully, but utterly failed to fit the distribution of responses in each condition, leading to a rejection of the model in favor of other models that would not have been considered, had the first model not failed.

To sum up, modeling is a tricky enterprise. The present work very nicely sets out a simple neural scheme and then follows the implications of that scheme for working memory development in the case of visual arrays of items to be remembered. Perhaps the strongest recommendation for the model is that it served as a motivator to get Simmering to test the same children on both the usual infant and usual child procedures, leading to an elegant set of results that in turn led to further refinement of the model. The model served as a very nice proof that one can go far with basic, elegant neural principles. In a similar manner, in the future, one could imagine that the modeling would help to guide further work on the nature of decay effects, the relation between items in working memory and precision of the representations, and potential differences between the rates of development of these concepts. It might lead to predictions about when and in what way working memory can be trained. In normal individuals, there has been little evidence that working memory training helps to improve tasks other than those similar to the one trained (e.g., Melby-Lervåg & Hulme, 2013; Redick et al., 2013), but there might be more hope in individuals with processing abnormalities. It is possible to impair a model and then see how it might be trained, leading to predictions that could be tested in real individuals.

The work illustrates that further progress depends on close communication between researchers with empirical and modeling orientations, as well as between researchers emphasizing development in infancy versus later childhood.

REFERENCES

Baddeley, A. D., & Hitch, G. (1974). Working memory. In G. H. Bower (Ed.), *The psychology of learning and motivation* (Vol. 8, pp. 47–89). New York, NY: Academic Press.

Bolton, T. L. (1892). The growth of memory in school children. *American Journal of Psychology*, **4**, 362–380.

Camos, V., & Barrouillet, P. (2011). Developmental change in working memory strategies: From passive maintenance to active refreshing. *Developmental Psychology*, **47**, 898–904.

Case, R., Kurland, D. M., & Goldberg, J. (1982). Operational efficiency and the growth of short term memory span. *Journal of Experimental Child Psychology*, **33**, 386–404.

Cowan, N., Hardman, K., Saults, J. S., Blume, C. L., Clark, K. M., & Sunday, M. A. (2016). Detection of the number of changes in a display in working memory. *Journal of Experimental Psychology: Learning, Memory, and Cognition*, **42**, 169–185.

Cowan, N., Nugent, L. D., Elliott, E. M., & Saults, J. S. (2000). Persistence of memory for ignored lists of digits: Areas of developmental constancy and change. *Journal of Experimental Child Psychology*, **76**, 151–172.

Cowan, N., Ricker, T. J., Clark, K. M., Hinrichs, G. A., & Glass, B. A. (2015). Knowledge cannot explain the developmental growth of working memory capacity. *Developmental Science*, **18**, 132–145.

Ebbinghaus, H. (1885/1913). *Memory: A contribution to experimental psychology*. Translated by H. A. Ruger & C. E. Bussenius. New York, NY: Teachers College, Columbia University. (Originally in German, Ueber das gedächtnis: Untersuchen zur experimentellen psychologie)

Estes, W. K. (1950). Toward a statistical theory of learning. *Psychological Review*, **57**, 94–107.

Hulme, C., Thomson, N., Muir, C., & Lawrence, A. (1984). Speech rate and the development of short term memory span. *Journal of Experimental Child Psychology*, **38**, 241–253.

Jacobs, J. (1887). Experiments on "Prehension." *Mind*, **12**, 75–79.

Keller, T. A., & Cowan, N. (1994). Developmental increase in the duration of memory for tone pitch. *Developmental Psychology*, **30**, 855–863.

Lin, P.-H., & Luck, S. J. (2009). The influence of similarity on visual working memory representations. *Visual Cognition*, **17**, 356–372.

McLaughlin, G. H. (1963). Psycho-logic: A possible alternative to Piaget's formulation. *British Journal of Educational Psychology*, **33**, 61–67.

Melby-Lervåg, M., & Hulme, C. (2013). Is working memory training effective? A meta-analytic review. *Developmental Psychology*, **49**, 270–291.

Miller, G. A., Galanter, E., and Pribram, K. H. (1960). *Plans and the structure of behavior*. New York, NY: Holt, Rinehart and Winston.

Oberauer, K., Lewandowsky, S., Farrell, S., Jarrold, C., & Greaves, M. (2012). Modeling working memory: An interference model of complex span. *Psychonomic Bulletin & Review*, **19**, 779–819.

Pascual-Leone, J., & Smith, J. (1969). The encoding and decoding of symbols by children: A new experimental paradigm and a neo Piagetian model. *Journal of Experimental Child Psychology*, **8**, 328–355.

Perfect, T. J., & Maylor, E. A. (2000). Rejecting the dull hypothesis: The relation between method and theory in cognitive aging research. In T. J. Perfect & E. A. Maylor (Eds.), *Models of cognitive aging* (pp. 1–18), Oxford: Oxford University Press.

Redick, T. S., Shipstead, Z., Harrison, T. L., Hicks, K. L., Fried, D. E., Hambrick, D. Z., et al. (2013). No evidence of intelligence improvement after working memory training: A randomized, placebo-controlled study. *Journal of Experimental Psychology: General*, **142**, 359–379.

Sowell, E. R., Peterson, B. S., Thompson, P. M., Welcome, S. E., Henkenius, A. L., & Toga, A. W. (2003). Mapping cortical change across the human life span. *Nature Neuroscience, 6*, 309–315.

Sperling, G. (1960). The information available in brief visual presentations. *Psychological Monographs, 74* (Whole No. 498).

Thomason, M. E., Race, E., Burrows, B., Whitfield Gabrieli, S., Glover, G. H., & Gabrieli, J. D. (2008). Development of spatial and verbal working memory capacity in the human brain. *Journal of Cognitive Neuroscience, 21*, 316–332.

Walley, R. E., & Weiden, T. D. (1973). Lateral inhibition and cognitive masking: A neuropsychological theory of attention. *Psychological Review, 80*, 284–302.

CONTRIBUTORS

Vanessa R. Simmering is an Assistant Professor in the Department of Psychology at the University of Wisconsin–Madison. Her research program focuses on understanding cognition and development from a dynamic systems perspective by considering how multiple factors influence behavior across timescales and contexts.

Nelson Cowan is Curators' Professor at the University of Missouri, Columbia. He has conducted NICHD-funded research on working memory, attention, and their childhood development since 1984. His work is shaped by a philosophical interest in human consciousness combined with the hope that the findings can be useful to educators and neuropsychologists.

DOI: 10.1111/mono.12258
© 2016 The Society for Research in Child Development, Inc.

STATEMENT OF EDITORIAL POLICY

The SRCD *Monographs* series aims to publish major reports of developmental research that generates authoritative new findings and that foster a fresh perspective and/or integration of data/research on conceptually significant issues. Submissions may consist of individually or group-authored reports of findings from some single large-scale investigation or from a series of experiments centering on a particular question. Multiauthored sets of independent studies concerning the same underlying question also may be appropriate. A critical requirement in such instances is that the individual authors address common issues and that the contribution arising from the set as a whole be unique, substantial, and well integrated. Manuscripts reporting interdisciplinary or multidisciplinary research on significant developmental questions and those including evidence from diverse cultural, racial, and ethnic groups are of particular interest. Also of special interest are manuscripts that bridge basic and applied developmental science, and that reflect the international perspective of the Society. Because the aim of the *Monographs* series is to enhance cross-fertilization among disciplines or subfields as well as advance knowledge on specialized topics, the links between the specific issues under study and larger questions relating to developmental processes should emerge clearly and be apparent for both general readers and specialists on the topic. In short, irrespective of how it may be framed, work that contributes significant data and/or extends a developmental perspective will be considered.

Potential authors who may be unsure whether the manuscript they are planning wouldmake an appropriate submission to the SRCD *Monographs* are invited to draft an outline or prospectus of what they propose and send it to the incoming editor for review and comment.

Potential authors are not required to be members of the Society for Research in Child Development nor affiliated with the academic discipline of psychology to submit a manuscript for consideration by the *Monographs*. The significance of the work in extending developmental theory and in contributing new empirical information is the crucial consideration.

Submissions should contain a minimum of 80 manuscript pages (including tables and references). The upper boundary of 150–175 pages is more flexible, but authors should try to keep within this limit. Manuscripts must be double-spaced, 12pt Times New Roman font, with 1-inch margins. If color artwork is submitted, and the authors believe color art is necessary to the presentation of their work, the submissions letter should indicate that one or more authors or their institutions are prepared to pay the substantial costs associated with color art reproduction. Please submit manuscripts electronically to the SRCD *Monographs* Online Submissions and Review Site (Scholar One) at http://mc.manuscriptcentral.com/mono. Please contact the *Monographs* office with any questions at monographs@srcd.org.

The corresponding author for any manuscript must, in the submission letter, warrant that all coauthors are in agreement with the content of the manuscript. The corresponding author also is responsible for informing all coauthors, in a timely manner, of manuscript submission, editorial decisions, reviews received, and any revisions recommended. Before publication, the corresponding author must warrant in the submissions letter that the study has been conducted according to the ethical guidelines of the Society for Research in Child Development.

A more detailed description of all editorial policies, evaluation processes, and format requirements can be found under the "Submission Guidelines" link at http://srcd.org/publications/monographs.

Monographs Editorial Office
e-mail: monographs@srcd.org

Editor, Patricia J. Bauer
Department of Psychology, Emory University
36 Eagle Row
Atlanta, GA 30322
e-mail: pjbauer@emory.edu

Note to NIH Grantees

Pursuant to NIH mandate, Society through Wiley-Blackwell will post the accepted version of Contributions authored by NIH grantholders to PubMed Central upon acceptance. This accepted version will be made publicly available 12 months after publication. For further information, see http://www.wiley.com/go/nihmandate.

Page numbers in *italics* represent figures.

CURRENT